MaiNtENaNt 19

A JOURNAL OF CONTEMPORARY DADA WRITING & ART

PETER CARLAFTES & KAT GEORGES

EDITORS

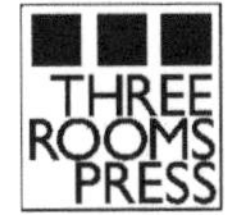

THREE ROOMS PRESS

NEW YORK

WWW.THREEROOMSPRESS.COM
EACH BOOK BORN IN GREENWICH VILLAGE

MAINTENANT: A JOURNAL OF CONTEMPORARY DADA WRITING & ART
ISSUE 19

Editors
Peter Carlaftes & Kat Georges

Design & Production
KG Design International

Inspiration
Arthur Cravan

ON THE COVER:
"THE SUNFLOWERS OF 2022"
Painting, oil on canvas
ADRIAN GHENIE
© Copyright Adrian Ghenie

One of the world's foremost artists, painter Adrian Ghenie was born in Romania
and is currently based in Berlin. According to Pace Gallery, which represents much of the artist's
work, "The Just Stop Oil demonstrations at the National Gallery in London are of particular interest
to the artist, having centered on Vincent van Gogh's iconic *Sunflowers*, a painting to which Ghenie
has frequently referred in his own art." Ghenie frequently shares his current work-in-progress
on his instagram account, @adrian.ghenie.

Special thanks to Emma Foley and Haley Scull, all the contributors,
and readers, museums, galleries, booksellers, and everyone who supports this journal.

Maintenant 19 is dedicated to the memory of
Walter Robinson and Chuck Connelly
(and the United States of America)

ISBN: 978-1-953103-61-1   ISSN 2333-2034   TRP-119

Copyright © 2025 by Three Rooms Press.

MAINTENANT: A JOURNAL OF CONTEMPORARY DADA WRITING & ART
is published annually by Three Rooms Press, New York, NY

Current and back issues of MAINTENANT are available at www.threeroomspress.com/shop

For submission details, visit www.threeroomspress.com or email info@threeroomspress.com

For inquiries about obtaining the MAINTENANT series for your educational or cultural institution
archives or classroom, please email editor@threeroomspress.com

To schedule a workshop, presentation, or dada salon hosted by the editors,
please email editor@threeroomspress.com

Distributed by Ingram / Publishers Group West (www.pgw.com)

INTRODUCTION:
ETHICS CLEANSING

In the face of right and wrong by the breed of weak or strong, humanity has placed far too much emphasis on belongings, not belonging.

There was a time when ethical behavior had a fixity of purpose: the prevention of corruption, favoritism, undue influence and abuse of entrusted power.

Yet it is those who commit these transgressions that prosper most, by completely dispensing with the need for ethics.

What exists is a philosophy where the only guiding principle is to ensure the greatest profits.

MAINTENANT 19 is a testament to the unflinching exposure of self-righteousness. We are no longer bred to be rational creatures. Denial is key. Freedom from blame is the promise. But if blame we must, then here we must first blame the face in the mirror that accepts this way of life.

These times of Ethics Cleansing enable some to think they are better than others, but if someone must be better, then let it be ourselves.

—Peter Carlaftes and Kat Georges, editors

CONTENTS

CONTENTS

MaiNtENaNt 19

BECKY FAWCETT

GOXHILL, LINCOLNSHIRE, UNITED KINGDOM

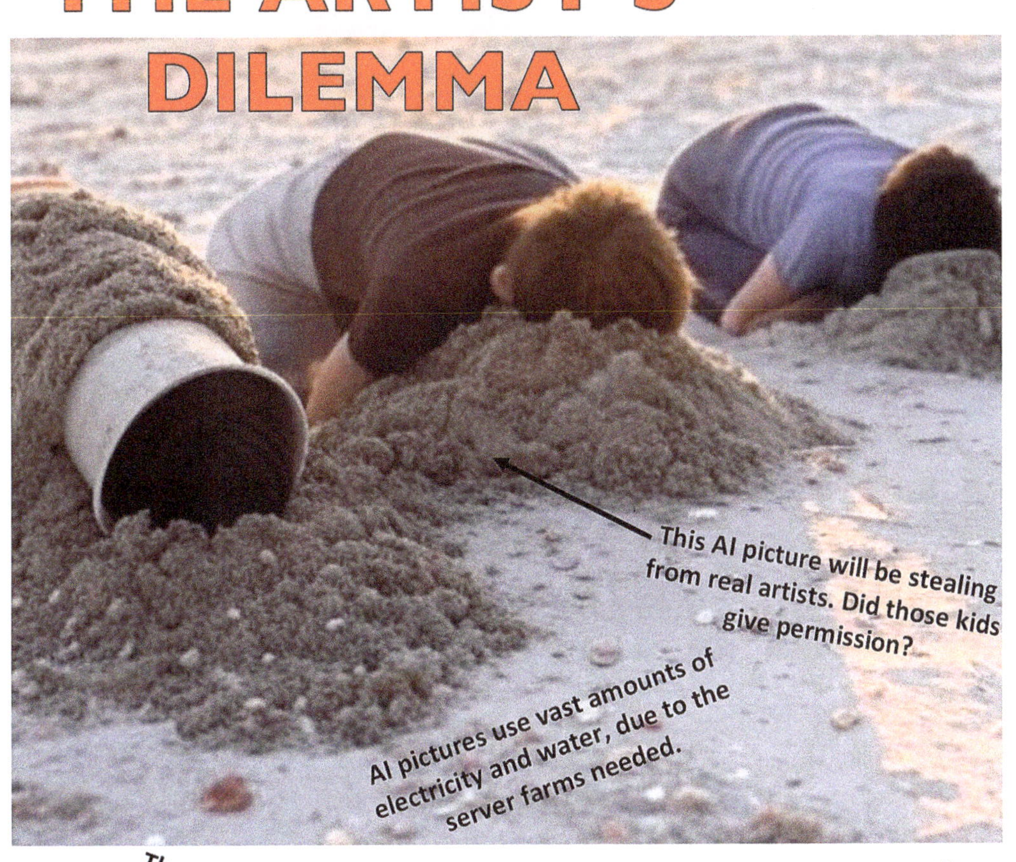

THE ARTIST'S DILEMMA

AI image and text, A4

KATHLEEN FLORENCE

LOS ANGELES, CALIFORNIA

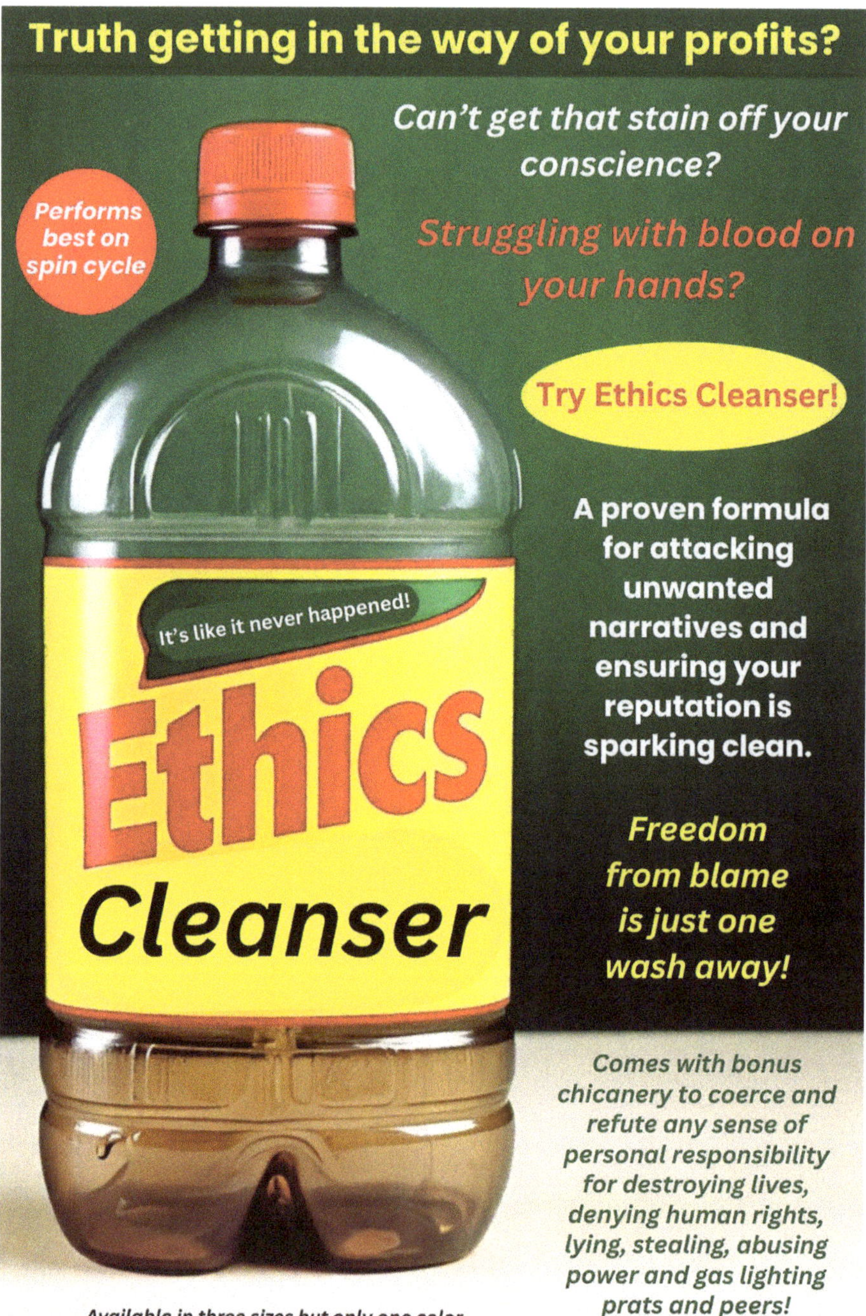

Available in three sizes but only one color.

A PROVEN FORMULA

Digital media, 6 in x 4 in

BIBBE HANSEN

HUDSON, NEW YORK

Pesky conscience got you down?
Remorse and guilt cramping your style?
Bewildered by the loss of standards and values?
Appalled at the current parlous state of so-called civilization?
Jump into the latest trend and say goodbye to all that nonsense
What you need is the newest handy-dandy Ethics Cleanser!
Our product is top-rated to consistently deliver the
brightest empty shiny minds
No more worries, no more fuss; break out TODAY
from the old-fashioned mold
And march backwards with the best of today's
newly carefree & liberated
Leave kindness and compassion
justice and human decency behind
on history's garbage pile – where it belongs!
Go about your daily life without a twinge of regret or worry
leave that for life's maggots and the great unwashed
When you are ready to turn your back on humanity
and breathe easy again reach out for:
The ONE, the ONLY, CRAZY & AMAZING Ethics Cleanser!
No need to wait--Don't hesitate!
Buy our product now and make TODAY
your date to ERASE the slate
Laugh as the principled and just
are dragged away and disposed of
applaud the death of GOOD!
Hurry to join the ranks of the latest, greatest rogues and
miscreants--unleash your most malignant and corrupt
Class A Inner Villain
Your freedom is our business!

**FRESH START CLEANSER
LEAVES NOTHING BEHIND!**

Text and image collage

LINDA J. ALBERTANO

1942–2022

BUSY (POLITICAL)

destruction of civil liberties

media manipulation

suppression of dissent

secret arrests and secret trials

corporate corruption

monopolies

cronyism

class warfare waged by the wealthy

the erosion of public services

infrastructure collapse

educational crises

public health meltdown

judicial malfeasance

election fraud

proliferation of nuclear weapons

regime-change wars

environmental degradation

global warming

I'd like to do something about it, but . . .

LOIS KAGAN MINGUS

NEW YORK, NEW YORK

CHATTING AT DINNER

There was another mass shooting today.

Pass the salt.

She left him so he raped her.

And the gravy.

He bullied him for the whole world to see.

Did you pick up the mouth wash?

DEI should be disregarded.

Your bra strap is showing.

Neo Nazis kicked the rabbi.

I should have put in more garlic.

He was in drag so they beat him up.

I'm too full for dessert.

I heard they videotaped it.
I heard she killed herself.
I heard he strutted and smirked.
I heard he said that's not important.
I heard no one cared.
I heard they took his dress as a trophy.

Pass the potatoes. I heard nothing.

PENNY ARCADE

NEW YORK, NEW YORK

A PLAGUE ON MY HOUSE

Our species has lived, survived plagues, the temporal, attacking our bodies. Here in America we are at the epicenter of a moral and ethical plague.

We watch war, outright genocide, famines, the thorny pain of others.

Empathy is being bred out of us. What were once the values of honor, of decency hold no

cachet in our current world. Right now, there is bombing and hunger in Gaza, an

incomprehensible war. In Congo, Myanmar, Tibet, Ethiopia other genocides, other wars.

I am on a train headed towards Rome.

I have lost the will to stay the course, to watch the news.

I have lost the means of imagination I need to envision peace,

to envision an end to internecine war,

Once during the Plague Years of Venice

Plague doctors wore masks with giant beaks stuffed with herbs rosemary and thyme

To kill the stench of physical decay, keep them at distance from sickness

What can I use to allow me to stomach what I see and hear?

This moral rot.

This is trickle down from Haliburton.

The excesses of the past 25 years

Has bequeathed us this dividend, we are paid in kind.

There is a plague on my house

What will spare us?

NICOLE EISENMAN

BROOKLYN, NEW YORK

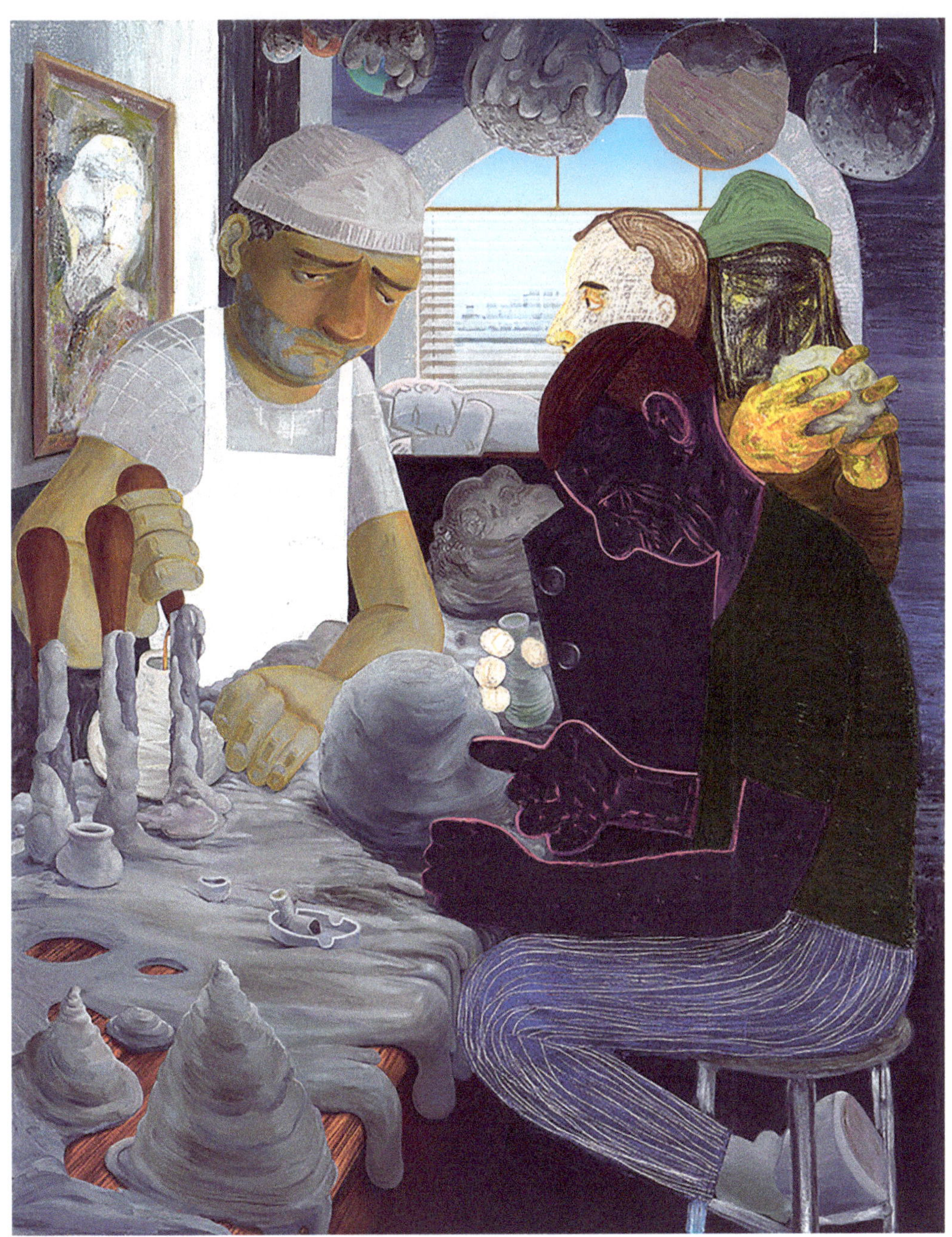

ACHILLES HEEL

Oil on canvas, 82 in x 65 in

MATHIAS JANSSON

ÅKARP, SWEDEN

weighs lightly on the scale of capitalism

a word, so kind
an act, so good
a thought for your next of kin
and a right decision

where every earned penny
every new status symbol
and every social media update

builds an impressive air castle
around your empty soul

THE SCALE

Digital image, 3671 px x 2937 px

MIKE WATT

SAN PEDRO, CALIFORNIA

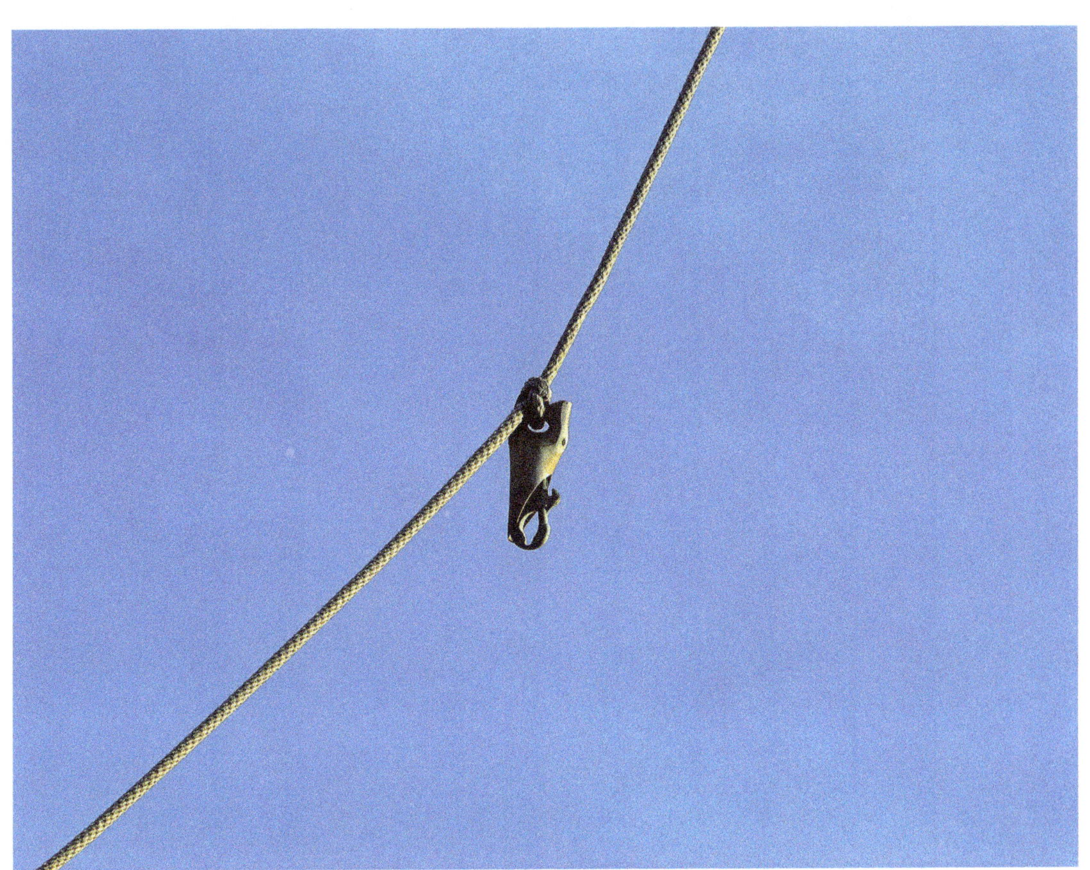

SEEN HERE IN PEDRO

Digital photograph

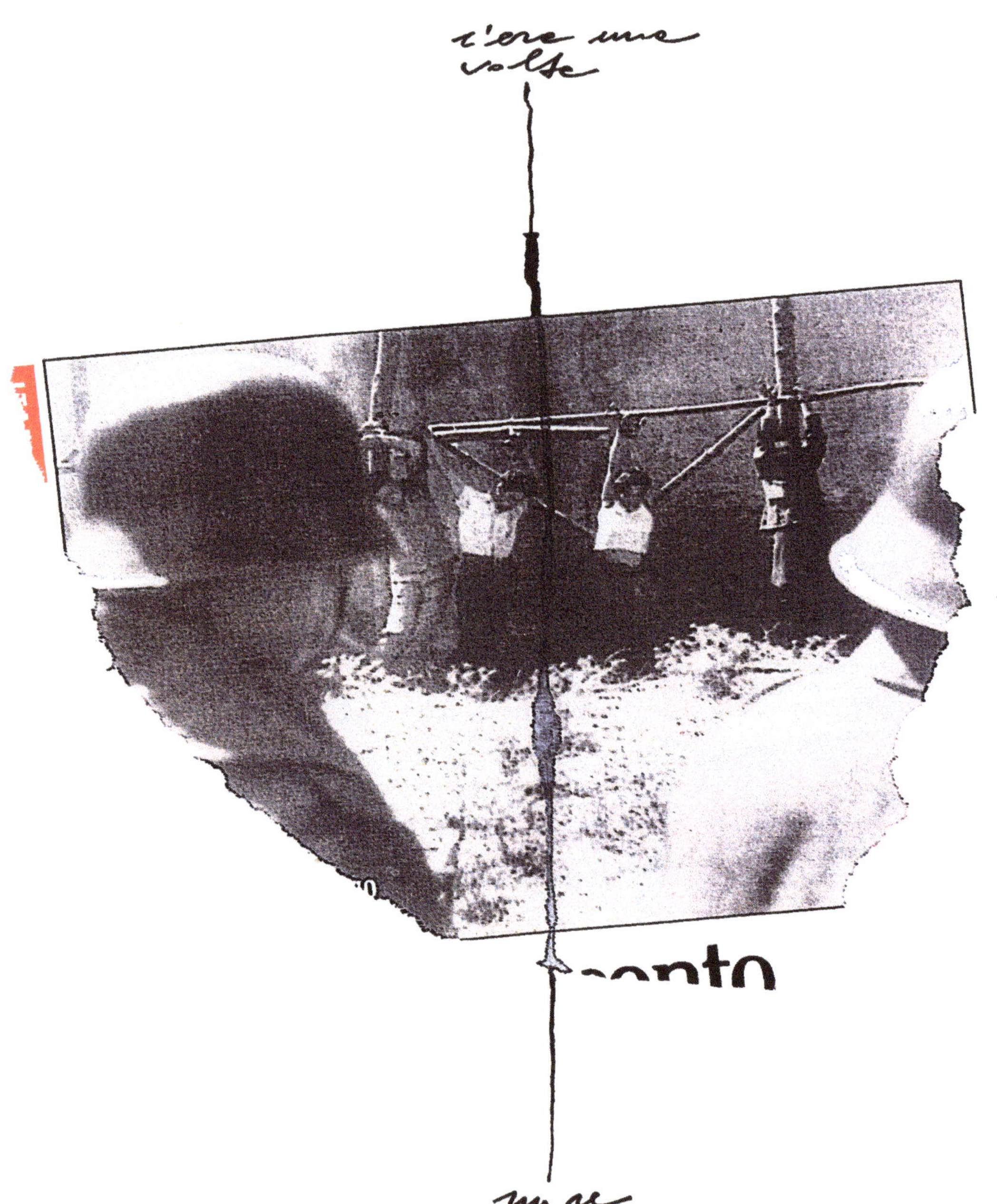

ONCE UPON A TIME

Collage and ink

FRED MARCHANT

ARLINGTON, MASSACHUSETTS

NIGHT IN THE MUSEUM OF HELMETS

one has a horsehair plume .... the other a bright green feather

one in the shape of a country .... this one sharp as a shark tooth

one smells of fear-sweat .... the other reeks of smoke

one as hard as bone .... this one soft as felt

a rusted visor duller than rain .... a new brass one shining in the sun

this one spins like a top on its top .... this one is still as an urn on the mantle

i was there where it happened said one ... i have been here dreaming it didn't

i say it saved the nation .... a bowlful of hollow words

i loved what i looked like .... i couldn't wait to get mine off

many have wondered how i felt .... they think we had no feelings

we thought we would live forever .... we prayed it would just be over

i aways felt better on the ground .... i longed for someone to pick me up

here is the hole the shrapnel cut .... here is a strap with nothing to hold onto

TERESE COE
NEW YORK, NEW YORK

SLAUGHTER

For the kings and armies of Ancient Greece,

vengeance came without caprice.

The murderous are unforgiving.

They simply do away with the living.

MARTINE BELLEN
KEW GARDENS, NEW YORK

RESILIENCE ERASURES

Enola Gay struck

As resiliency symbol.

No Little Boy bomb

Hit Hiroshima.

No feminism needed.

No identity.

ROBIN TOMENS

LONDON, UNITED KINGDOM

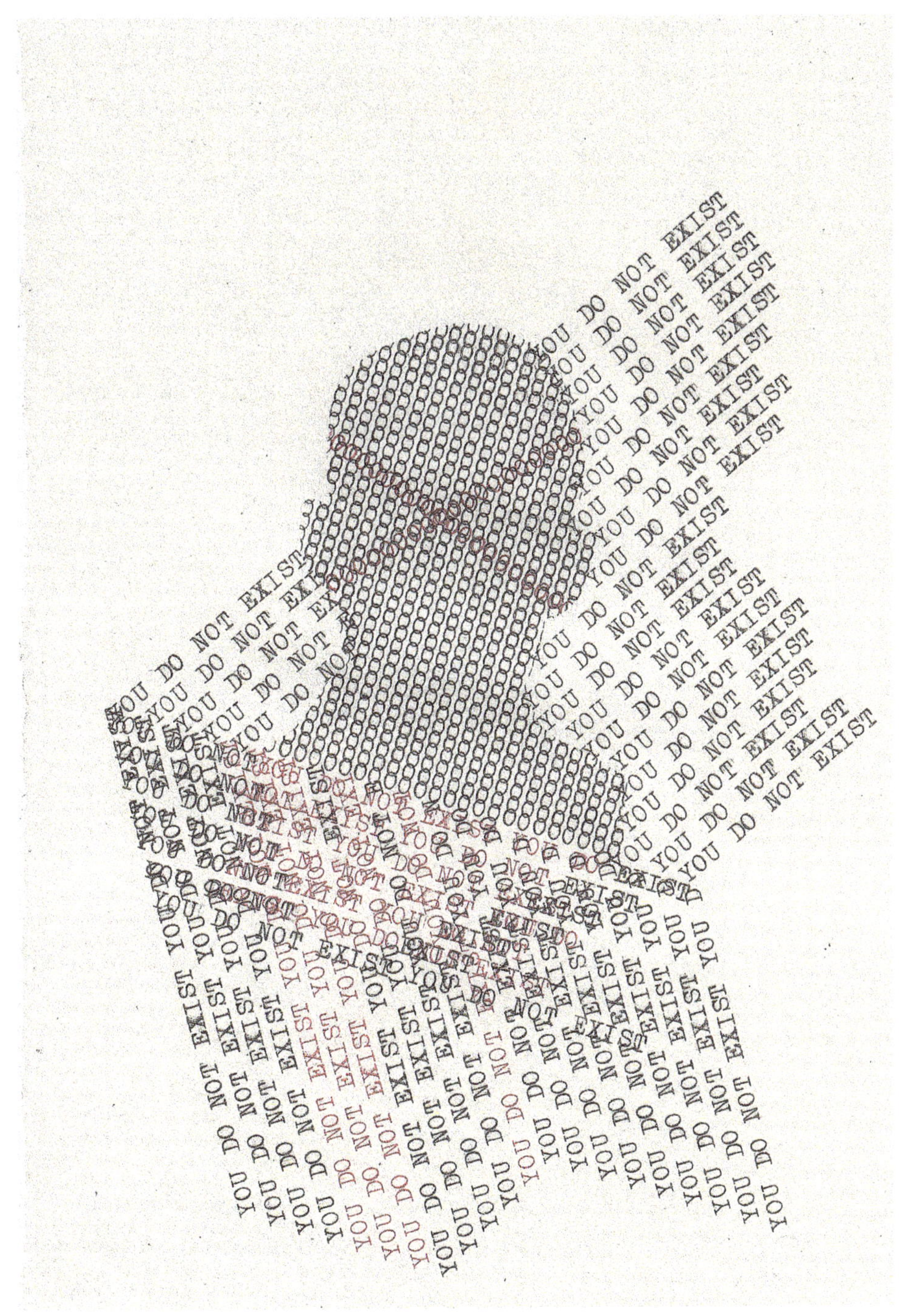

CEASE TO EXIST

Typewriter; 14.8 cm x 21cm

VOLODYMYR BILYK

ZHYTOMYR, UKRAINE

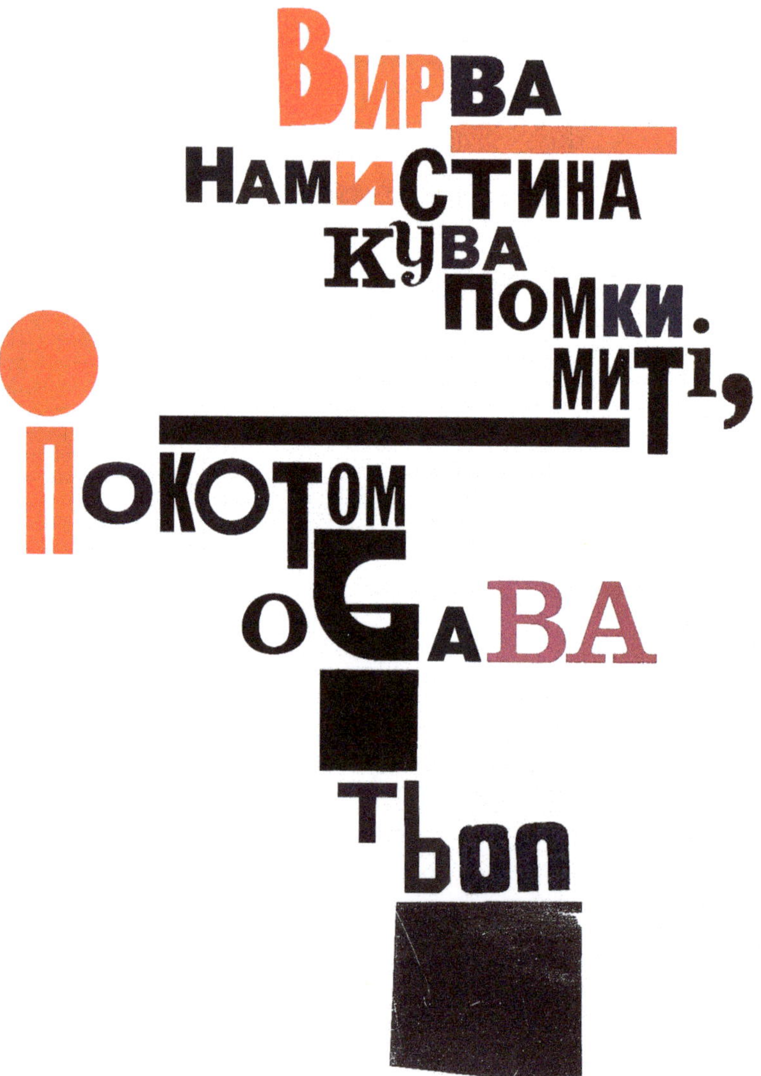

one's explosion crater is another one's bead on a necklace
– an instant reminder that goes with a pang
followed by a river of dread overflowing its banks
only to snap back once you get used to it.

BOOM GALORE

Digital text

FRED HARPER

BROOKLYN, NEW YORK

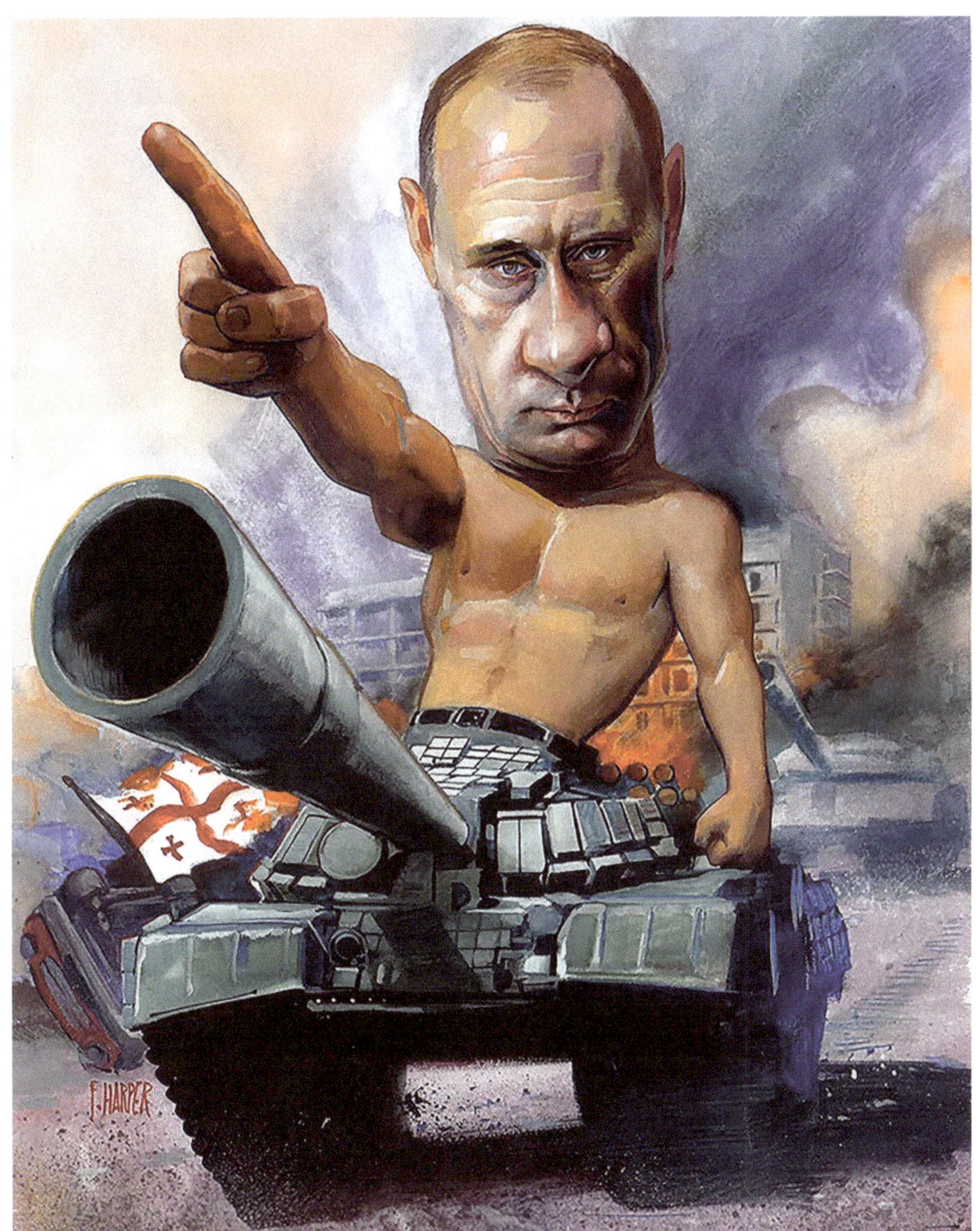

EXTENSION

Gouache on paper, 10 in x 12 in

DEREK ADAMS

STANSFIELD, SUFFOLK, UNITED KINGDOM

MEASURING THE VOLUME
OF AN ELEPHANT

A thousand people

    walk in different directions.

Metal boxes contain

    repeated images,

    repeated images

on a glass canvas.

A million people,

paid to move numbers,

    move numbers

        around.

A child disguised,

    disguised as a skeleton.

Dies with flies on his eyes

    and nothing,

nothing in his distended stomach

but the truth

    the truth.

LUIZ MORGADINHO

LISBON, PORTUGAL

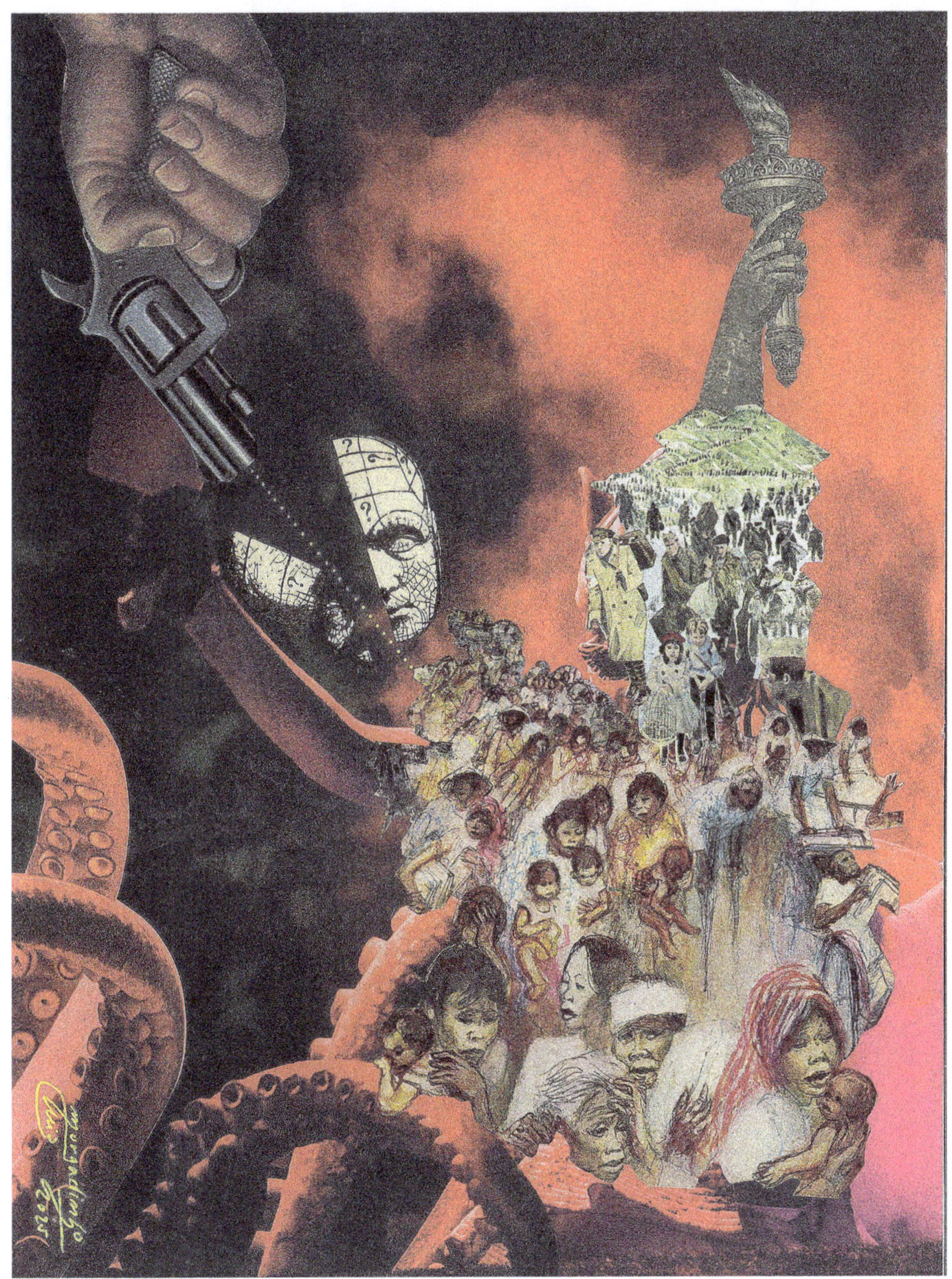

ETHICS CLEANSING

Collage, 27 cm x 21.5 cm

ANDREI CODRESCU

BROOKLYN, NEW YORK

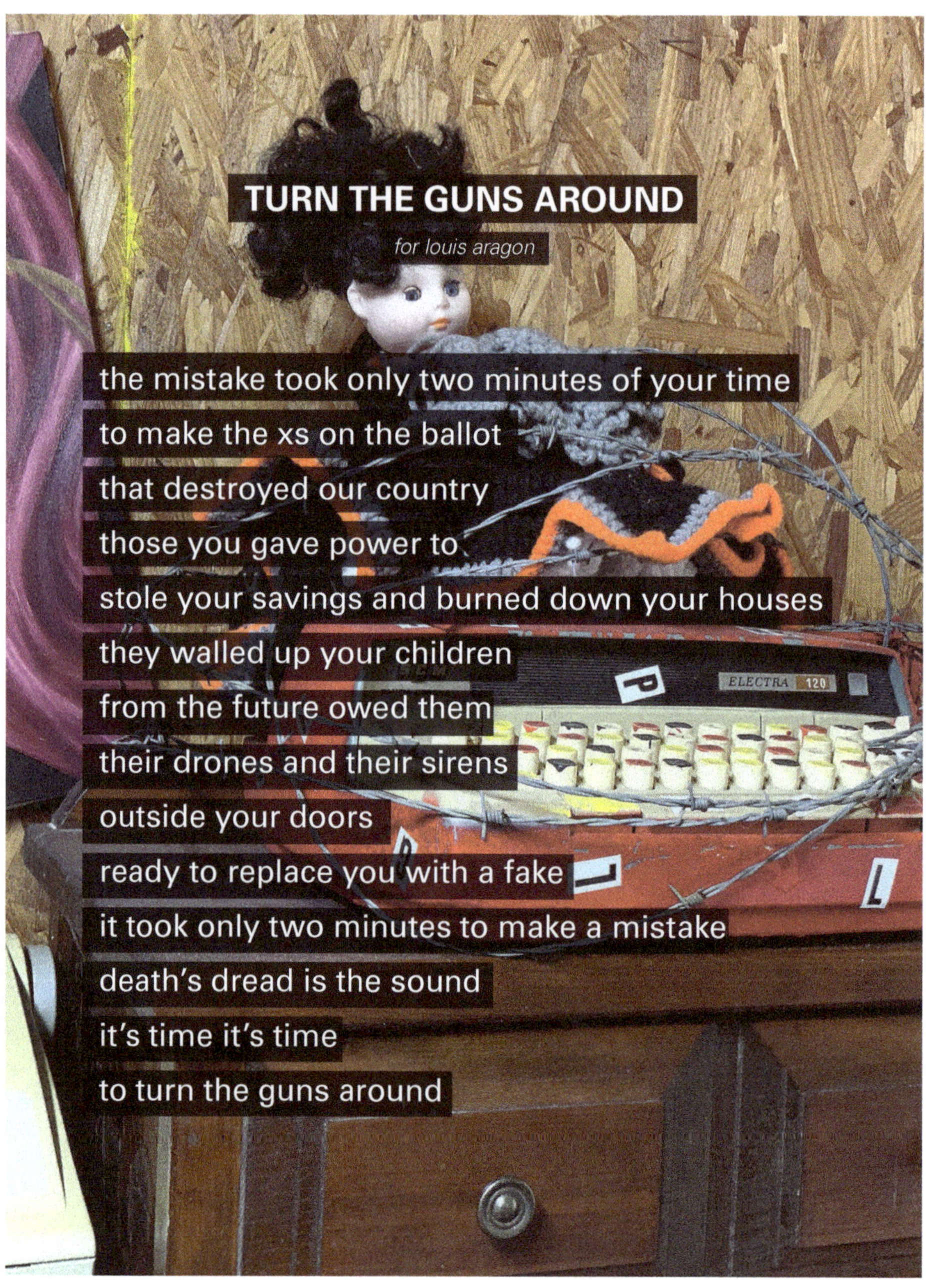

TURN THE GUNS AROUND

Poetry on photograph

EVA HELENE STERN***

GRAZ, AUSTRIA

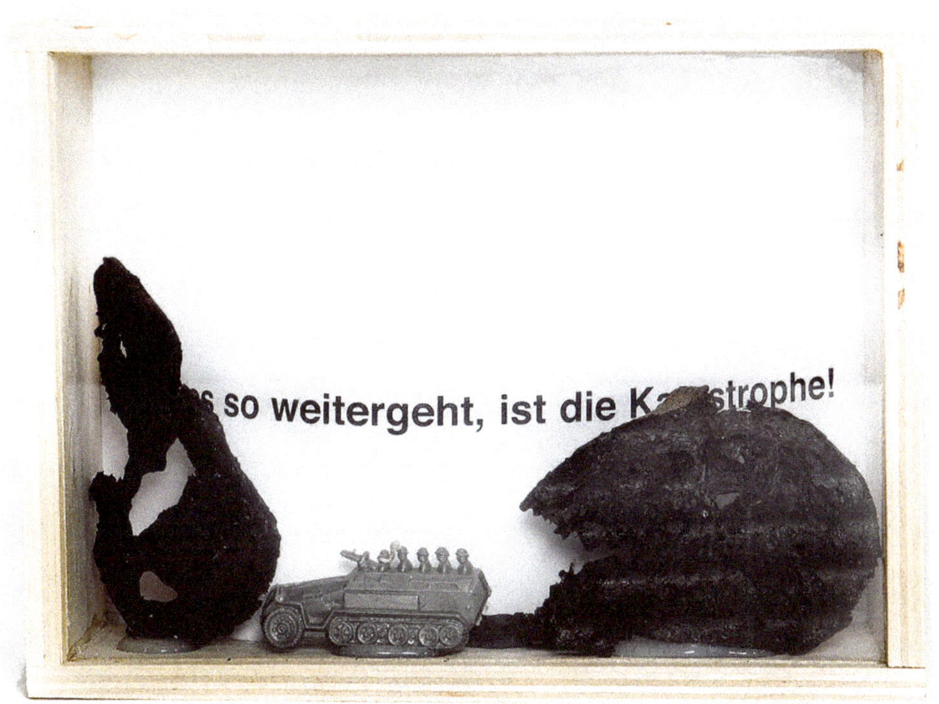

**"DASS ES SO WEITERGEHT,
IST DIE KATASTROPHE!"**

Quote Walter Benjamin
Collage, burned bread, plastic children's toy, postcard, wooden IKEA Box

RENAAT RAMON

BRUGES, BELGIUM

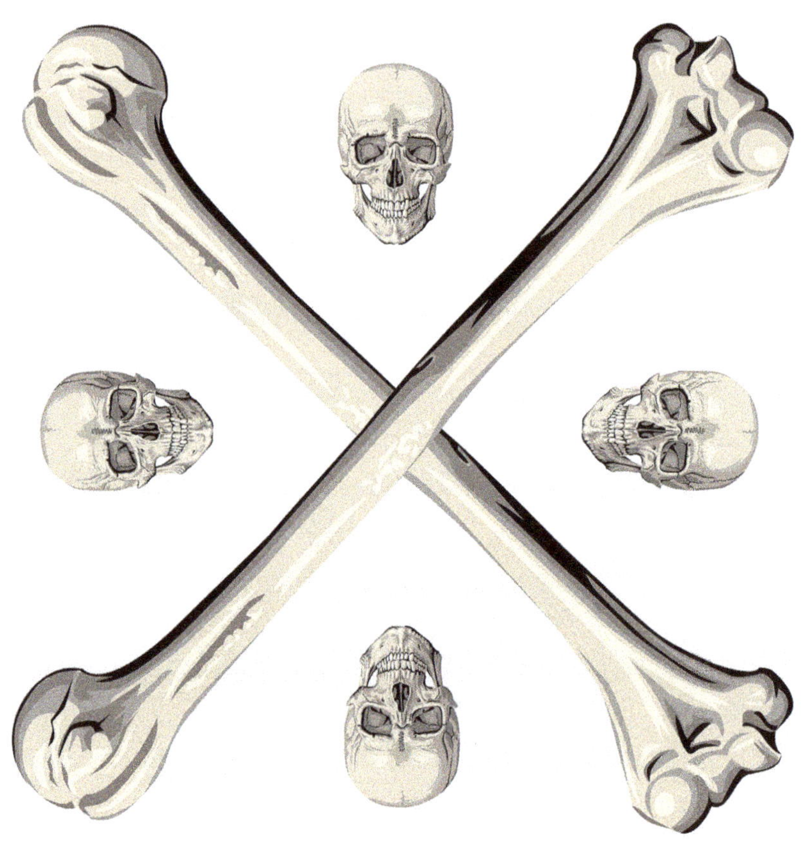

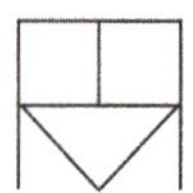

SHAMROCK

Digital print

CARLI MUÑOZ

SAN JUAN, PUERTO RICO

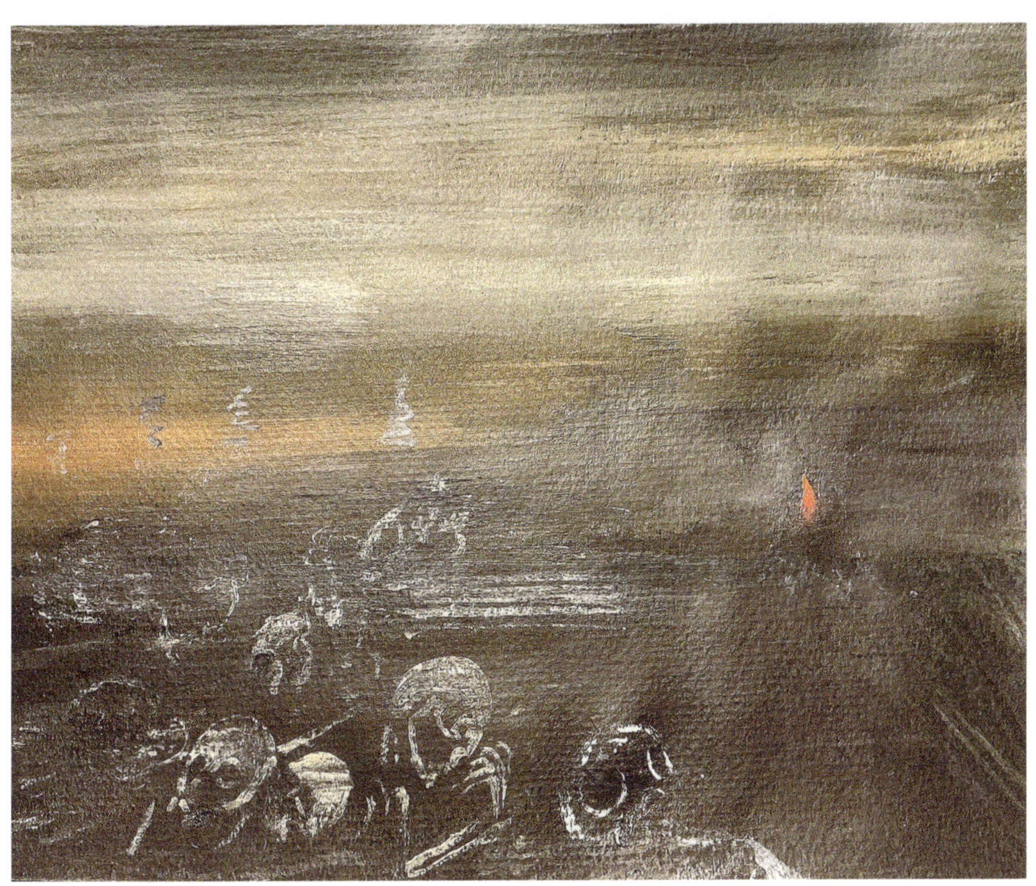

AFTER THE LAST WIAR

Acrylic paint, 8 in x 8 in

VIDYA HARIHARAN

MUMBAI, INDIA

FUGUE

The gentle rain falls,
a fine mist,
on the soldier's limb.

Miles away
harsh sunlight
kickstarts
a brutal war.

Mothers sit on stoops
Waiting for spring.

The ignoble sit at grand tables
Feasting on the cornucopia.

PATRICIA LEONARD

THE BRONX, NEW YORK

OBEYAH

Heart ripped out of chest

the obeyah man cyan't fix mi now

No potion or tonic could cure my broken heart

No blood sacrifice or chant could bring him back

No

Sheh

Love was destroyed by humans

Parentals who call themselves beings

DARIO ROBERTO DIOLI

LANDRIANO, PAVIA, ITALY

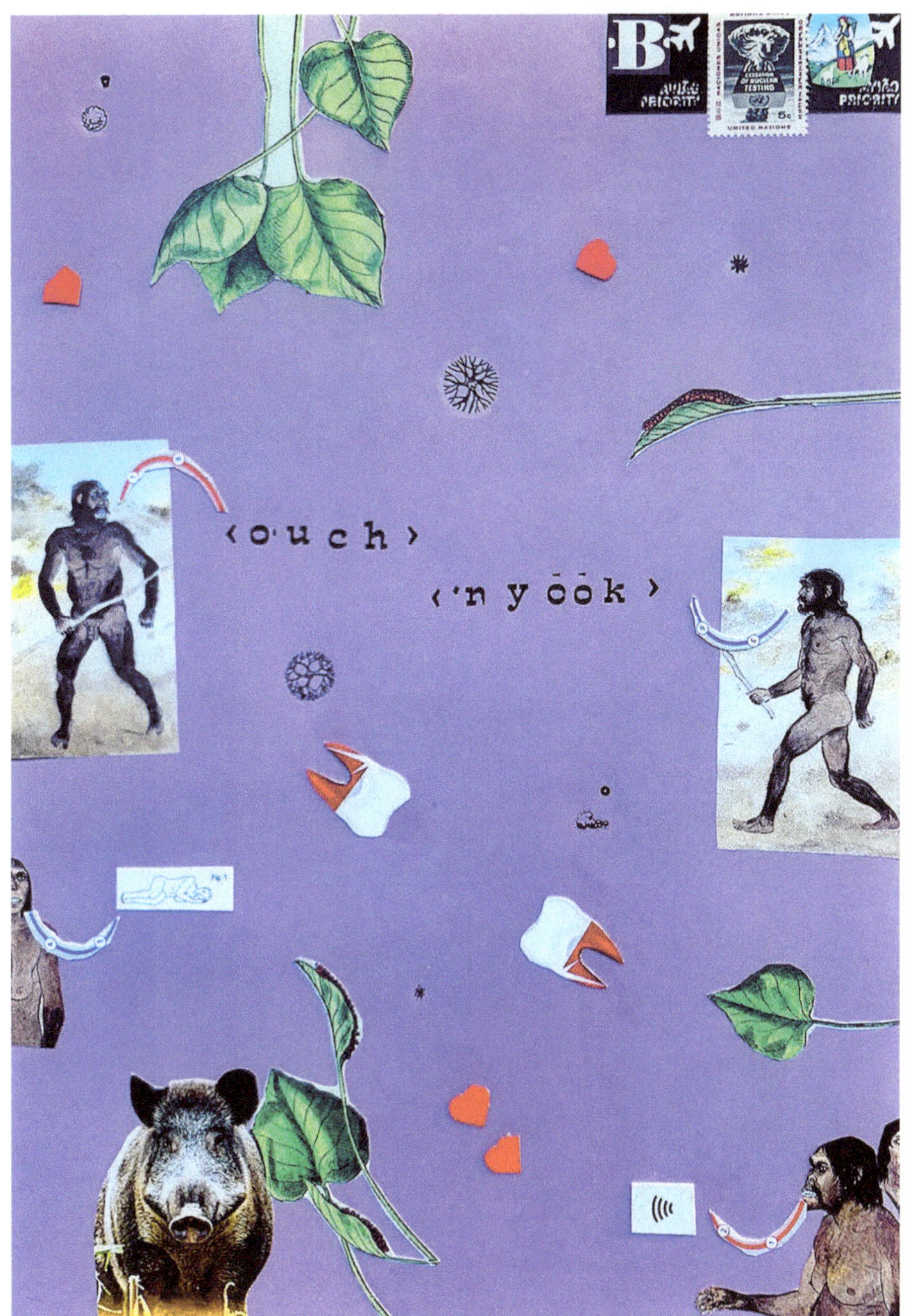

ANY NUKE IS ALREADY TOO MUCH

Collage, stamps, and Letraset, 34 cm x 24 cm

WAYNE ATHERTON

DOVER, NEW HAMPSHIRE

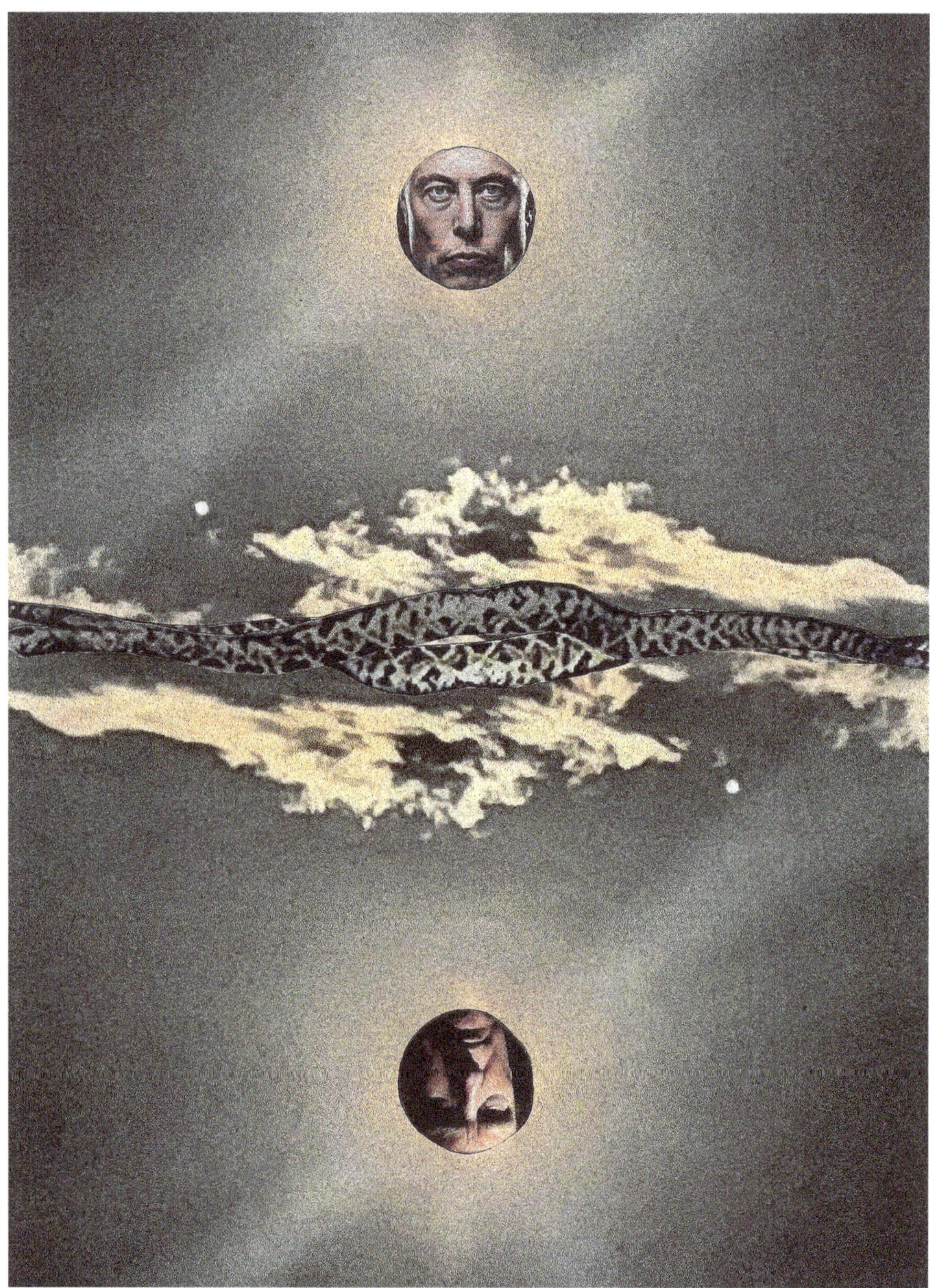

I SEE A BAD MOON RISING

Photomontage on paper

BOB HOLMAN

NEW YORK, NEW YORK

THE IDEA OF REALITY

These are dark times. Fascism is alive and growing,

its body like a snake, lovingly unwinding, welcoming,

then constricting around those who believe they have found

a warm, safe space… and then their breath is squeezed out.

The IDEA of safe and warm stays as long as you believe

the lies of the tyrant, but REALITY is a joyless monotone

of gray with clouds for eyes. What do we do? I dunno.

No Sé

In Bolivia, not voting is against the law.

Don't vote and you lose access to your bank accounts

while you formally report your excuse.

Now that's democracy –Vote or else!

Only problem is deciding which crook to vote for.

In Peru, they have a special jail just for Presidents,

where there were five of them locked up at the time.

In Bolivia, they had a gasoline crisis –cars lined up

for hours to get fuel, yet you could see petroleum

gushing straight from the ground. All Bolivian oil

is exported as crude for fast bucks, though

100% of their refined gasoline is imported.

En Bolivia, voto por

la Orquesta Experimental Indígena.

SOPHIE DUNÉR

GOTHENBURG, SWEDEN

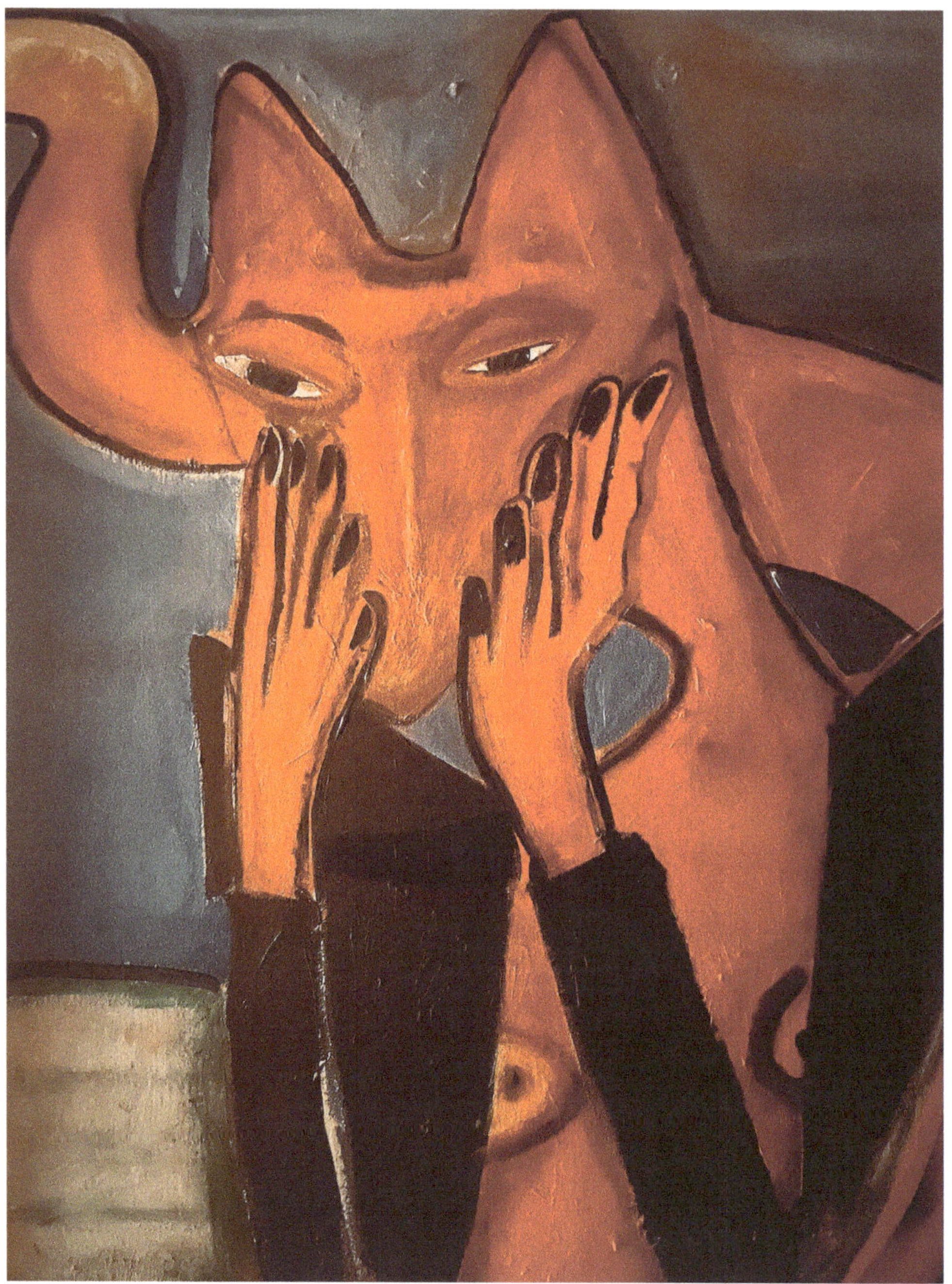

BRUTALLY BLAMED

Acrylic on masonite, 1280 cm x 1686 cm

DOUG KNOTT

1943–2022

THE AWARE WOLVES

To the aware wolves belong
The space between ghosts
And night of eggplant dark

The moon, itself a wandering soul,
Peers through tree-tops
At my heart – a deer frozen
In a forest of eyes, lupine
And shaped like leaves

I know they are near
I hear them when they call
My name. Summoning me
Is entertainment
At my own expense

They lope alongside me
And when I look at them
Their eyes get bigger

I treat them now as my children
Feed them everything I have.

And at night I draw these friends around me
and look up at the moon
Awash in darkness, and all that hunger is
A long wail in the night

LILY DESPIC

WINNIPEG, CANADA

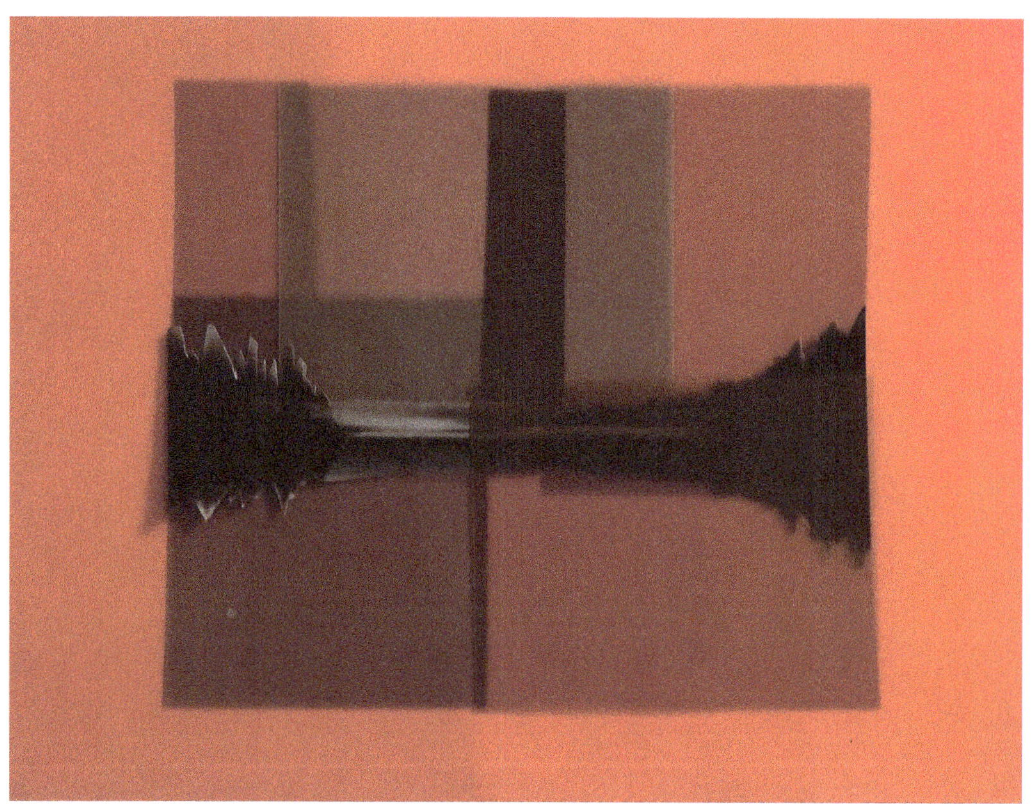

RED SKY AT NIGHT

Color transparanices on cardboard, 11.5 cm x 75 cm

ANNE WALDMAN

NEW YORK, NEW YORK

PATHETIC PARENTHETICAL

LOSAR, 2025 YEAR OF THE WOOD SNAKE

"As fountains sob in ecstasy"–Baudelaire

[path
         least
   taken   mementos
least
ally in the norm
                         Of walk, I lean

He said
 I screen as if from straw already dead
She said
I exclude the matter that once was
    rough takes

        & Master They told me *watch an ember, make look like dead*
alighting. Gone on gone, then you can disappear, I'd forgotten
you write too
And don't go sleeping around with the adjectives
Hurts. like
Treason

   What lineage are you on?
To thy inanimate form aside
old Trobaritz?

        Abject fallacy!
I once loved your resemblance to wit and surprise inebriants

Jerry Hiler calls from the Barbary coast in my scenic plight
"While I know my Greek & Latin so nice..."
"It's just celluloid" Nathaniel chimes over another century
"Many courtyards and jesters for our plaints..."

  Ship on O wave, human as helm & crime, crucible poet

  & for the plucked leaf, afloat, reject thy silence]

CORNELIUS EADY

BROOKLYN, NEW YORK

SOMEONE ELSE

(song for the people of Ukraine and Palestine)

The water
Cannot be shot
The water cannot
Be killed
From under the soldiers
Boot

I rise

The water
Cannot be shot
The water
Cannot be killed
Unfinished business

I rise

The water cannot be
Shot
The water cannot
Be killed

What will they try
To stop me now?

The water cannot be
Shot

The water cannot be
Killed

Beneath the tank's
Tread

I rise

The water cannot
Be shot
The water cannot
Be killed

A bomb leaves
A crater
And now I'm a
Pool

The water cannot
Be shot
The water cannot
Be killed

What will they try
To stop me now?

The water cannot
Be shot

The water cannot
Be killed

Between their brutal
Fingers
We rise

The water cannot
Be stopped
The water cannot be
Killed

From their
Rusted engines
We rise

The water cannot
Be stopped
The water cannot
Be killed

What will they try
To stop us now?

It's what they'll
Never learn;
Eventually

The darkness
Must turn

The water cannot be shot
The water cannot be killed
How do you slaughter
The rain?

The water cannot be shot
The water cannot be
Killed

From the ruined soil
We rise.

Someone will rise up
From the murder soil
Someone will
Rise up
From the murder soil

They'll always be
Someone else.

We rise.

ISRA CHEEMA

AUSTIN, TEXAS

ANGEL JIBRAEL STRIKES A HEEL INTO MY GRIEF

An earthquake in me

trembles the terrain of my body

hairs on the surface of my skin quiver

    from left shoulder to right hip a fault

    line forms diagonally like a single seam

    pull a loose thread wrong and it falls apart

        I hook my right hand around the left side

        of my body to grip skin tightly

        try to keep the fracture from widening

            from splitting me apart into two but

            my sweaty fingers slip

            the skin splits open

                clavicle cracks

                ribs are pulled and snapped apart

                bone shatters

                    the flesh of my torso is ripped

                    A canyon opens to the heavens like

                    a mouth that greedily swallows the expanse

                        of my body but I don't bleed

                        The deluge erupting from this cavern

                        from the brown dirt of my body

                            is water

                            Zam! Zam! I say

                            Stop flowing

                                I place my palms into the chasm

                                at the bottom of the basin but

                                the gorge surges and overflows

                                I am abundant

MALAK MATTAR

LONDON, UNITED KINGDOM

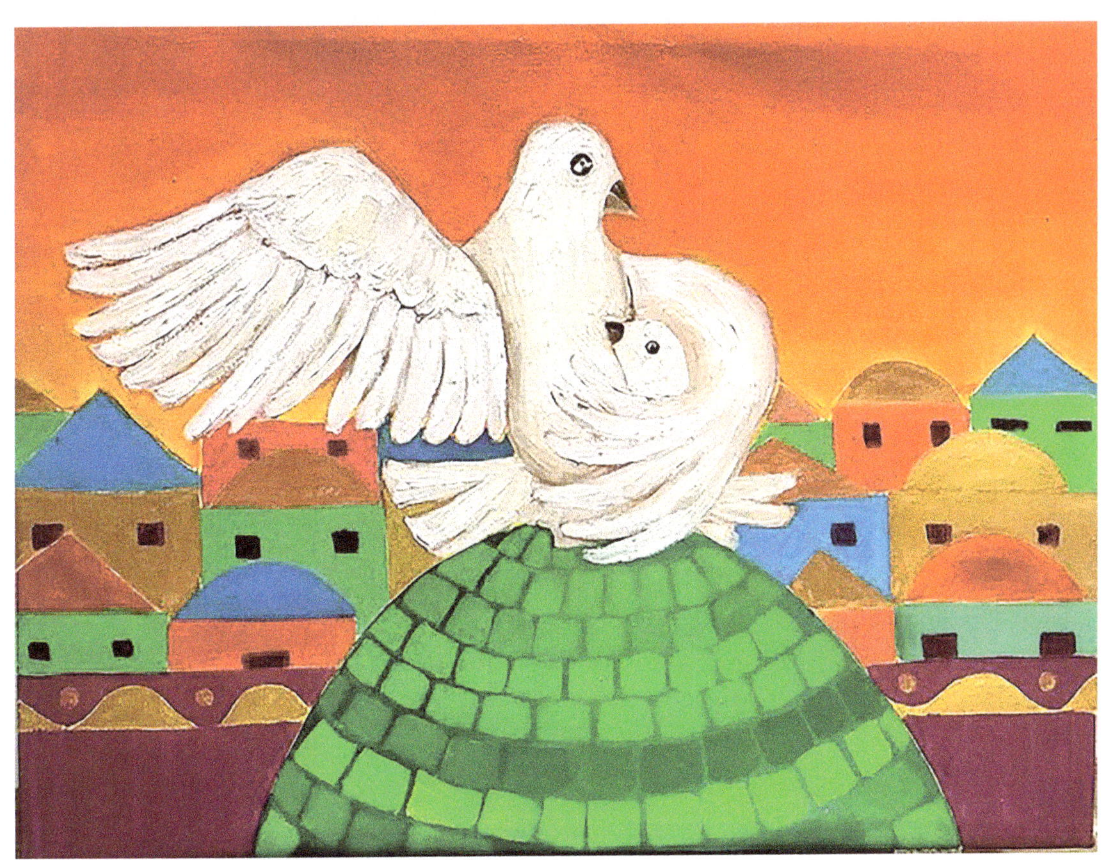

JERUSALEM

Oil on canvas, 60 cm x 50 cm

MAHNAZ BADIHIAN

SAN FRANCISCO, CALIFORNIA

یگناوید

،دنزیم مخز ار اوه نم رظن
دنکیم چچ مغ زا هک نییگنس نانچنآ یدرد
—دبسچیم گرم هب هیاس نوچ یگدنز
دنوشیم وحم هانگیب یاهناج زور ره

،دناهدشمگ یاهشفک زا رپ اههداج
،هدشمگ یاهاپ
،دنراد رس رب یگزره یاهاجات اههکلم
و اههمامع هک یلاح رد
دنناشوپیم نامیا مان هب ار بیرف اهابع
،دننکیم مظعم تمکح ناونعهب ار نونج نیوناناحور
،دشکیم یگتفشآ هب ار نامیا ،نید
دنکیم نفد اهاسیلک و دجاسم ریز ار اههنذ
دناهدش اه نامناخیب رتسب اهنابایخ
خرس گنر هب ار دوخ ار اهتلم
—دننزیم گنر ناکدوک نوخ اب
هیرگ و ون یرنه
،دنشوجیم رادغاد ناردام کشا زا اهدور
خلت یاهمشچ
؛دننکیم رپ کیتسالپ اب ار تعیبط
.دنوشیم هفخ ییایمیش یاهلابز نایم رد یاههام
ملاس نادازون دلوت هب ام و
میراد دیما مومم یاهمحر زا
،دننزیم هسررپ بیریش مدرم
دوخ یگدنز اب هبیرغ
،دنشکیم نمشد نوچ ار ناشنارداپ ناسرا
—دنوشیم هده زد ندرگ قرش رد ناراترخد
دننادیم دنلب دح زا شیب ار ناشیادص
؛مدرک گرزب ار منادنزرزف هک مدوبن نم
،دنتفرگ شوغآ رد ار اهنآ اههناسر
هک دنتخومآ اهنآ هب و
دننک شومارف ار دوخ ریصوت یتح
،دن،هدیم رییغت لوپ لیم اب قباطم ار اههرهچ ناحارج
میمانیم تخانش ار نآ ام و
،دنوشیم نفد گذرا یاهزور راوآ نایم رد ناتسود
ییاهتعاس ماحدزا رد هدشمگ
دنربیم هجوم ییادرف یوس هب هک
.میسریمن نآ هب زگره هک
تسا ارذگ یحبش اهنت زورما
؟میوریم اجک هب
—تسا هدرک هناوید ار ام قالخا دوبن
،تسام یامنبطق نونکا یگناوید
،دخرچیم راوهناوید هک
هاگترپ یوس هب هشیمه

MADNESS

My opinion wounds the air,
a hurt so heavy it drips with sorrow.
Life clings to death like a shadow—
each day, innocent lives dissolve.
The roads are littered with lost shoes,
lost feet,

Queens wear crowns of whoredom,
while turbans and
cloak deceit in the name of faith.
Clerics preach madness as wisdom,
religion jumbles beliefs,
buries minds beneath mosques and church
Streets stretch out as beds
for the homeless.
Nations paint themselves red
with the blood of children—
a grotesque new art form.
Rivers surge with tears
of mourning mothers,
a bitter wellspring.
Nature is force-fed plastic;
Fish choke on chemical debris.
We dare to expect healthy newborns
from poisoned wombs.
People stroll unrooted,
strangers to their own lives.
Boys kill their fathers as foes,
girls beheaded in the East—
their voices deemed too loud.
It wasn't me who raised my children;
media cradled them,
teaching them to forget
even their reflections.
Surgeon's mold faces to money's impulses,
and we call it recognition.
Friends are buried
in the rubble of passing days,
lost to the crowd of hours
that rush toward a tomorrow
we can't catch.
Today is just a fleeting ghost.
Where are we going?
Lack of ethics drives us mad—
its madness now a compass,
spinning wildly,
always toward the brink.

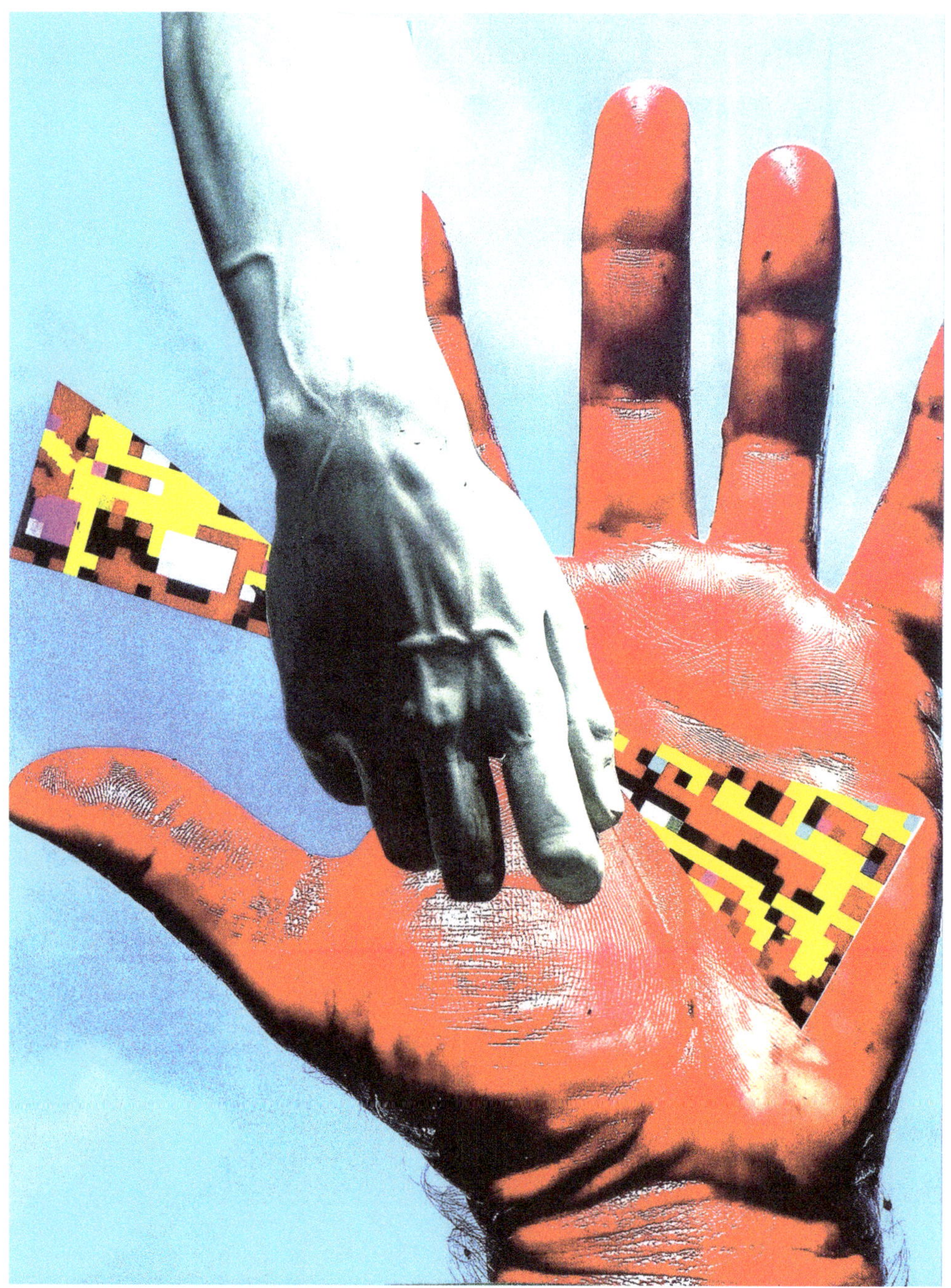

QUESTION

Digital print, 21 cm x 29 cm

CHERYL J. FISH

NEW YORK, NEW YORK

UNDER THEIR SKIN

Standing in rubber boots, North Koreans, mostly young women
work in Chinese seafood factories near the border. Shrimp and
squid on American plates processed by women who signed
contracts. Standing for 16-hour shifts in their own sweat, in rubber
boots. Taste their own raw breath, shoulder-to-shoulder cut off
from communications with home and family. They stay for two to
three years.

The fish sticks at McDonalds. Your restaurant shrimp scampi.
Walmart frozen fish pulled, cleaned and sorted by workers chosen
from among many applicants. No faces. Global economy, profits
to industry and overlords.

We are expected to scorn North Koreans. In tight aprons, with
flexible hands, the most efficient women smell and stab. No
matter if they're sick, lonely, madness creeping up their legs like
crabs or flinching squid. Standing in rubber boots on blocks of ice
sea death in their nostrils. Worrying about some man's hands, one
of the bosses, groping them.

How long do cracked shells live and scream under their skin?

MILO STARR JOHNSON
SAN FRANCISCO, CALIFORNIA

BONFIRE OF THE ANCESTORS: PRELIMINARY INSTRUCTIONS

Take a bag of whitest ashes

To the woods of family trees

Sprinkle 'round the edges

Do it on your knees

Return again at night

A candle in your hand

Let the forest whimper

Stories of the land

Come back in the morning

Swing your sharpest axe

Cut down all the trees

Pile them up in stacks

Drag off all the stumps so

The understory's clear

The space is now ready

Your fire goes here

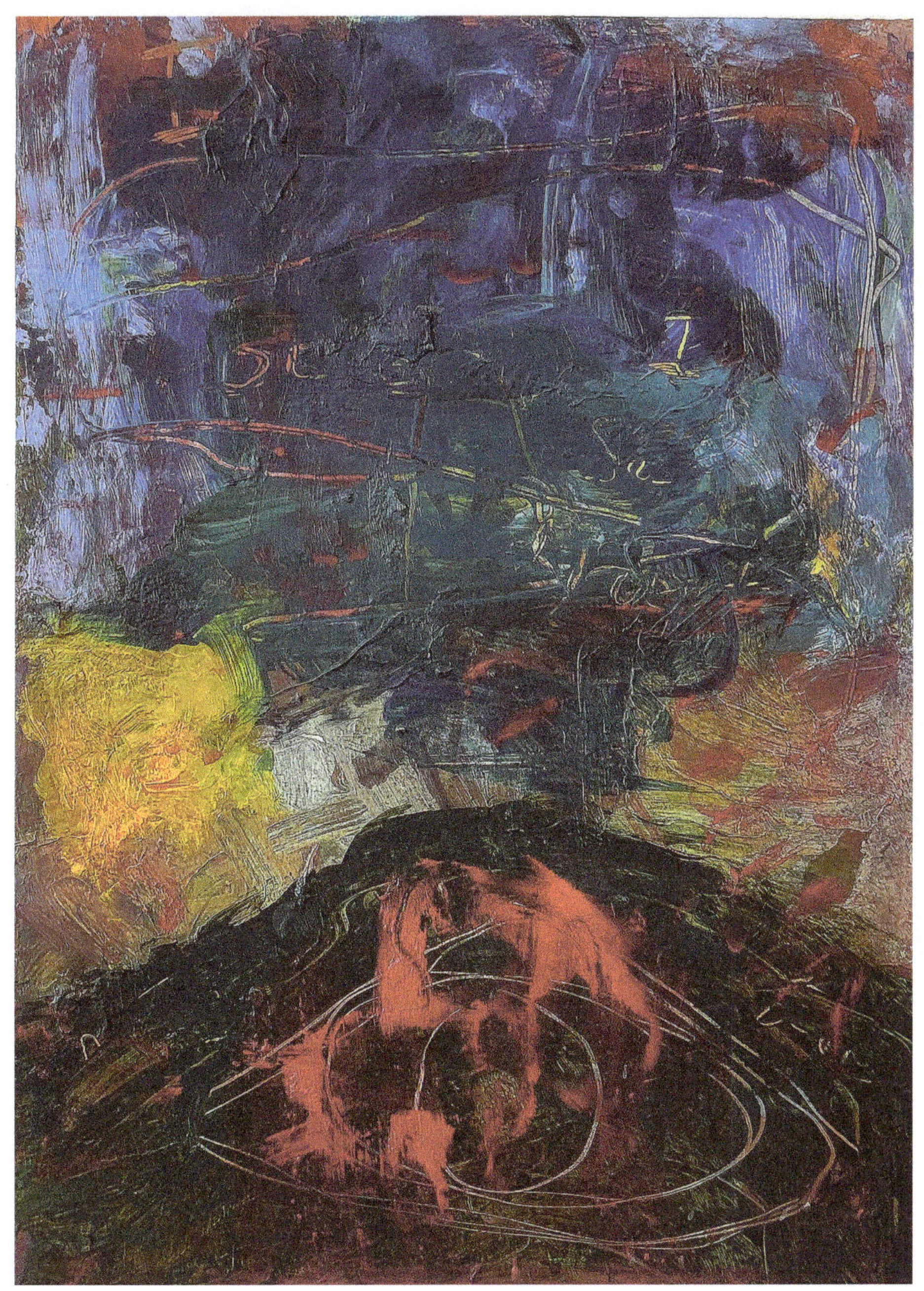

VOLCANO

Painting

THADDEUS RUTKOWSKI

NEW YORK, NEW YORK

IMMIGRANT

My mother left China

a year before it came under Mao—

before her family landed on the wrong side.

The chairman cleared the country

of the unconverted.

She was lucky to get out when she did.

She arrived in the US

before China's borders were closed

and the rest of her family was trapped.

Years later, she found her siblings:

One brother was fixing bicycles in LA,

another was a student in Saskatoon.

Her brothers didn't speak English

and she'd lost her Chinese,

so her brothers' children translated for them.

AMY BARONE

NEW YORK, NEW YORK

RÉTTIR

At the end of summer in Iceland,

groups of farmers and friends gather

to lead sheep home after a summer

spent lounging in the mountains.

On horseback and foot, they guide the animals

from the highlands, where they fed on berries, grass

and flowering plants, to sorting pens on farms.

The tradition dates back to the Vikings

when welcoming sheep back to the city

guaranteed winter survival for city folk.

Echoing a spiritual and emotional ethos, the practice

underscores Icelanders' sense of community in aiding

each other during disasters, upholding a fading activity,

and leaving no one behind.

KATHY BRUCE

DUNOON, SCOTLAND

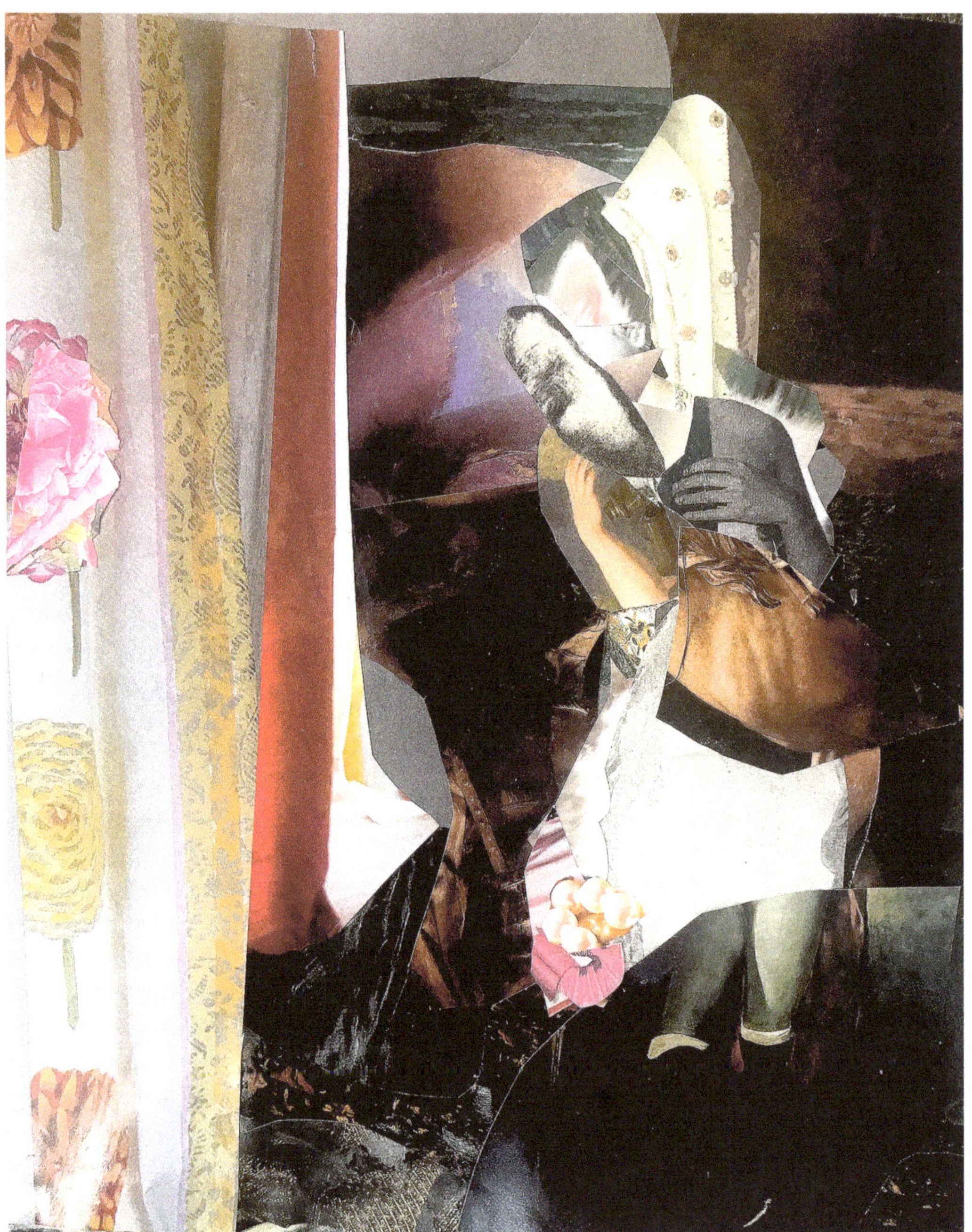

RISING HYSTERIA

Collage, 12 in x 17 in

SOPHIE MALLERET

NEW YORK, NEW YORK AND PARIS, FRANCE

WORD BUBBLE EMPTY

Word bubble   Empty
Cheers Chews Cheers the fat & the chat
                    Man with no leg
                    Crosses street on his knuckles
Your knuckles/   yours   bleed with
Your hands and   imaginary knees
                    Clapping left & right
                                    Fanning the invisible
                                    Vacuum cleaner on speed

          Roams your brain
          Night & day
          Might this be
                    The last full moon   from   hell
Greets all   there is left   to greet
We lost   language
When we   lost   words   turned baby food
                         For the brain / neurones lagging behind
                                        Because
We   *all*   wanted to be   *all*   the same
A wanna be clown
Dressed like a king
Criss cross sing song my/   yours   afternoon breeze
                                You love the crown clown

And the clown
Makes you laugh
                    With your hands
                         Fanning the improbable
Wishful thinking   hanging by a feather
From/   On Margaret's knees
                    Who is Margaret
                    There is no Margaret
          He just likes the name
So   we call everyone Margaret
                    Might as well be a number
Big brother sister
          Collecting prime numbers
Not knowing what it is / they are   / what/ who they are
And where the imaginary salmon
Laid his eggs   the last time
                    Last time I checked
                    There was none / no last time
          Now   It's always the last time and
                    Never
                    All the same
                    It's a /   *What a Beautiful World*

JIMMY VEGA

LYNWOOD, CALIFORNIA

X TELLS ME SHE'S TIRED OF TRYING

tired of everything constantly shattering—
someone threw a brick to the window
of her irises & now everything she tastes
is colored blackish blue. she hardly stains
her lips these days—nothing matches
the fear of her father being deported

but she gets up every morning anyway
despite the taste of metal that lingers
in her mouth after she's stopped dreaming
—x tells me she's tired of listening
to slowdive songs, whispering melodies
inside the hem of sleep, trying to erase

cacophonies like amber rain—
i can have my world destroyed, i'm used to it

she sighs, as if heartache was a private soliloquy
to god, dust-stained knees on the verge of fragility
mumbling invocations like reading a laundry list
to herself, tasting salt of casted sigils

x tells me she's tired of trying—
tired of sleeping, tired of eating, tired
of dealing with differentials, tired of dreaming,
tired of collecting letters from the department
of justice, tired of cheap wine breath, staining
her voice red, tired of 1:08 a.m. phone calls

tired of feeling defeated, x tells me she's
tired of pressing keys—chopin won't cure
her heartache or hide her father from ice—
she's tired of circling cloud corners inside
her ruminations like heavy sleep lids during
nocturne no. 20 in c-sharp minor like
nocturne no. 20 in c-sharp minor—

GENE PRITSKER

NEW YORK, NEW YORK

Ethics Cleansing

Graphic Score

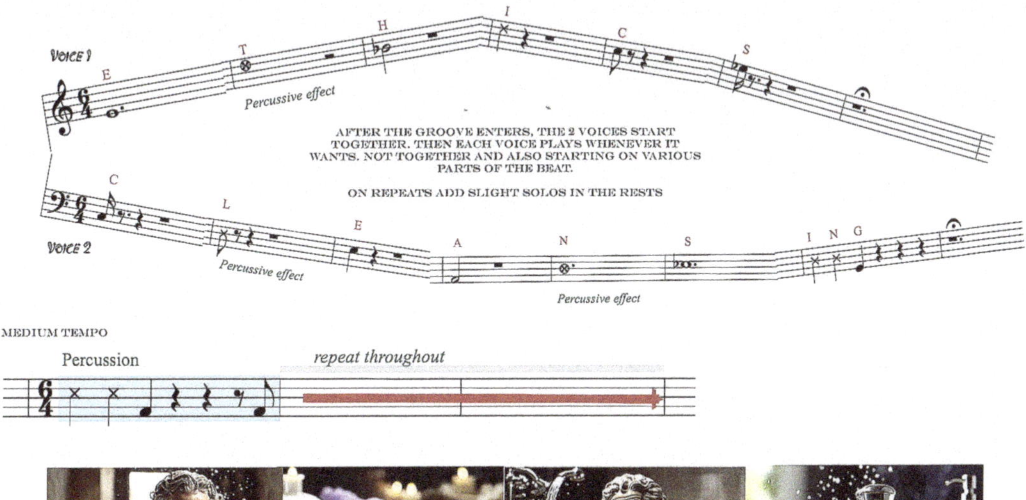

ETHICS CLEANSING

Paper, musical graphic score, 8.5 in x 11 in

RAYMOND PETTIBON

NEW YORK, NEW YORK

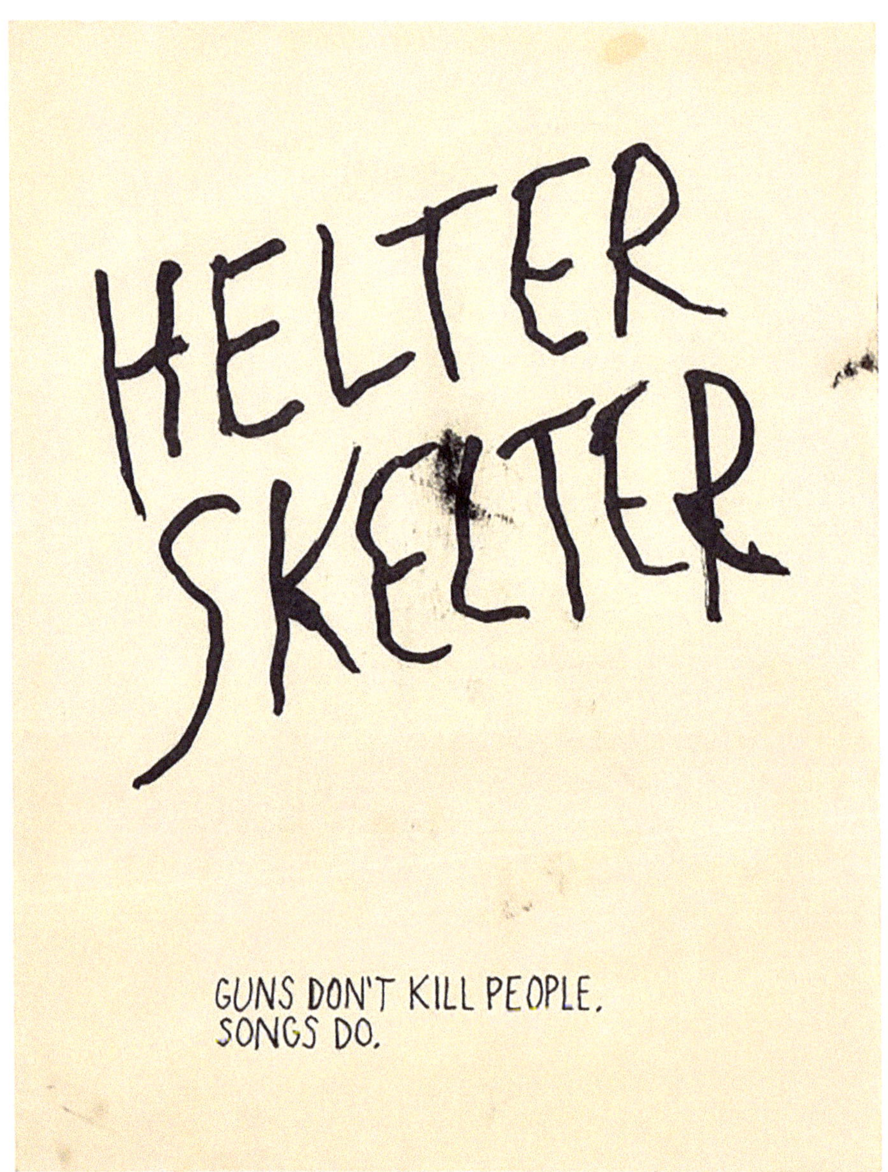

No Title (Guns don't kill . . .)

Pen and ink on paper
© Raymond Pettibon, courtesy the artist and David Zwirner

THURSTON MOORE

LONDON, UNITED KINGDOM

DUE FOR SERVICE

swung by yr house earlier
light was off so i sat in my car
scratched to hell cd of steve lacy on the floor
cold aroma of empty coffee cup
i miss smoking
we used to smoke, drink, play records
granola and yoghurt with all the trimmings
ten bucks worth of gas
should get me home

VINCENT KATZ

NEW YORK, NEW YORK

I'M GLAD

I was getting tired. Now I'm glad they're wandering around my city.
I was getting tired of seeing them in their medallions, looking dazed
and holding maps. Now I perceive a skinniness in all, and I'm proud
and alive in this city. The city lived its life again last night, has survived
its latest loss, is born again in bodies and flowers and pizza at 11:30
am.

It is a day, and as such, people go about it, do their shopping, enlist
advice, suck a fruit, and drop it in the garbage. They are dressed —
for the weather and their part in it. They are champions who have
lost, and today are born.

SUSAN SHUP

PARIS, FRANCE

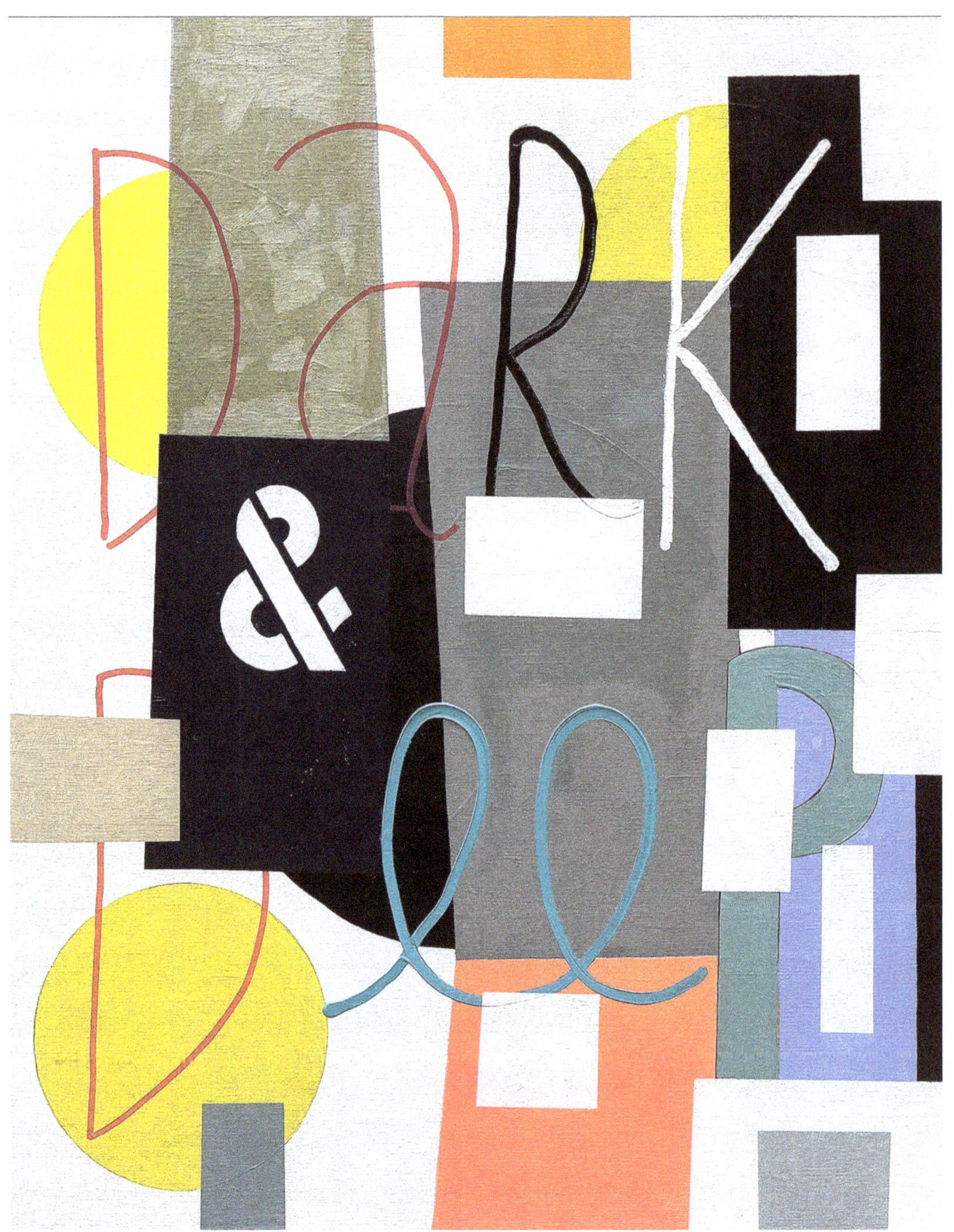

DARK & DEEP

Acrylic and oil on canvas, 100 cm x 81 cm

CHARLES PLYMELL

CHERRY VALLEY, NEW YORK

MANNA

I got those Armageddon

rapture headed

end times blues

flyin' round the globe of

a kaleidoscopic deja vu

like in a big poster

making love to you

fighting against a

melancholia of spirit

when night air is swift

around a fossilized past

and echolalia of the stars

satisfies savant harmonies

deep in scattered abysses

and distant Mars

like burned beauty

from men and wars

while the moon shined a

beacon into a black cave

of PreCambrian leaders when

engines roar & billionaires rave.

ERIC DROOKER

BERKELEY, CALIFORNIA

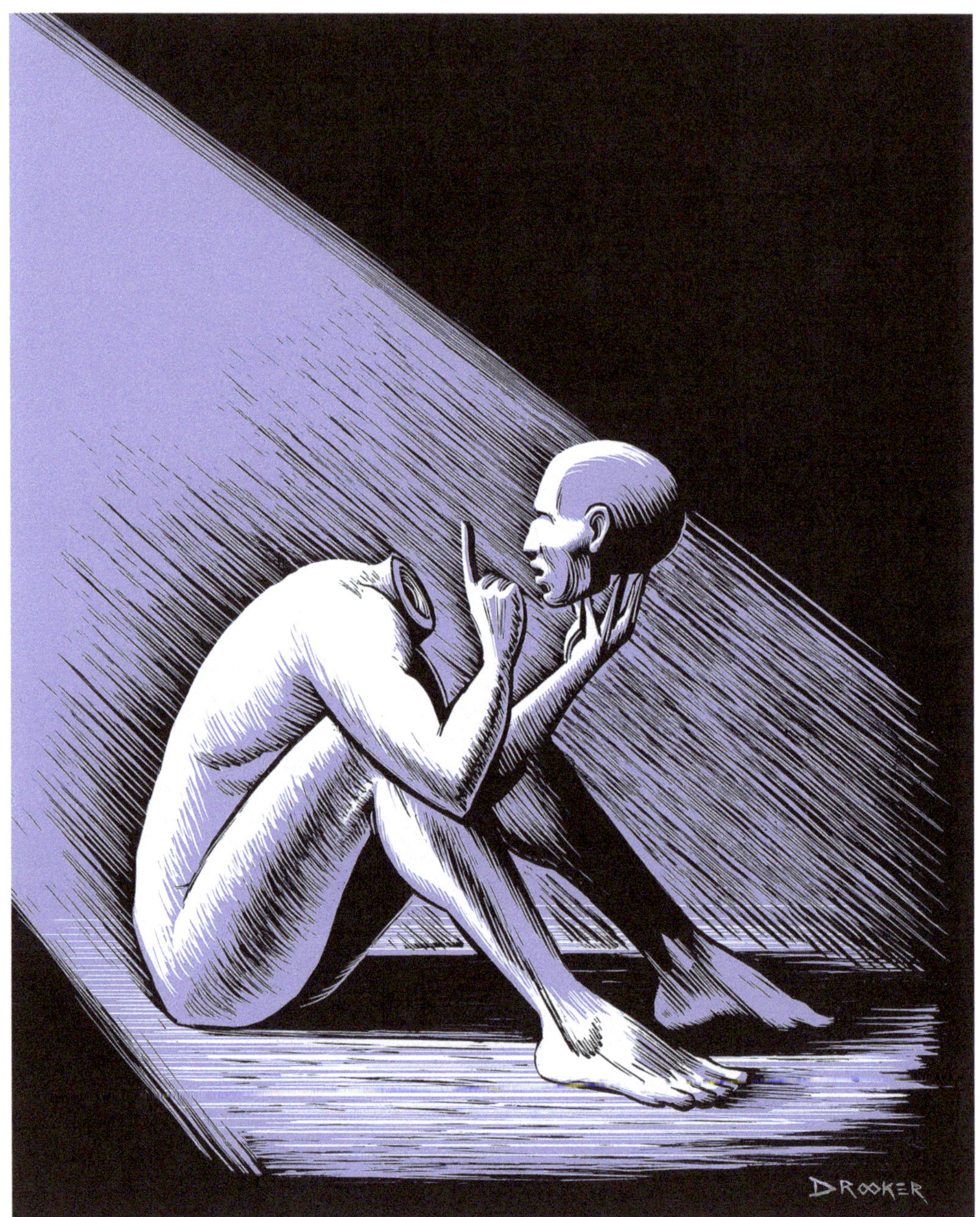

SELF CONTEMPLATION

Scratchboard (with digital color), 6 in x 8 in

HARRY E. NORTHUP

WOODLAND HILLS, CALIFORNIA

A CALLING

I am my own shield
It's what I have
A willingness to study
A devotion to night's calling

Memories of acting in good films
A lifelong devotion to the study
Of acting, movies, poetry
A lifetime of acting in movies

& composing poesy
I am the shield of rambling voices
Of men & women alone among others
Wanting attention

I am the shield of two geese flying
Alone, away from the flock
I am the shield of numbness
Of receiving love greater than

Ever imagined
I am the shield of nothingness
Of love within, whole but broken
I put my shield down

PETE DOLACK

BROOKLYN, NEW YORK

CORPORATE CRIME IS SYNERGY NOW

The old is new again it seems

So the television and the White House tell us

We're going to skip the 20th century and return to the 19th

Or maybe the 16th

I am not sure what we should call a mix of feudalism and fascism

Ah, there is a piece of the 20th century after all in our cowardly new world

That is not so new

It was harder to keep people in their place in the 20th than the 19th or the 16th

And here in the 21st people insist on noticing that kleptocracy is worse than ever

Plunder? Inequality? Financial swindles? Get with the program, it's the 21st century!

What to do about corporate crime?

Put the criminals in office; it's synergy now

What should we call a country like this that doesn't grow bananas?

The Orange One Man Crime Wave might tempt us to call it an orange republic

But even the ultra-mendacious never do it alone

You need a rapacious gang who believe they deserve all you have

And a propaganda machine to tell you that's what's good for you

You'll love it, trust us! Would we lie to you?

Not that they have to rely on convincing you down is up and night is day

There is always force lurking in the background ready to be unleashed

The fist and the gun were more open in the 16th or the 19th century

We are so more modern today demonizing those Other people to keep you safe

Until you notice, too late, your Medicare, your Social Security is gone

And then the force is applied to you, too, and you find you aren't exceptional after all

Of what use are ethics when force is on your side?

MARK KOSTABI

ROME, ITALY

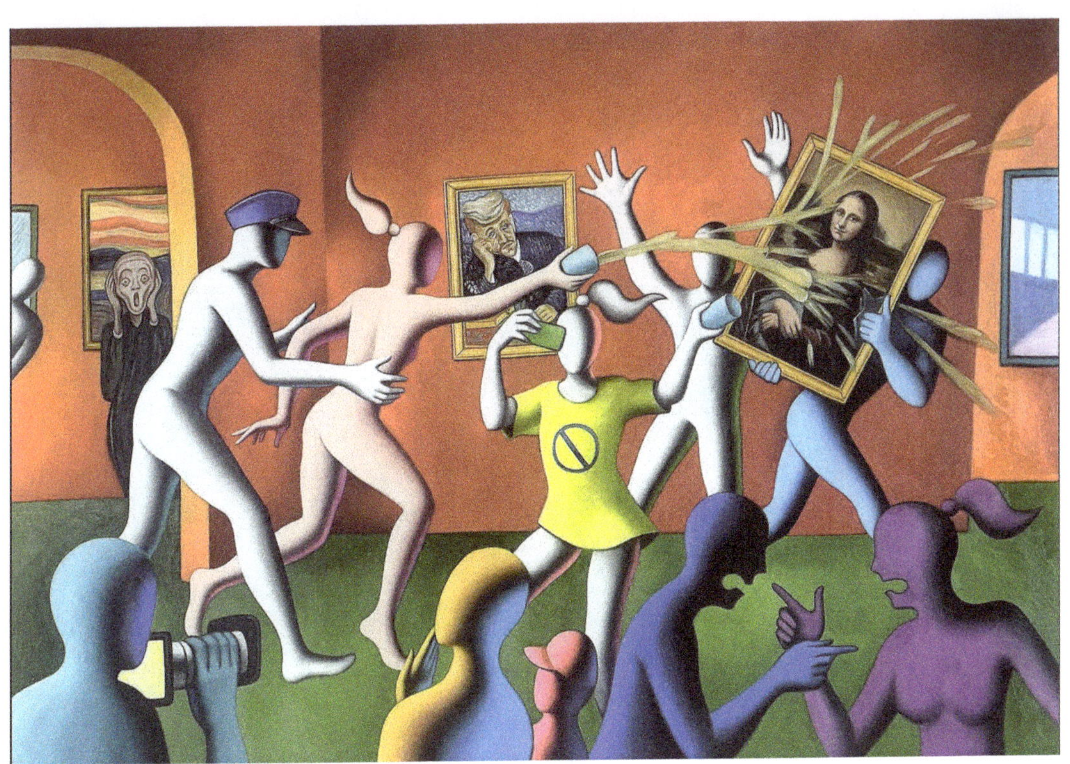

DISRUPTED BEAUTY

Oil on canvas, 102 cm x 130 cm

CHUCK CONNELLY & ADRIENNE CONNELLY

1955-2025 | PHILADELPHA, PENNSYLVANIA

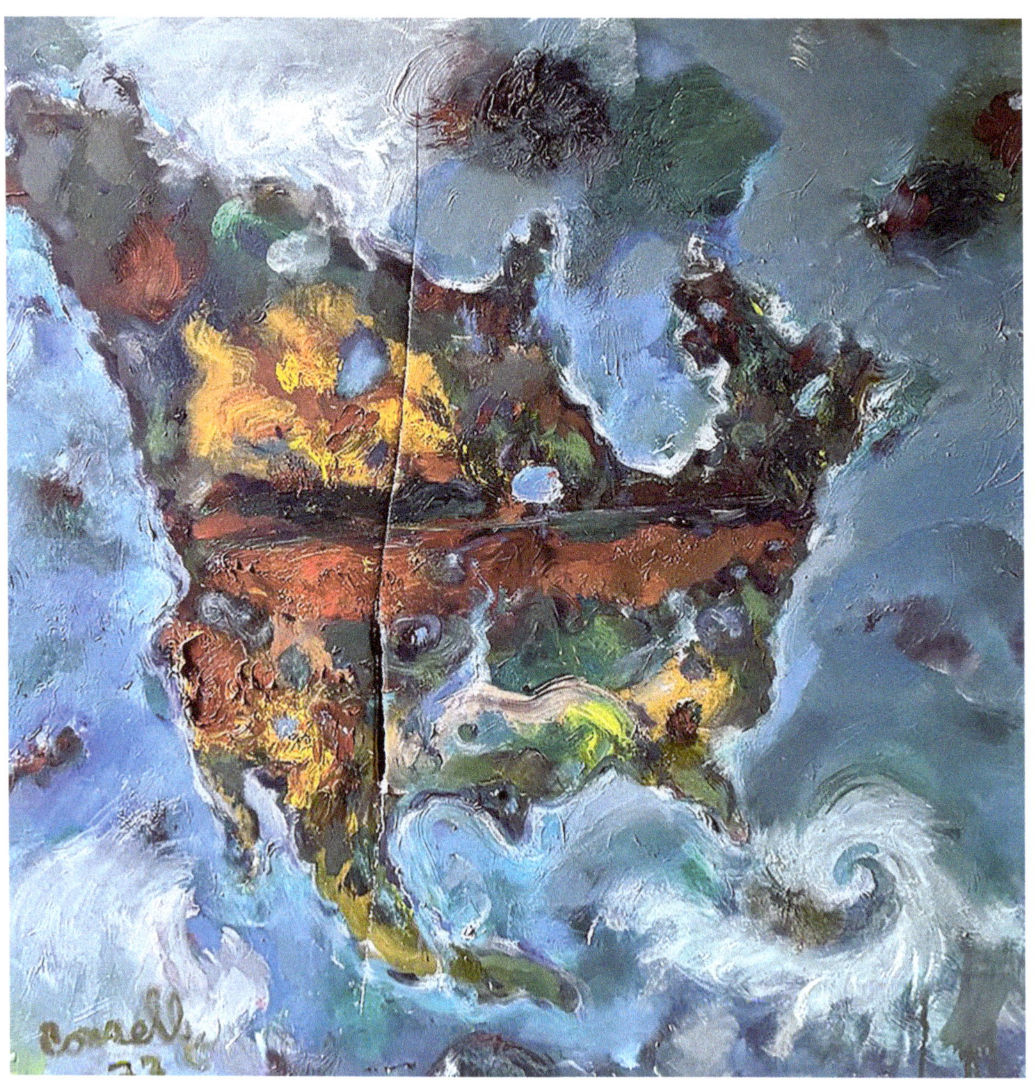

DECONSTRUCTING AMERICA

Oil on canvas, 36 in x 36 in

ANAÏS BUCHER

LUCERNE, SWITZERLAND

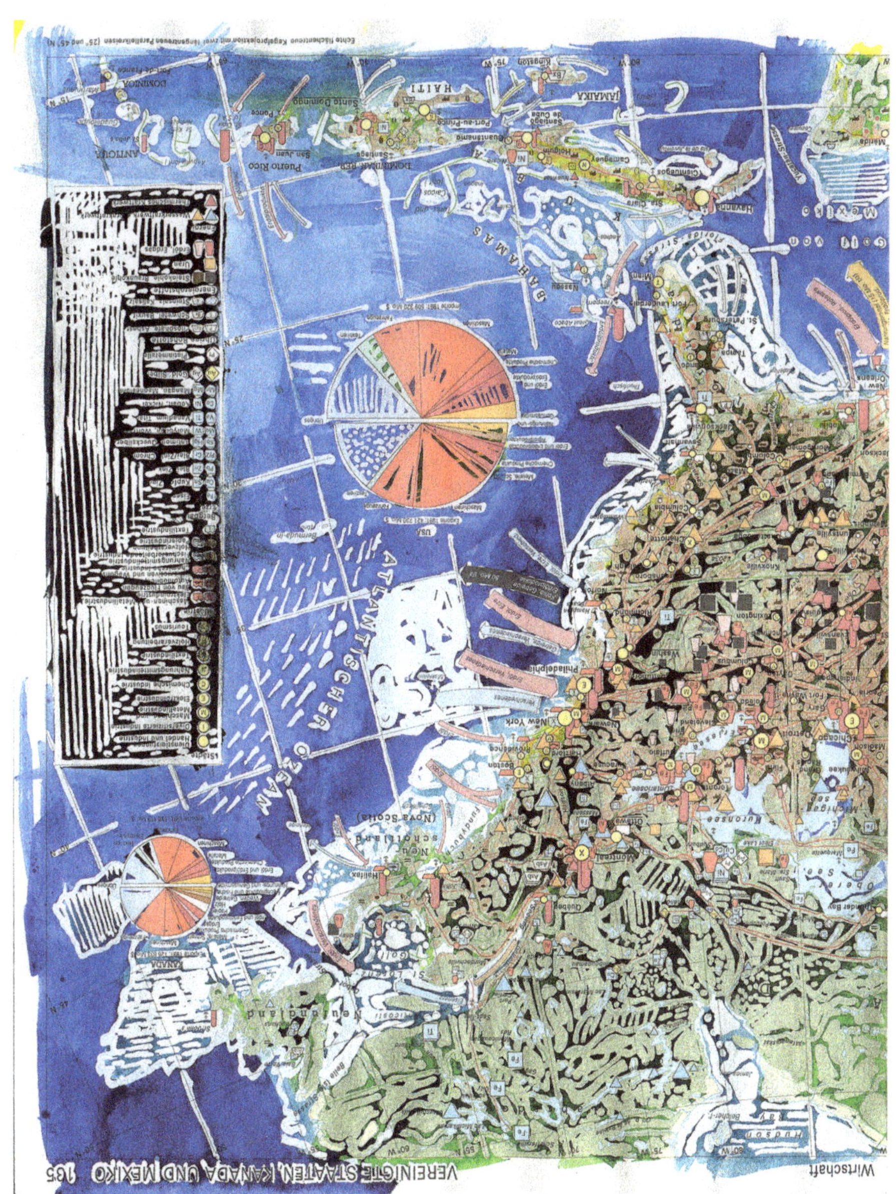

GULF OF MEXIKO

Ink on printed material, 23.8 cm x 31.2 cm

STEVE DALACHINSKY & YUKO OTOMO

NEW YORK, NEW YORK

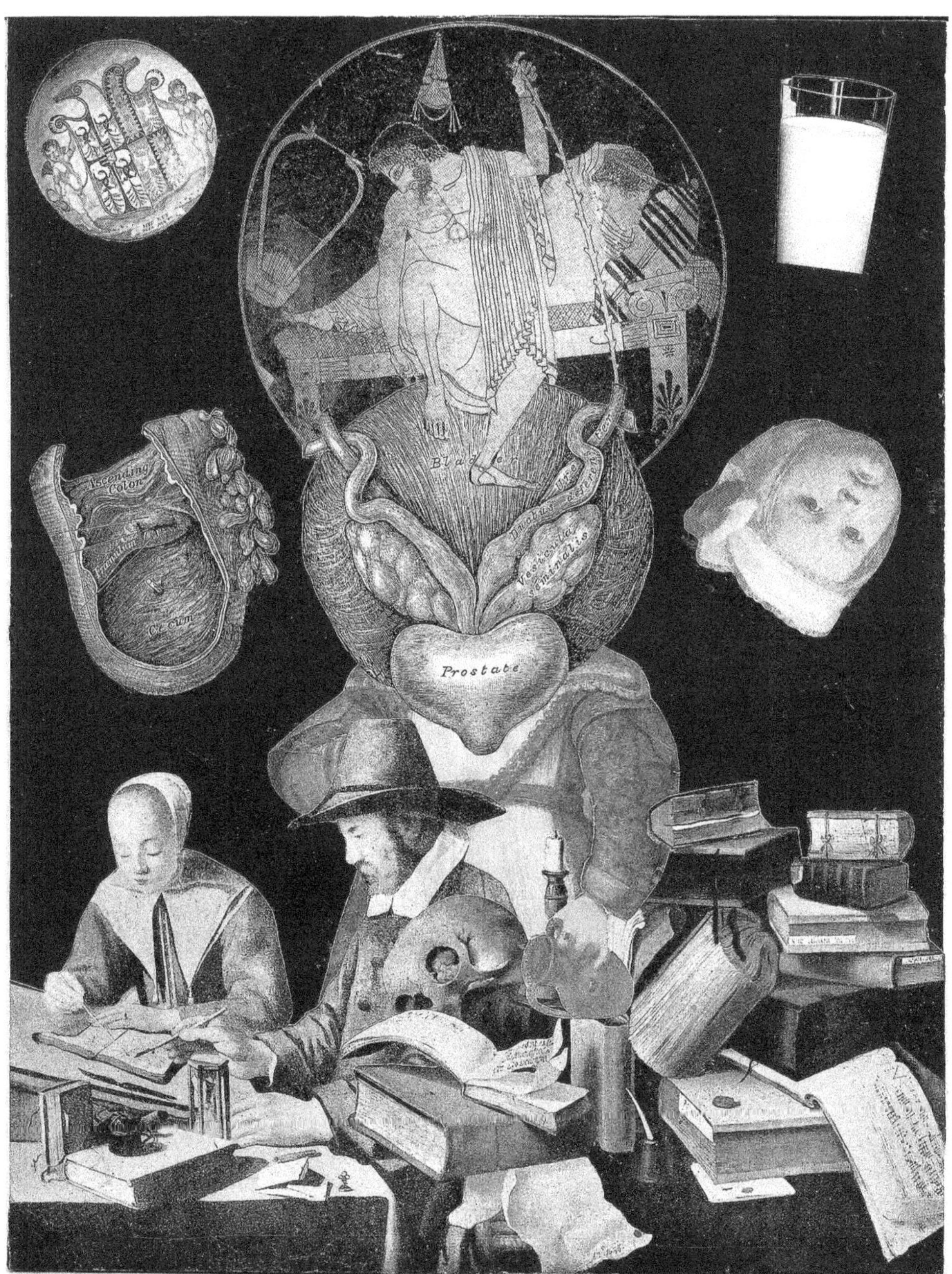

EXECUTIVE ORDERS

Collage, 8.5 in x 11 in

ROGER CONOVER

FREEPORT, MAINE

EXECUTIVE ORDER 207

By the authority vested in me as President by the Constitution and the Laws of the United States of America, it is hereby ordered that the Department of Preferred English (DOPE) shall remove all place names and visual signifiers acknowledging the presence of women, people of color, people with disabilities, people of non-heterosexual persuasion, and immigrants of non-European heritage with proper place names consistent with America's traditionally white, Anglo, hegemonic English-speaking culture, as codified in the 2025 edition of the Dictionary of Correct National Names and Standards. With this Executive Order, President Trump affirms that America's towns, cities, counties, territories, municipalities, lakes, rivers, mountains, islands, parks, and other features of the American landscape will forthwith be identified according to the language the President himself speaks.

By way of example, the state of Montana will henceforth be known as "Mountain". Colorado becomes "Red".
Florida becomes "Flowery".
Illinois becomes "Ordinary".
Nevada becomes "Snowy".

In the case of some place names, such as Oregon and Tennessee, where the origin of the name is unknown or disputed, the President hereby authorizes the board of the super-pac MAAA (Make America American Again) to coin a new name—subject to the President's approval.

Note from the Undersecretary of Language: When EO 207 goes into effect, these place-name changes will be reflected in publications and other media including but not limited to maps, software systems, textbooks, and apps. A future Executive Order (EO 212, still in draft) will apply these corrected place names to a much broader range of cultural settings and contexts (such as songs, literature, sports teams, etc.). Thus when the new Executive Order goes into effect, Credence Clearwater Revival's "Born on the Bayou" will be titled "Born on the Stream". Michael Jackson's "Chicago" will be titled "Skunk" (or "Onion", at the discretion of the MAAA board). "Save me San Francisco", by Train, will be renamed "Save Me Saint Francis". Leonard Cohen's "First We Take Manhattan" will become "First We Take a Thicket Where Wood Can Be Found To Make Bows." Under the President's new policy, many professional sports teams will be renamed. The Cincinatti Reds will become "The Curly-Haired Reds"; the Utah Jazz will be renamed "High Jazz", etc.

You get the idea. A much simpler, more pronounceable, more spellable, and more American approach to how we communicate our image of homeland to ourselves and others. The purpose of this policy is to Make America American Again! In the words of the President, the re-Americanization of America is long overdue.

RICH FERGUSON

LOS ANGELES, CALIFORNIA

DEAR AMERICA,

Where are your papers to show your citizenship?
What are your thoughts on democracy?

America, your erogenous zones have become hot-button issues. Your blood is poisoned with racism, radicalism, misinformation, and political polarization.

America, stop melting down bullets to make crowns for your molars. Stop building playgrounds for new Hitler youth.

And what about your thoughts on education? Can you read my letters or calculate the difference between your richest and poorest citizens?

Dear America, is that a knife in your back? A ticking bomb beneath your powdered wig? Your pork barrel politics are stuffed with trichinosis. Your eyes have gone freedom blind.

Dear America, why haven't I heard back from you? Are you in prison? If so, I'll send you a cake with a pen inside
      so you can write back.

JOHN S. PAUL

BROOKLYN, NEW YORK

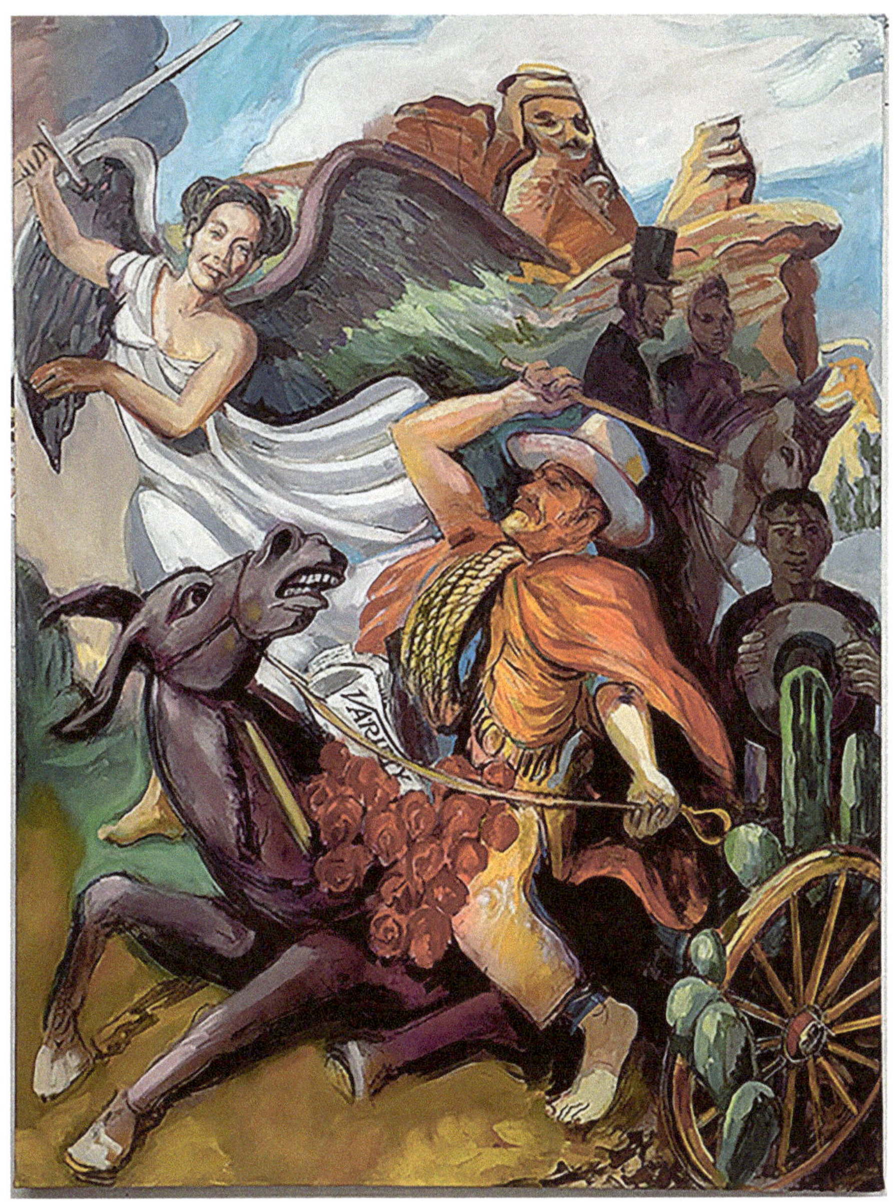

TURN BACK AT MOAB

Oil on canvas, 52 in x 80 in

CAROL DORF

BERKELEY, CALIFORNIA

SO EXACTLY WHAT ARE YOU AFRAID OF

I'm more afraid of the slow decline than dying.
Of losing my forward momentum   being stranded sans sticks
You're on your own   baby

I'm afraid of the oligarchs   buying all the papers
and shutting down   the news

I used to be afraid of dogs   was running then bitten   once

I used to be afraid of my father   though the shrink claimed he was
                              a paper tiger
He never hit the shrink   though the depressing abstracts in his office
                    would have been cause enough

I used to be afraid of my dreams   not the chase
                        but odd unpleasant interactions

I'm afraid of the line-up of billionaires
who believe they know more than any expert

Once when we finished the trail   in Yellowstone
                        the ranger warned us of the bear

I wasn't afraid of the bear   because it never crossed my path

I used to be afraid   of my mother disappearing   dying
Now that she's dead   and my father is long   gone   dead

I'm afraid   of breathing other people's   air
Of what it carries   one sister couldn't stop washing her hands
              touch the faucet and   now we all understand

I'm afraid   of what I'll learn   while scrolling

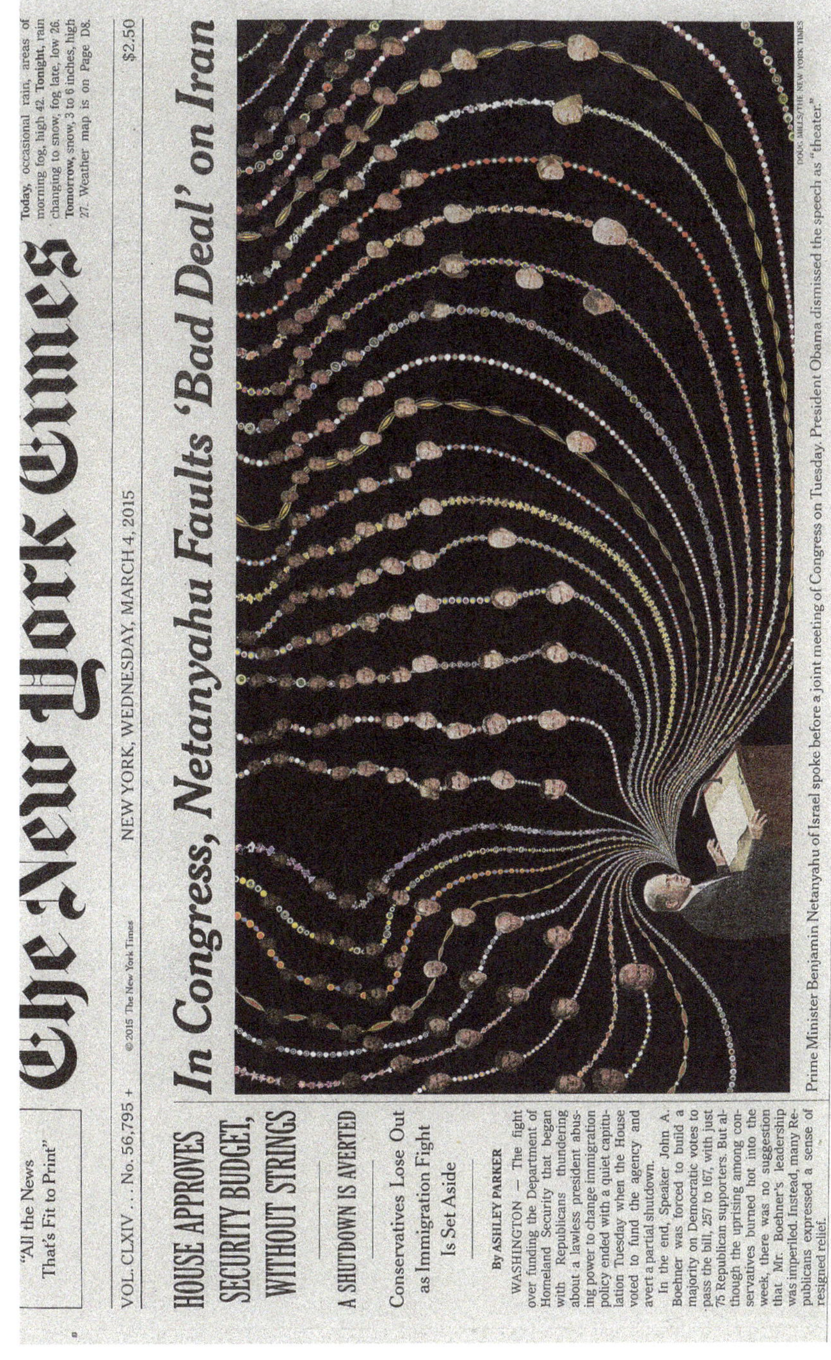

MARCH 4, 2015

Photo collage, acrylic, leaves, and archival inkjet print on paper, 50.75 in x 81.875 in

LET'S MAKE AN ART OF THE DEAL OR NO DEAL

Only a fool wouldn't accept
a luxury gift like this from Qatar
says the former AND current US Prez

and while the time might seem interminable
one day the orange debris will be cold in the ground
but for right here and now, he sits proudly in his seat with
co-fElon Musk right there by his side, ready to take off

DJT: The Qataris are fools for giving me such a plane.
EM: (wants to say it's a jet, but takes a hit of Ketamine
            instead.)

Cut to the Qataris (Saudis)

Note: #1 supports Hamas, #2 helped to fund 9/11

Q(S)1: So you are sure the remote pilot system
            will control the direction of the plane?
Q(S)2: It's a jet –and yes, we can fly the jet to any
            location we decide to target.

*Cut to the Department of Homeland Security with
Kristi Noem and VP J.D. Vance.*

KN: So you really think there is no security breech if
            we give the go ahead to the President to take off?
JDV: Absolutely! I see no problem whatsoever with him
            accepting their gift. Let'er RIP!!!

Back to the plane uhm—jet

DJT: I'm glad they were able to put toilets in each seat
EM: You can say that again! *(pees in seat)*
DJT: *(says it again)*

Back to the Qataris (Saudis)

Q(S)1: So exactly where do you think would be the most
            effective target?
Q(S)2: At first, I was leaning toward the Pentagon again,
            but the more I think about it—either Tehran or
            Tel Aviv would be most beneficial. You decide.

Back to the jet

DJT: I want a second plane to keep for myself.
ETM: Keep this one. Listen—I need to get out of here.

KAT GEORGES

NEW YORK, NEW YORK

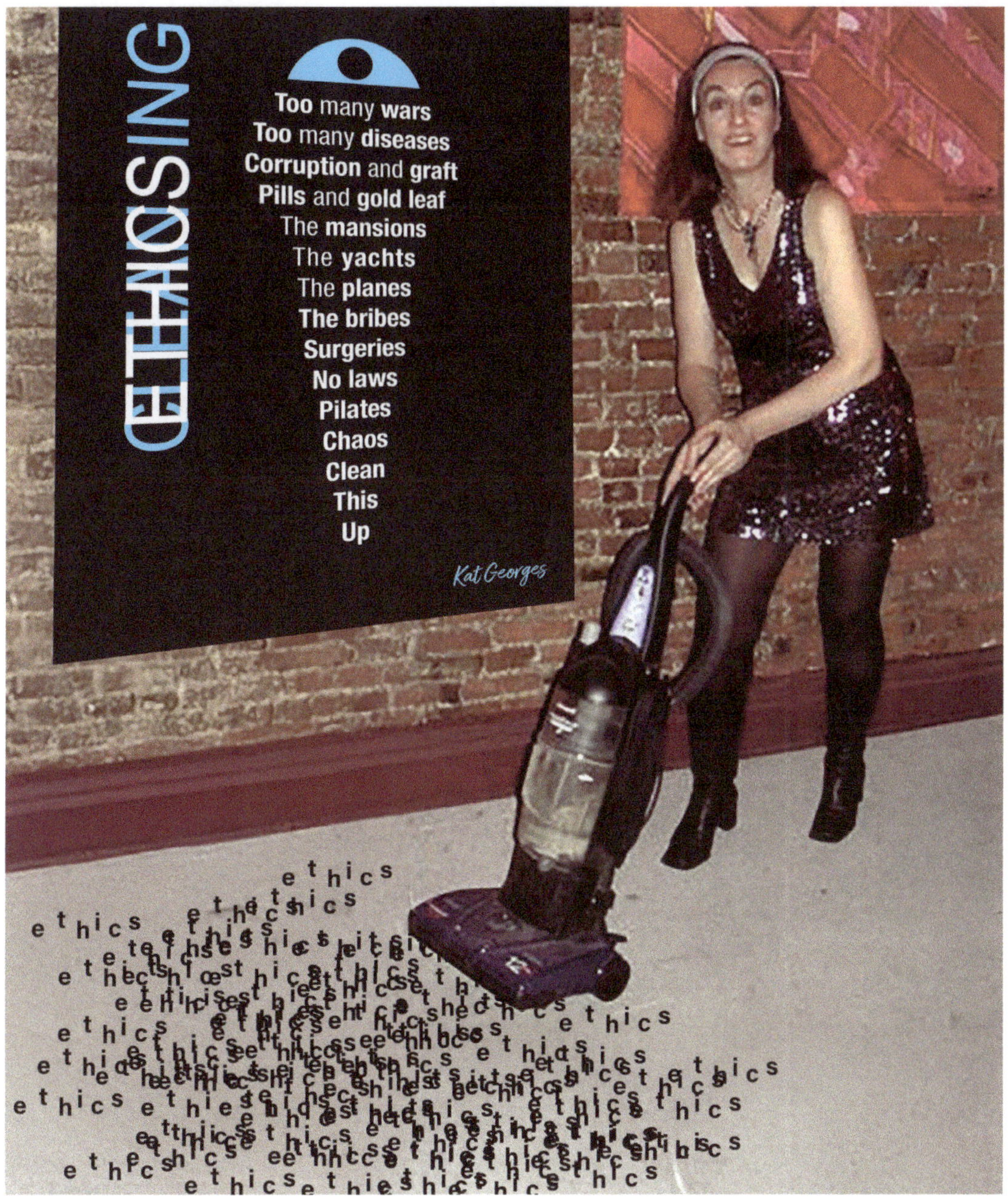

CLEAN THIS UP

Digital collage

JESSE McCLOSKEY

NEW YORK, NEW YORK

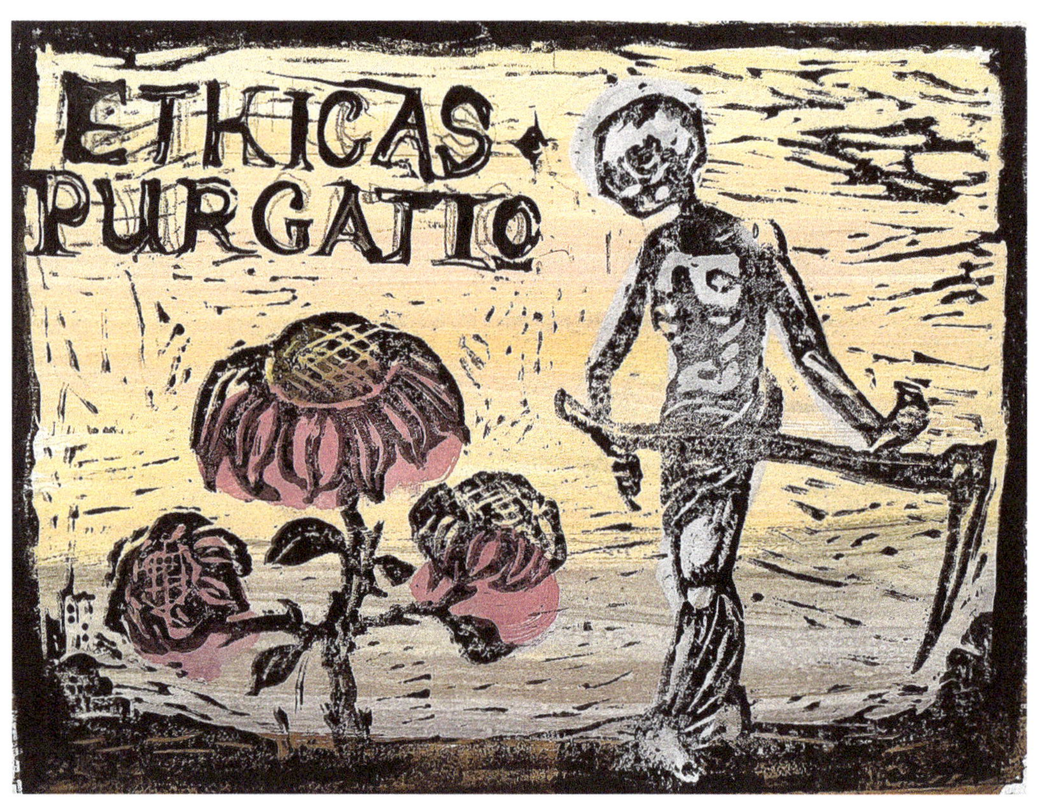

ETHICS PURGATIO

Mixed media, block print, 9 in x 12 in

NICCA RAY

NEW YORK, NEW YORK

ETHICS ARE THE WHISPER

ethics whisper through the corridors

of the buildings where

the men abandon rule of law

and women

walk the halls

taking notes

of what's been said before

their papers falling

from folders

onto the floor

a men's shoeprint

blocking out the question

where have ethics gone

and a child of the future

asks his mother

mommy what are ethics

and she stares blankly at the wall

and says i used to know

but for the life of me can't remember

it was so long ago.

NINA ZIVANCEVIC

PARIS, FRANCE

BROKEN HEART

I met an old New York friend the other day

And he was delighted that we could still laugh it out

We sat in a café near Luxembourg gardens until 5 and we were

Laughing non-stop under the winter sun

I forgot how we used to laugh and we got along so well

And what's the problem with your heart, he asked.

Well, it's been broken several times in my life but this

Time it's not a metaphor but quite a physical thing, I added

You did well not to go to Madagascar and become a lemur, he said

But true love is hard to forget

The invisible depression settles in and you lose desire to buy fruits

To buy shoes   to laugh with friends in a café

On we go and start new movements new faces old new stars

Yes it has something to do with desire

And its loss . . . it kind of slipped down through the crack

Of your broken heart, it's good to know

It is still there, hidden in that cavity

My heart I mean, or is it?

GORAN LIŠNJIĆ

OSIJEK, CROATIA

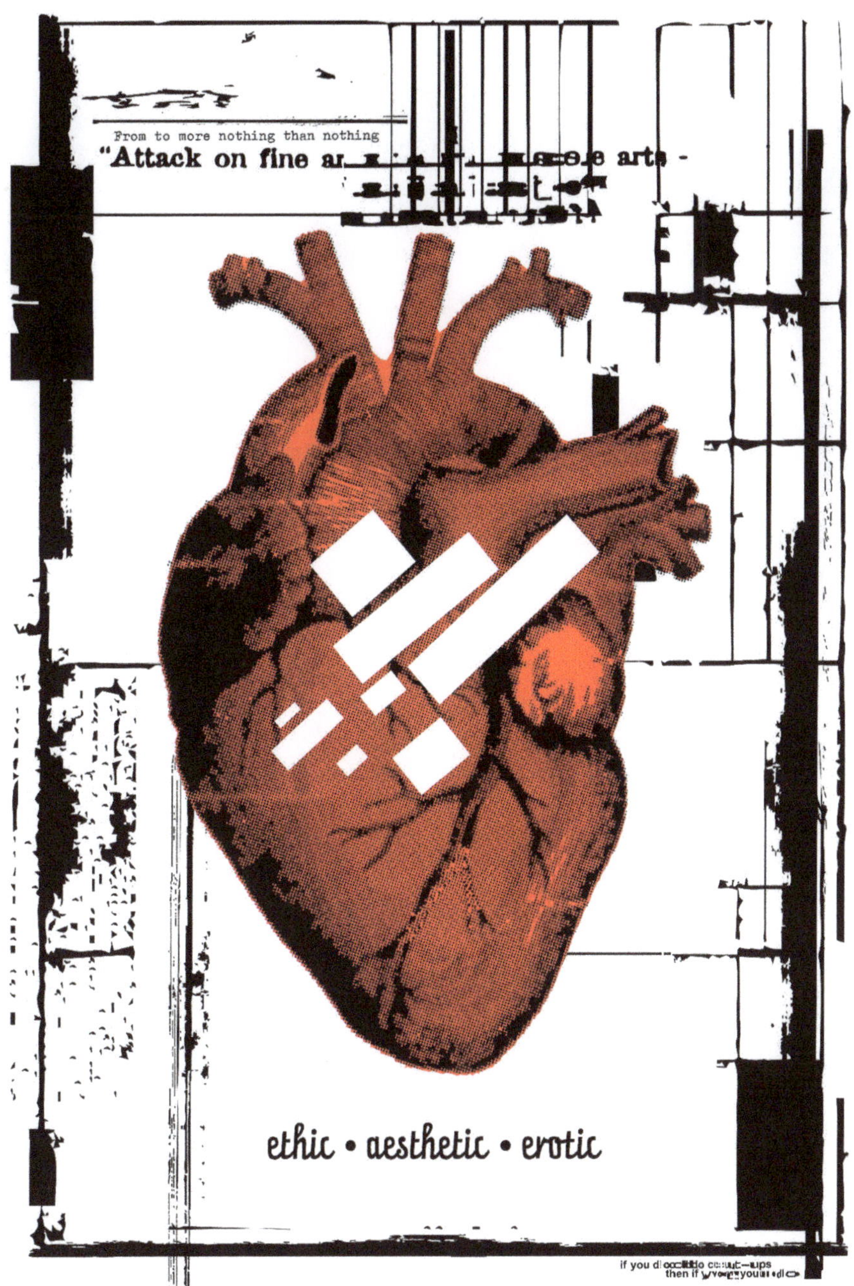

ETHIC / AESTHETIC / EROTIC

Graphic, 297 mm x 420 mm

W. K. STRATTON

ROUND ROCK, TEXAS

ETHICS

and so I remember a friend Laura Nyro

obsessed/thought she was better than Dylan

though I see no point in such

comparisons/artists sculpt what they

sculpt/leave it at that/a Carolina wren

mother's favorite bird

teaches me a whole new definition of

aggrandizement as an infected dawn gray

spreads

lightless

I stand naked in protected seclusion on my clean

back porch and sip black Folger's/lava hot, as I

like it/offensive to all coffee snobs, as I like

it/and celebrate morning breeze on my skin/I

recall Eli's Coming as a good song, even if it was

too often buffed to cubic zirconia, making it

meaningless/it is the flaw that makes the

diamond perfect, a lesson I learned way back in

high school/likewise ethics must be marred to be

ethical/In my mind I hear not Nyro but Johnny

Cash's cover of Dylan's Wanted Man and recollect

getting lost in Juarez when I could still sing.

MAUREEN ALSOP

QUEENSLAND, AUSTRALIA

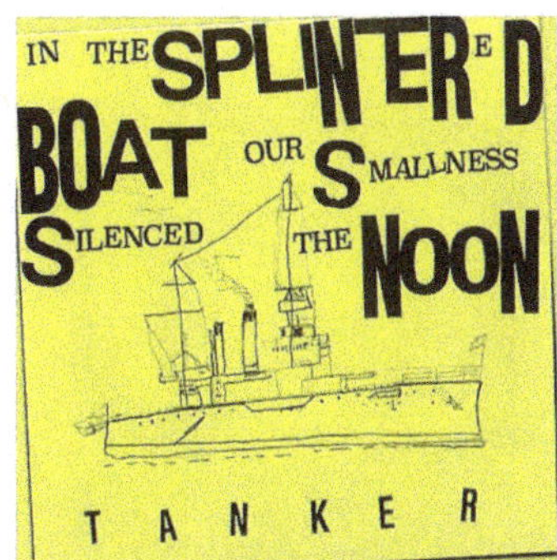

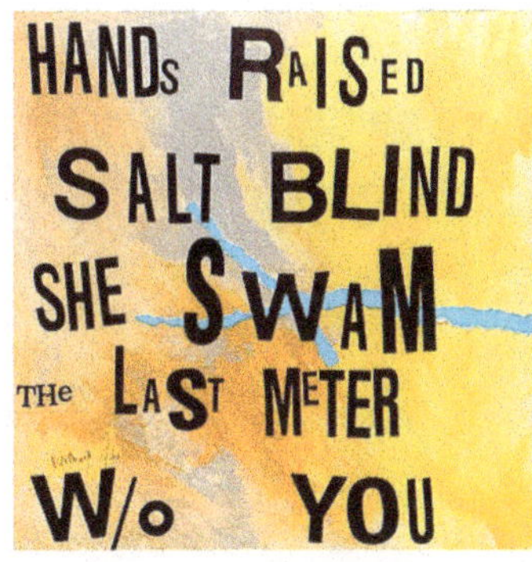

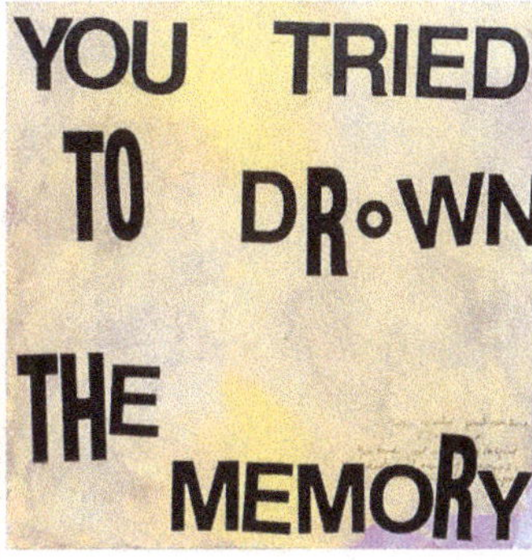

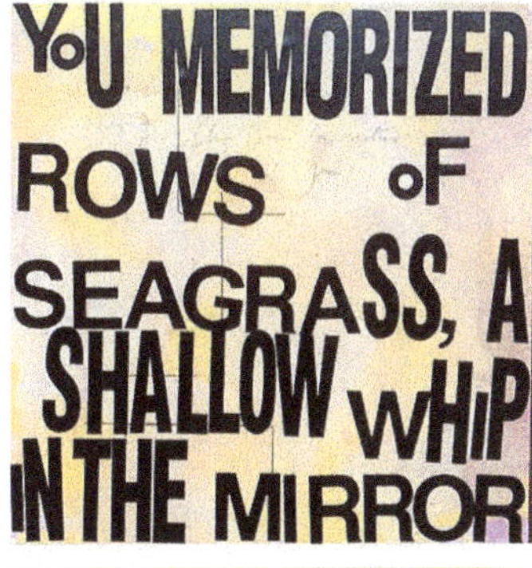

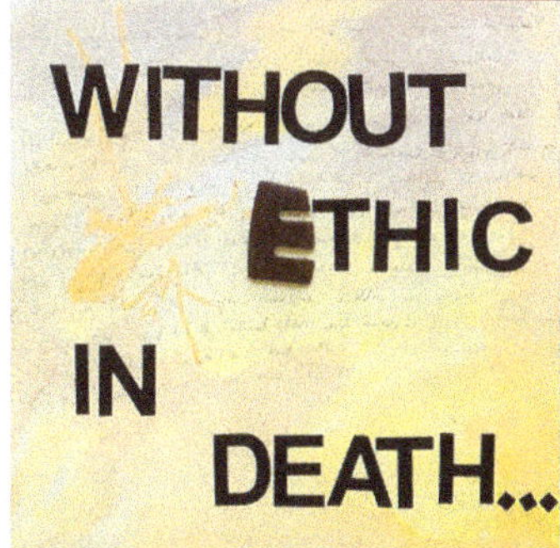

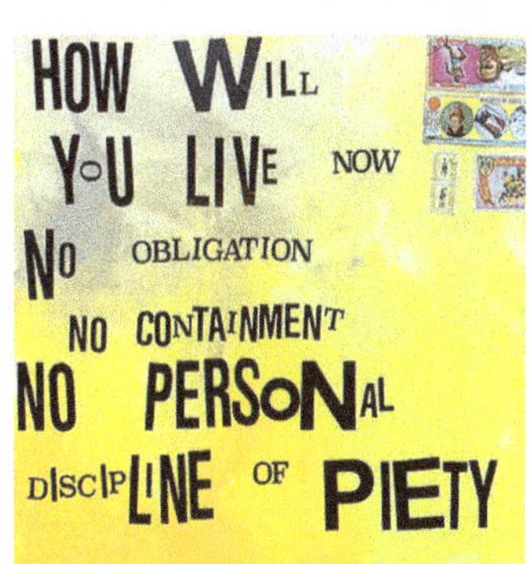

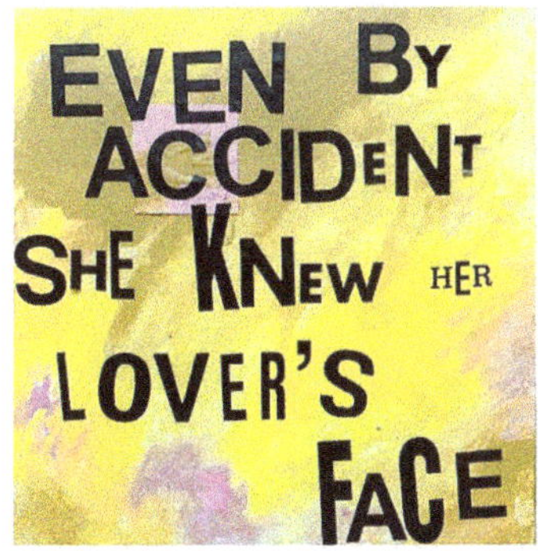

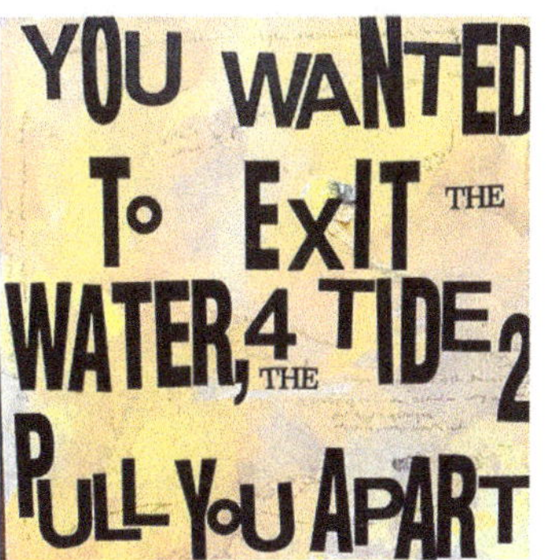

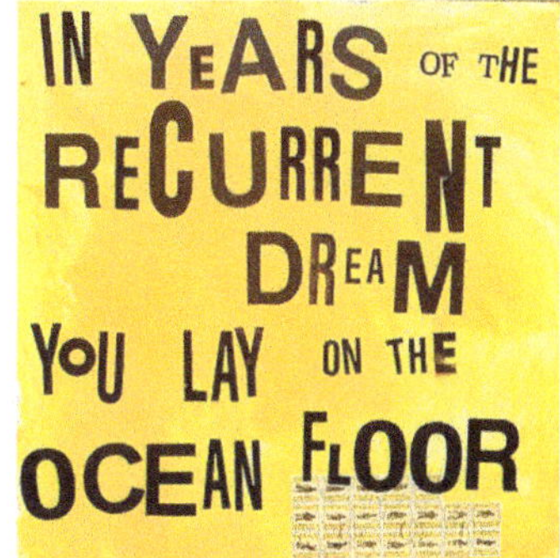

WITHOUT ETHIC

Visual poem, mixed media, 40 cm x 40 cm

MATTHEW HUPERT

NEW YORK, NEW YORK

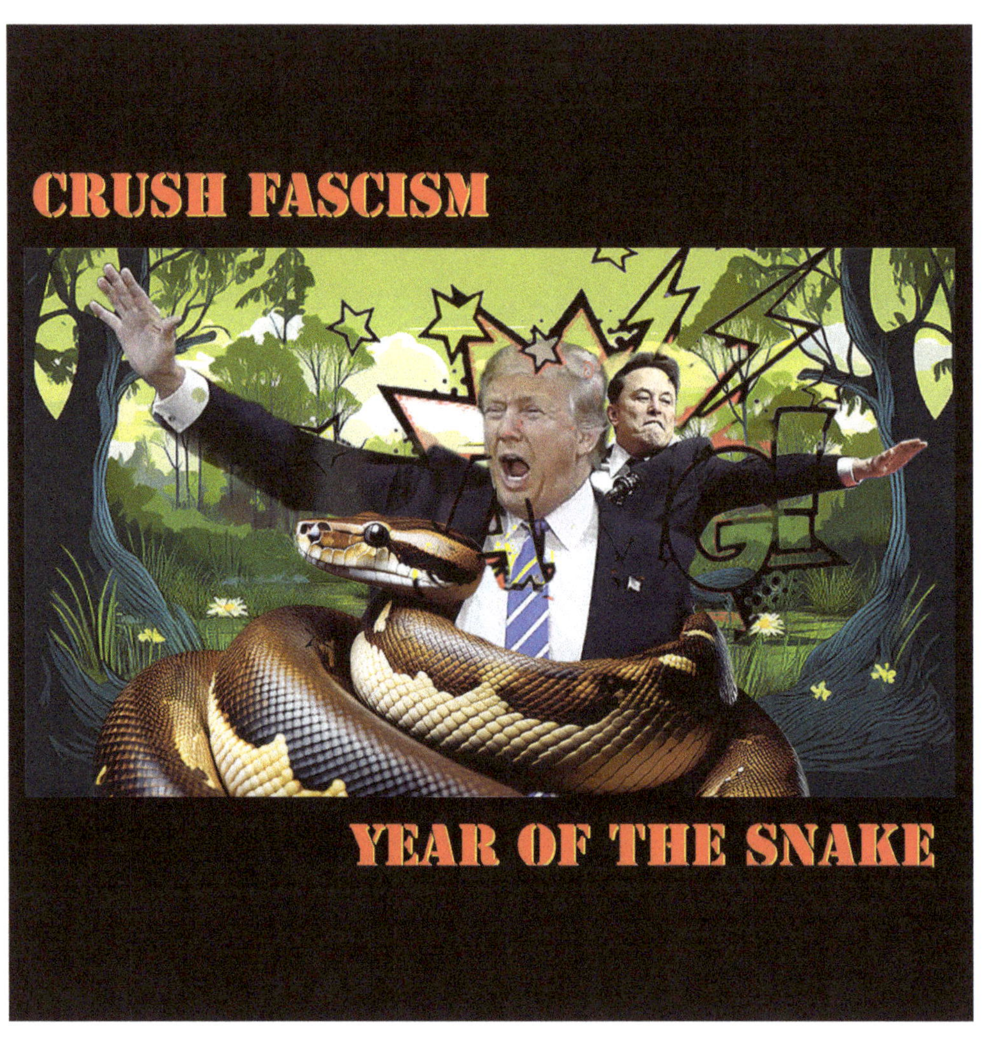

YEAR OF THE SNAKE

Digital collage, 2700 px x 2700 px

C. MEHRL BENNETT

COLUMBUS, OHIO

IS IT A DREAM?

On the first of February
She slept and dreamt of
Ink draining into the sink
Heart shapes drawn with
The ashes of burnt books
Money piles on Wall Street
An increase in homelessness

On the first of March she awoke to
Government agencies flattened
Birds tangled in electric cords
No more glaciers in Alaska
Her head is shaved and he
Stares at her, smiling close,
He says, "No more woke folk."

VOXX VOLTAIR

LAS VEGAS, NEVADA

DEATHICS

The words simmered
For months, in my mind

I could not seem to find meaning
In the world
In the actions of inhumanity
Towards humanity
The Insanity of sanity

Lachesis, the thread
Unraveled by Clotho
Cut by Atropo

This botched web
Of reality
Birth of the Schizoid Spider
Wrapping itself into
Its own victim

The Worm Ourbouros
Finally makes sense
The snake that eats
Its own tale

GERALD NICOSIA

KNOXVILLE, TENNESSEE

POEM FOR THOSE WHO HAVE
LIFTED THEIR VOICE

for Lawrence Ferlinghetti

It is a time of total lostness

When the soul of America lies frozen

In a powerless homeless shelter in Dallas

Or abandoned in the hallway

Of an overfilled hospital in L.A.

When I look to every mailbox

For offers of help

When the numbers on gas stations

Echo like the body count in Vietnam

When a PEN executive tells me

"You can't read a poem against injustice

Because you haven't paid your dues"

When a Marine sergeant in a wheelchair

Who says "Don't kill"

Knows more than The President of the United States

When Kenneth Rexroth lies buried

Under blood-red leaves

And the grass no longer grows and

The rivers no longer flow

For all the petrochemicals

You cannot write lyric poems

In a time of utter hatred and mean spirit

I have only my heart to offer

However little it matters—

But if I did not offer it

The sin would be compounded

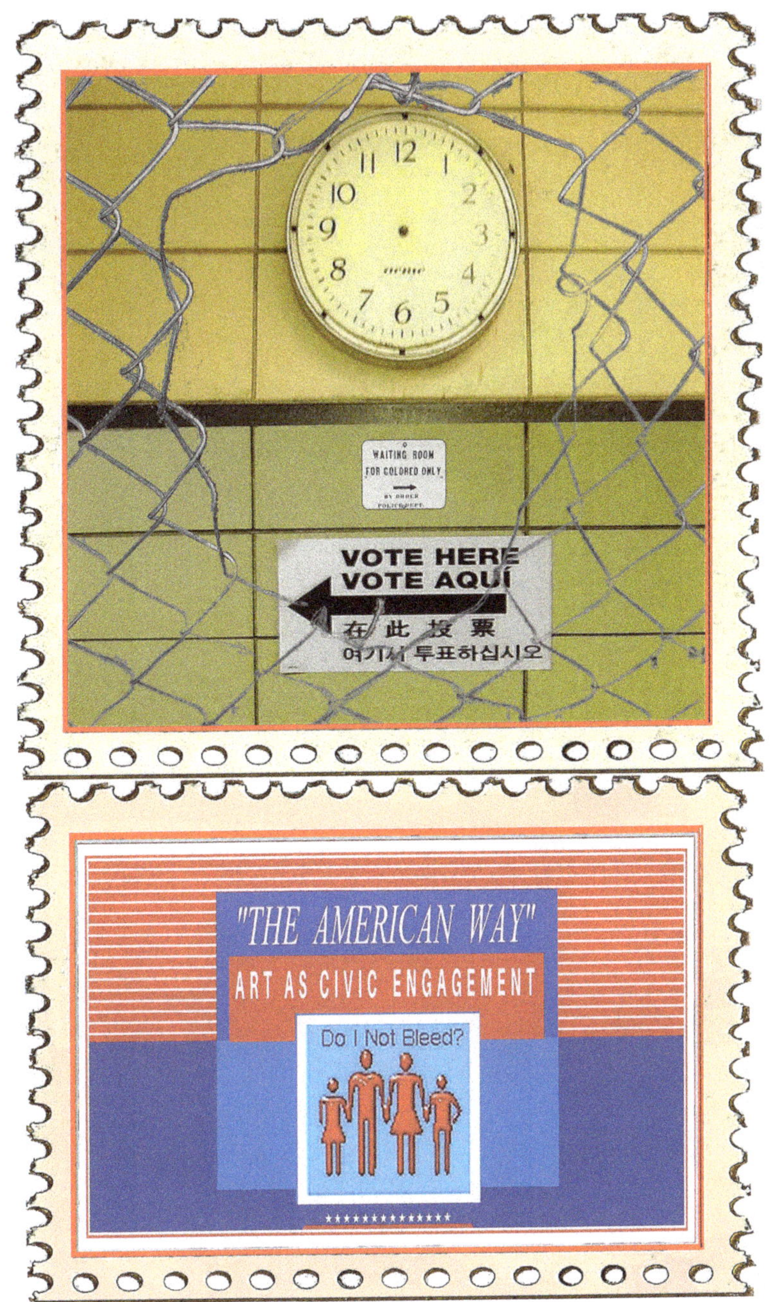

ALMOST OUT OF TIME

Collage

ELZBIETA ZDUNEK

BERLIN, GERMANY

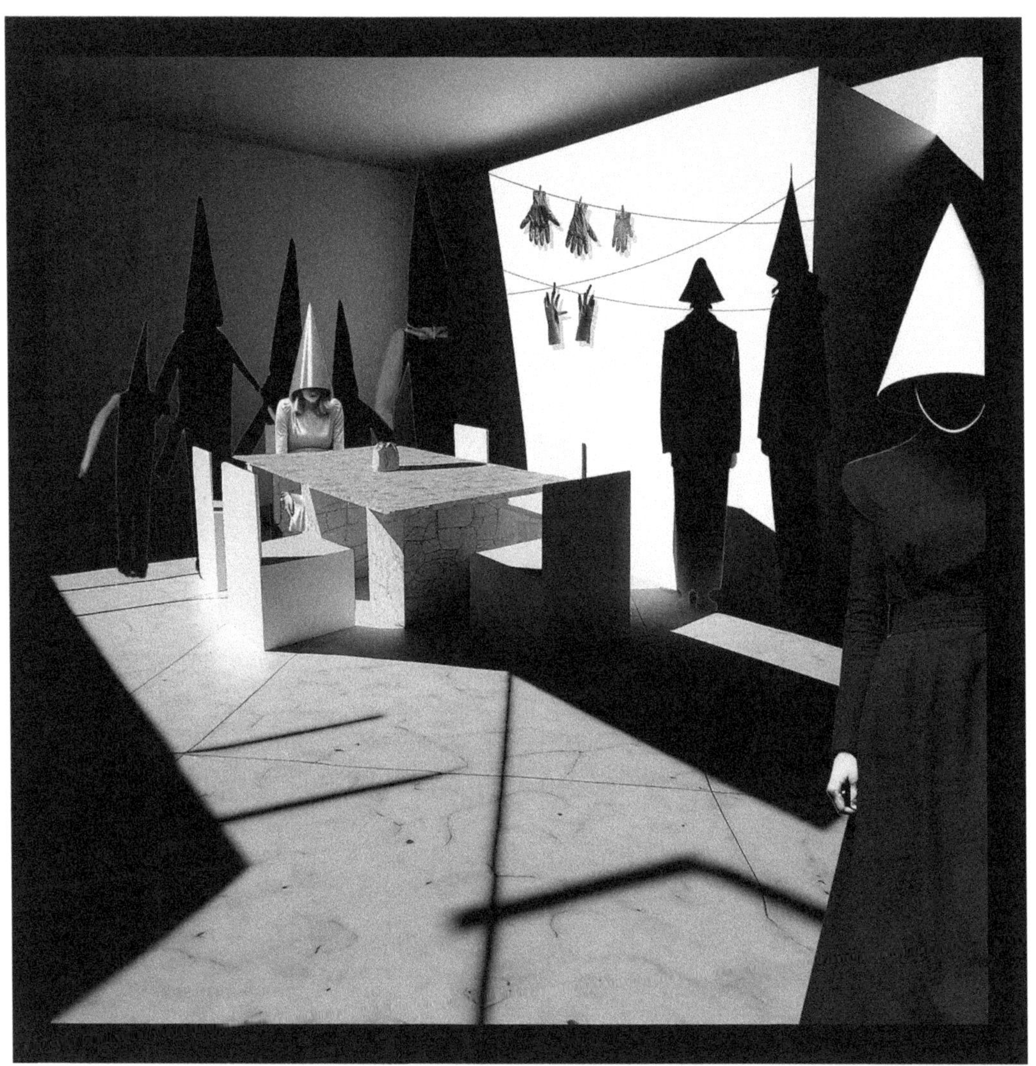

RECOIL

Collage, 30 cm x 30 cm

JeFF STUMPO

LITCHFIELD, NEW HAMPSHIRE

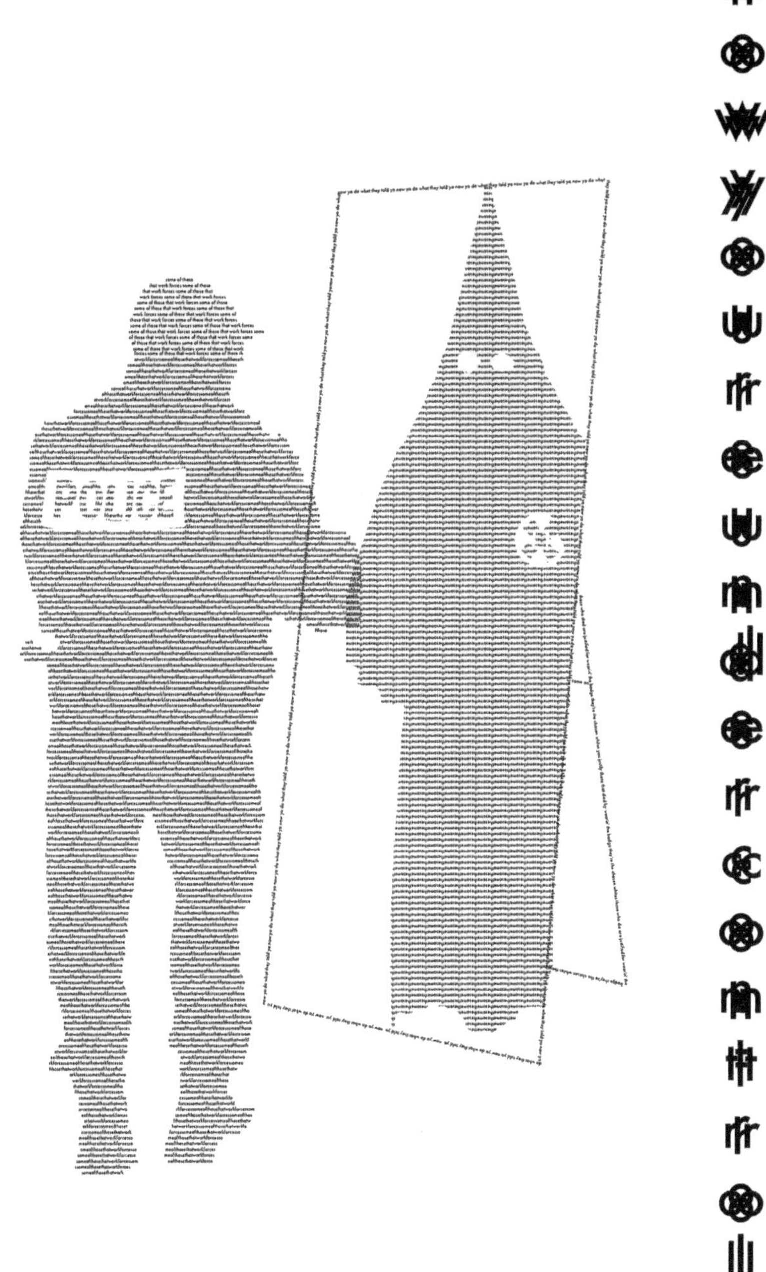

UNDER CONTROL

Concrete poem, 2400 px x 3600 px

A. D. WINANS
SAN FRANCISCO, CALIFORNIA

MAKE AMERICA GREAT AGAIN

I will not pledge allegiance
to the flag of the U.S.
And every thing it no longer
stands for.

I will not bow down
to corporate America
and its religious right.

I will not can not accept
your moral bankruptcy
your greenback God
buying and selling lives
on the stock exchange.

I will not bow down to a country
where assassins determine
the course of history
whose papal church has its own bank.

America you have become
one big insane asylum
your manic-depressive innkeepers
waging war on the masses.

Your henchmen stand proud
on your purple majestic mountains
kiss the cold stone faces
on Mount Rushmore
you a Mafia Don
with the cold kiss of death
on your breath.

SILVIO SEVERINO

CORK, IRELAND

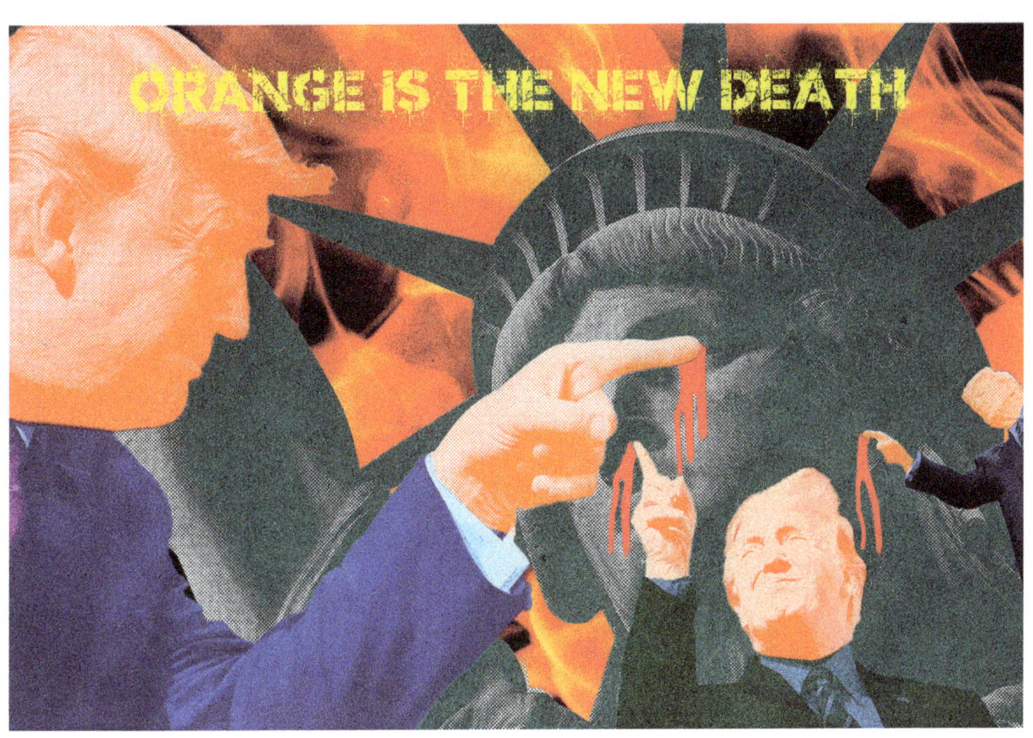

ORANGE IS THE NEW DEATH

Digital collage

S.A. GRIFFIN

LOS ANGELES, CALIFORNIA

COMBOVER THE BARBARIAN

My fellow Americans, what I say is what I say. We need to build walls. Lots of beautiful walls. And trust me on this; we have a lot to tear down.

I have a massive plan, because frankly, I have a massive brain, one of the biggest and most beautiful in the world. Nobody has ever seen such a big, beautiful brain. My brain can tell the difference between a lion and a rhinoceros. Imagine that! I can promise you that I will have very stupid people working on behalf of the American people that won't know what they're doing, and I ought to know.

I can also promise you that I have no point, and no point of view, and that is the point. My administration will be one disaster after another, making less and less sense with unbelievable foolishness and historical arrogance. Frankly, the list of humiliations goes on and on.

As a leader with huge hands, and believe me, they are huge, probably the hugest ever, I will have no obligation to honor governments or agreements. Through the art of the steal, my scorched earth values shall continue to inspire military interventions. I will bomb the shit out of everything, including Greenland, and they will love me for it bigly. The embarrassment of any longstanding peace will not be tolerated anywhere I can build hotels.

Led by Tech Bro President E-Wrong, our Dogebag team with their big balls, I mean these guys have big balls, you've never seen such big balls dragging on the ground, but not as big as mine, are working tirelessly to dismantle all our institutions, helping chaos grow and prosper, firing and institutionalizing countless federal workers and veterans, who I love dearly. Nobody loves our suckers and losers like me.

I look forward to a long history of failed policies and continued conflict creating political vacuums, suffocating democracy like a weak little kitten. Because quite frankly, I don't like weak little kittens, do you? They are weak and little, and I like big strong kittens, like my beautiful immigrant wife Melanoma. I also don't like the horrible Haitians who eat them, they are all kitten killers, gang members and drug lords and should be deported. Can you imagine that, eating helpless little kittens when you can drown them in your gold toilet?

I intend to build great Bitcoin pyramids, like they did in Egypt a long, long time ago using their big brains, but not as big as mine, and those pharaohs didn't do too badly with their big pyramids, you know? Well, maybe you don't, but they sure loved their gold! But nobody loves gold more than me, especially my lovely gold toilet where I can sit and read top secret documents and then wipe my great white butt with them. I am thinking about renaming my ass the Gulf of America. My huge Bitcoin pyramids will be the hugest in world history, just like my huge ass, taking advantage of America and the world, making it all more unstable than ever when my beautiful pointy pyramids finally fall.

Without diplomacy, war and aggression will be my first disorder of business. So, believe me when I say that I will surround myself with some very horrible people that are friends of mine. I love stupid, horrible, people. I really do, and they love me.

I will be a ratings machine! My face will be a beautiful live stream twenty-four hours a day. And here's the good news, I will look so good in those pictures, especially my mug shot on the $250 bill.

Lacking any coherent foreign policy, I will engage in industrial espionage supported by nation building lies, selling oil based on hostility, singing my false song of globalism reinforced by many, many magnificent tariffs, especially tariffs against 'Gina. I hate 'Gina, they are all very nasty people over there. I would like to grab every one of those nasty 'Ginas with my huge hands.

I will turn my back on our allies and refuse refugees that don't have millions of dollars for an American Depressed Gold Card, denying anyone without money entry into my More Lumbago Country Club.

Under my administration, and with the help of my Faux News cabinet and the Supremes, and I do love my Supremes, aren't they amazing? They're just the best, they do whatever I tell them, no consumer will ever again view the world through a clear lens. I will fully embrace the Heritage Foundation that doesn't exist, inspiring me to risk radical violence. Think of it, senseless policies desperately in need of global warming, fooling ourselves with artificial intelligence to mount the worst attacks on democracy in history.

These are my goals as leader of America the Super Luxury Store, with two baby dolls in every household. I challenge anyone who plays by the rule of law because as ruler of America and the world, I don't play by any rules except my own.

I will watch while the country falls apart. There is no victory.

I alone can fix it, because I alone can break it.

Thank you for the opportunity to thank me.

ORCHID SPANGIAFORA

WYNCOTE, PENNSYLVANIA

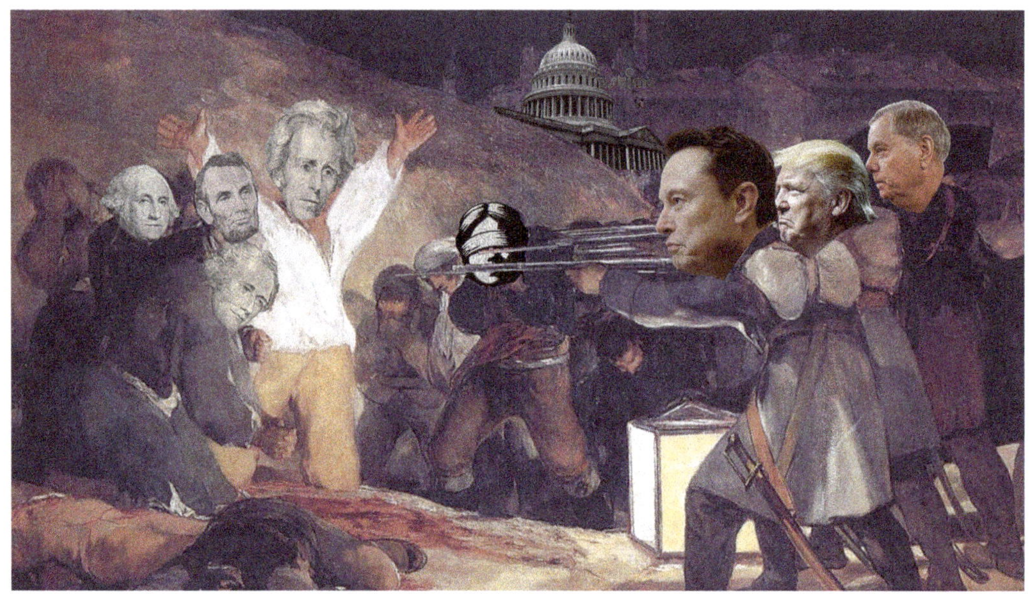

YOU'RE FIRED

Jpeg, 1575 px x 873 px

THOMAS FUCALORO

STATEN ISLAND, NEW YORK

GOD SAVES CERTAIN PEOPLE

Pork belly futures and other bellies
rely on the determination of those who have
very little in the tank but a lot in the gusto.
My table runneth over. My salivary
glands stink. Porked belly futures basted
yellow fist right this animal of syntax
an ocean of getting it wrong in the name
of making it look right. It all looks right
in the name of wrong. This god is hungry.
I say this god is hungry. Bite down on this
coin, feed this drain, my tuxedo has a numb
stain. Blunder what is coughed up. Fly to the
handle. Off with its head. This food here is
not enough. These fools here are not enough.
Let the pork bellied futures know you are doing
just fine. Swine if you're nasty. What I am
learning is that god is on their side, god is
what they say, he got that bullet to sway,
it nipped his ear it heightened the muting
of calm and care, and the Dow hit a record
high the following Monday and poork belly
futures and other bellies rely on the determination
of those who have very little in the tank but
a lot of gusto. I believe god controls the
economy. And certain people's fates.
Protects some. Not all. But I believe.
That's all that matters. What I believe.
My table. My. My. My. My. Me. Me. Me.
But I believe, yes, I believe. I believe in.

*

You know what I really believe:

The devil made that bullet sway

And God was holding the rifle.

VALERIE SOFRANKO

PITTSBURGH, PENNSYLVANIA

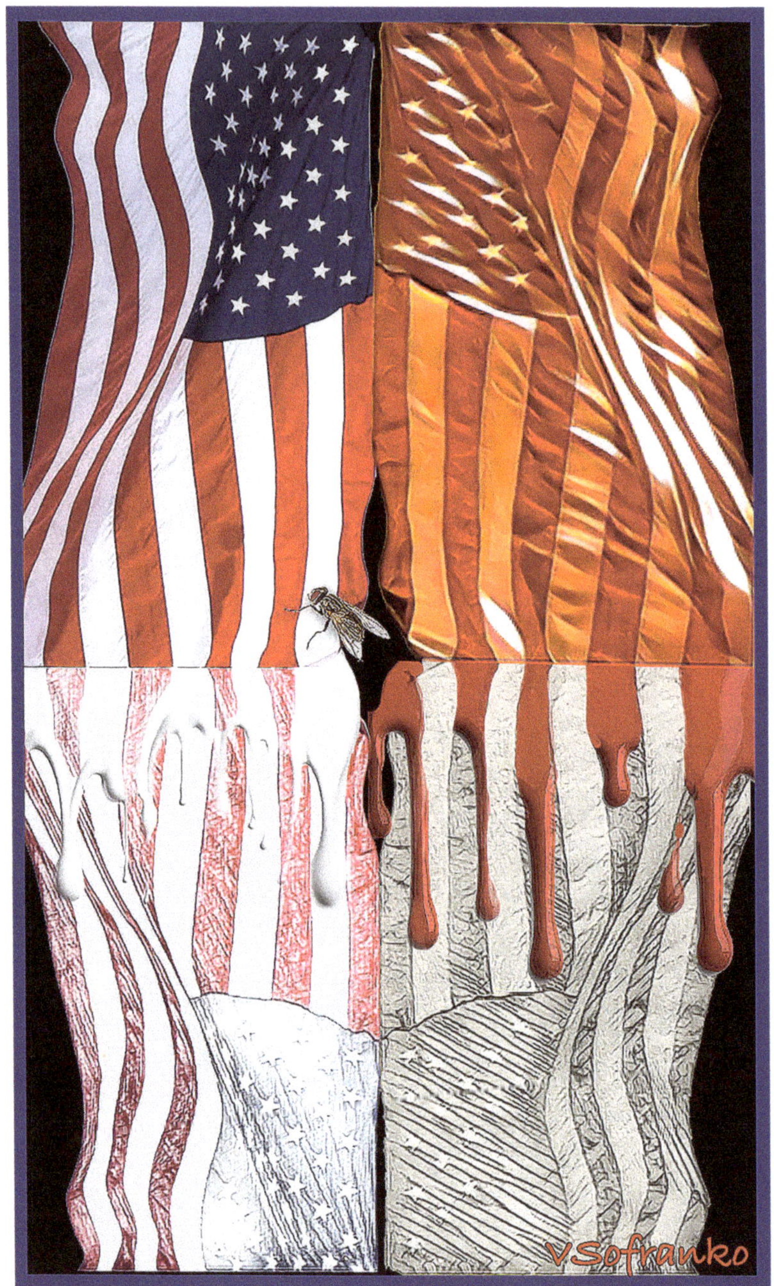

ALL FOR THE PRICE OF EGGS

Digital collage, 10 in x 16.5 in

LINDA KLEINBUB

MIDDLE VILLAGE, NEW YORK

ARE WE A NATION BRAINWASHED?

Are we a nation brainwashed?

Has our short-term memory failed us?

Are we a nation living in fear because another

immigrant is looking for the American dream?

How did we become a nation so divided by hate?

Afraid of our neighbor because his

skin tone doesn't match our own?

Why are we so fearsome of the same-sex lovers?

Or the transgender person who struggles

To find a peaceful existence living in their skin?

America, my grandfather came to you illegally.

At the turn of the century working on a boat from Poland,

He jumped ship in Canada, walked for months to New York City.

Unable to speak English, very little money in his pockets.

He struggled to make a living here.

America, what happened?

Doesn't Lady Liberty still stand

in the harbor welcoming the tired and poor?

America, will you remain

the land of the free, the home of the brave?

MIKE CALLAGHAN

TORONTO, CANADA

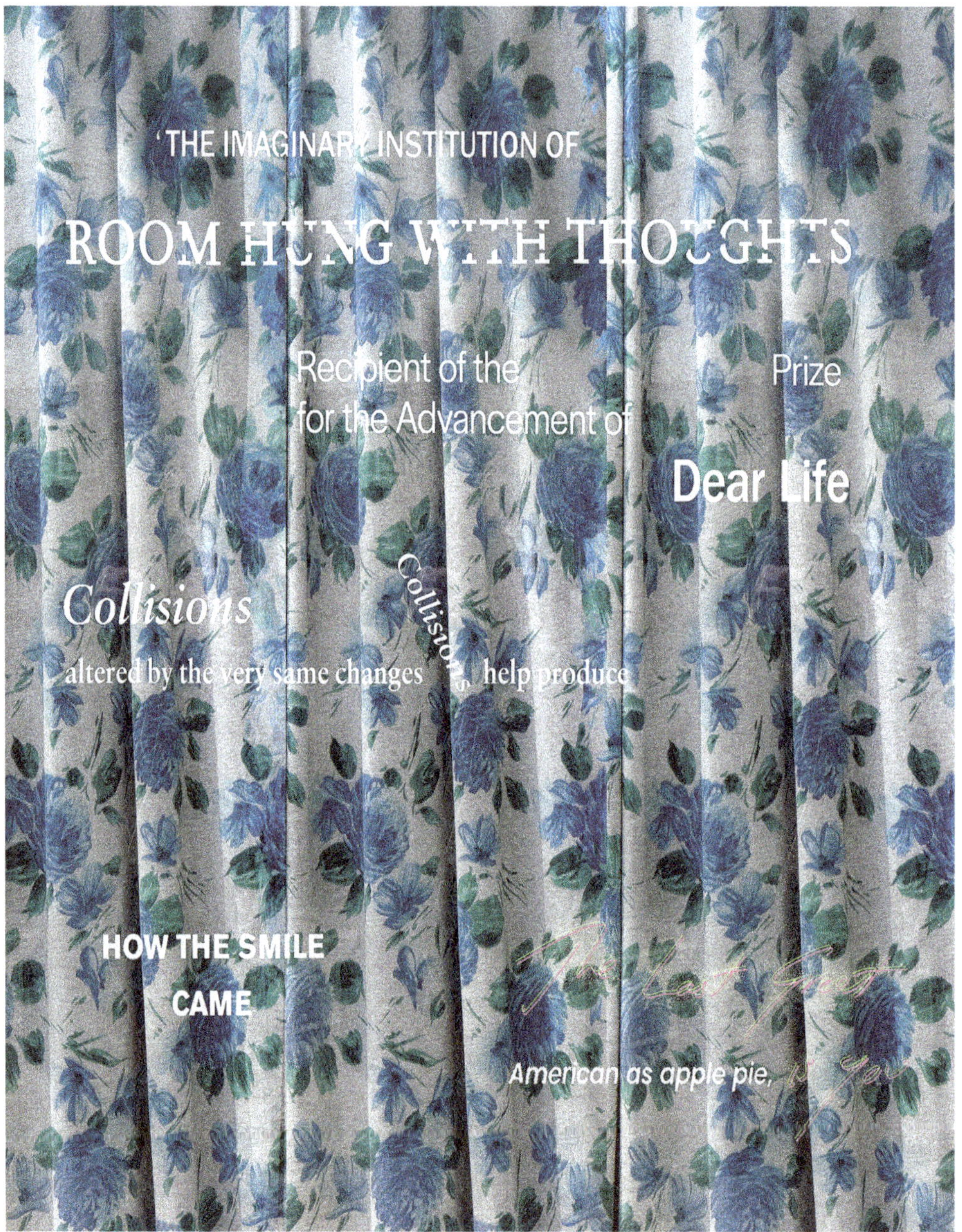

THE LAST GREAT IS YOU

Digital collage, 8 in x 10 in

PAUL DORN

ZURICH, SWITZERLAND

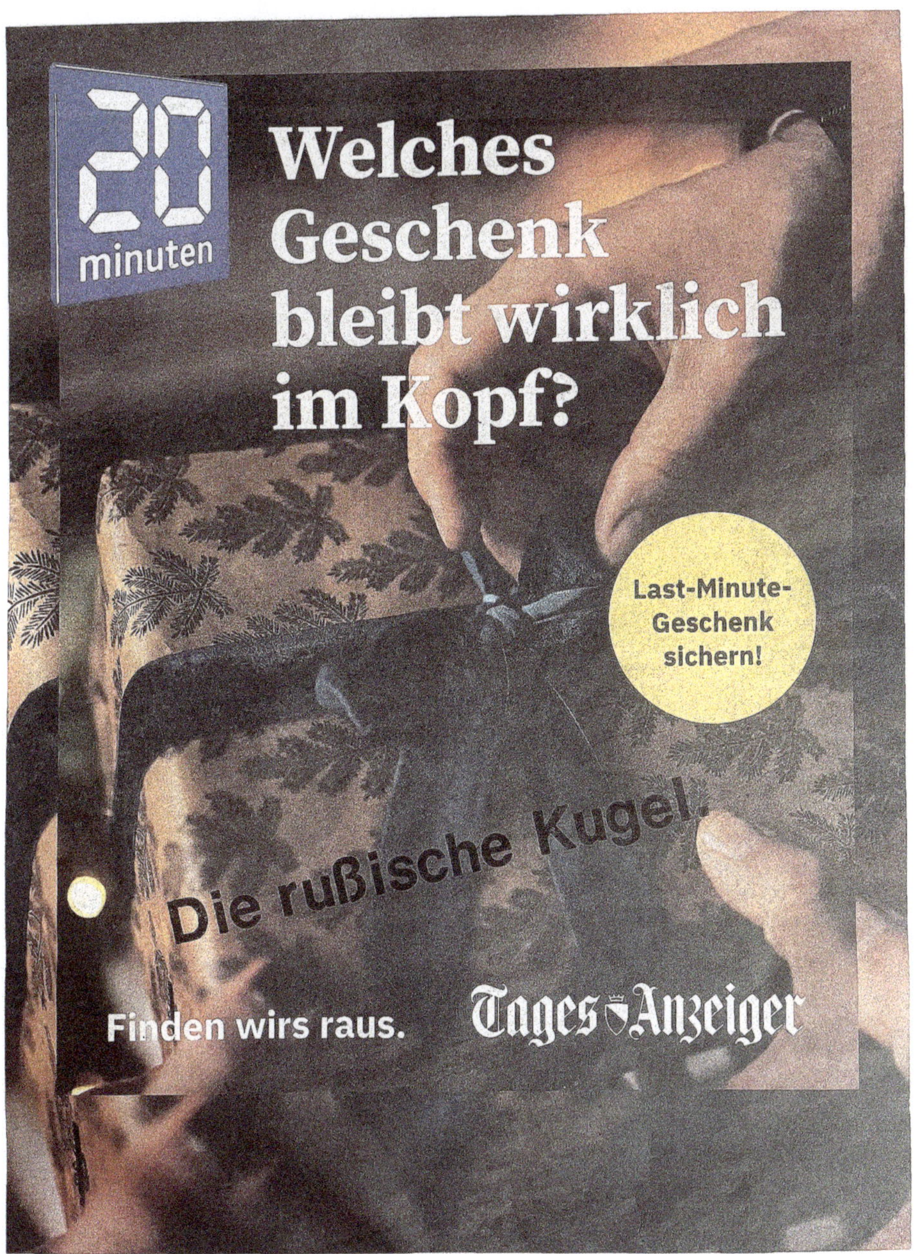

RUSSIAN BULLET

Collage, newspaper page, stamps, 22 cm x 28 cm

HANNAH BEHRENS

HEILOO, THE NETHERLANDS

LITTLE GAZAS EVERYWHERE

this is the dust of disappearing
worlds gone in fractions of second
broken glass and falling walls
buildings split open
revealing the levels of their former lives

crushed sons and daughters
just left there under
dust and smoke
with their nervous system collapsing
teeth chattering like skeletons
into splintering silent sadness

the empty sky spies on everyone
including the dead
down
to the last breath
buzzing toward the ground
a whole nation
massacred by a blackened horizon
it might take a thousand years
to rebuild what is lost

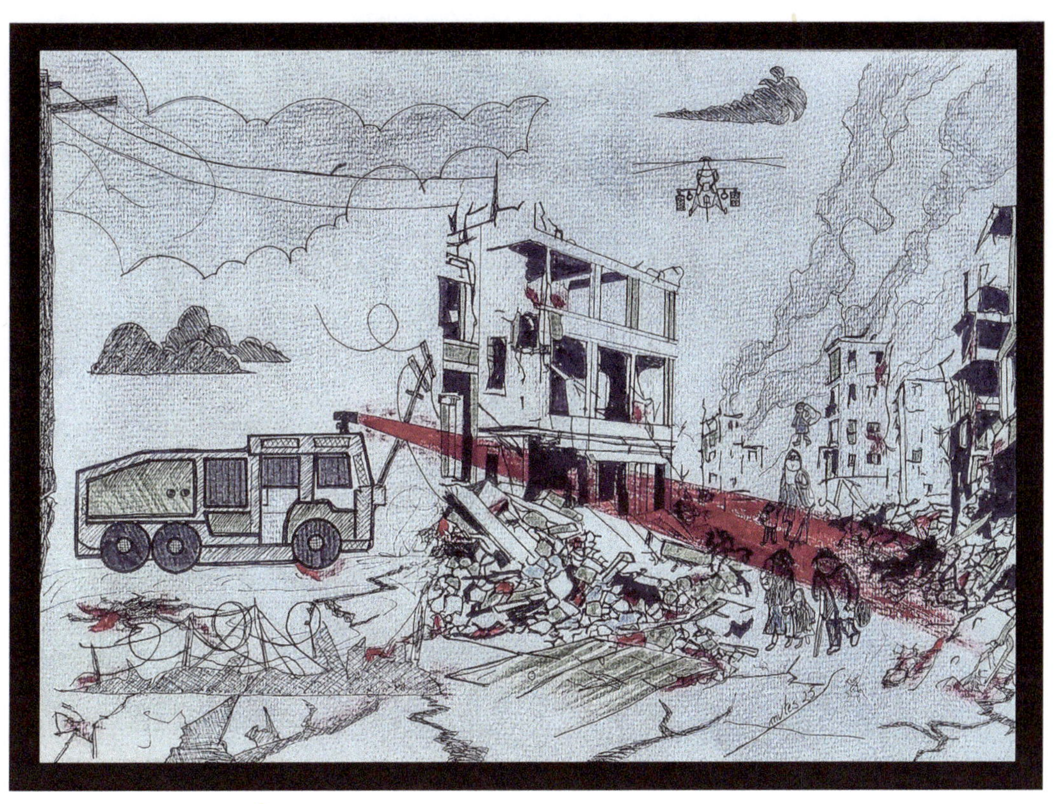

BLOODTHIRSTY CLEANSING

Drawing on paper, 29.7 cm x 42 cm

BRIDGET CHEBO ENGGASSER
WINCHESTER, VIRGINIA

HOMELAND INSECURITY

What is a homeland?
is it a choice that your parents made?
or their parents? was it even their choice?
or did someone choose for them
is it a memory? One you feel
or one you were told to feel
one you saw in a picture

is it somewhere you were born?
where you plant yourself
or somewhere you travel to?
a place you have to escape

or is it a whole planet?
a pre-pangaea crust
of the same rocks and dirt
that exist everywhere in the world
and is in itself just another piece
of a bigger rock from somewhere else
far away in outer space

LINETTE RABSATT
TORTOLA, BRITISH VIRGIN ISLANDS

A REFUGEE WHERE I PAY TAXES

I am my ancestors' seed
I have DNA from a strong breed
I am a Black Diamond in the blood I bleed
I work hard to give my children all they need
yet I stand today
where millions chill and relax
as a refugee where I pay taxes

ROBERT GIBBONS

BINGHAMTON, NEW YORK

LIMPOPO

I may disappear from the ink, did not have a South African childhood,

but what is in a name not the gold mine of the Transvaal nor the relics

of old collieries, the huts made of dung and mud but the transported muck

in my feet, north yellow cornfields, but the apartheid of the sugar cane and

the celery field, the same peonage of breath, the same ruin of swamp nor

goats or donkeys, but the rain will not quench the fires, and it has nothing to do

with the lie it is the name of another bush, of another time to be romantic, or

pedantic, and some may know of the inequalities, the folly

of the burning countryside, the burning of the sugar the displacement

of the diaspora, the name changes but the latitude connects, the dust

clouds travel equatorially, so I will remain a black shebeen, a cinderblock,

a subdivision of a neighborhood and try to mimic real earth, in this berth

of fire so in our lifetime, the telling times, if you had Mandela then

I have Obama; the change of old.

JERRY JOHNSON
NEW YORK, NEW YORK

LIBERTY GAGS

need detergent, need bleach. the stain is deeply woven
into the threads of your garments.

need deodorant, need perfume. your stench pervades the halls
of justice, of government,

Liberty gags and pukes. avenues, boulevards
and streets are blemished.

where once was clean air is now smoke, fog and ash.
we are masked again.

and you lie so much that your mouth needs potassium
hydroxide for mouthwash.

we entertain your words so much. our ears now
clogged with deafening wax.

facts and truth bounce off our hearing like handballs
slapped hard against brick

walls. walls, walls, our walls are built. our walls stand tall.
and Liberty gags and Liberty pukes and Liberty mourns
and Liberty weeps.

RUTH OISTEANU

NEW YORK, NEW YORK

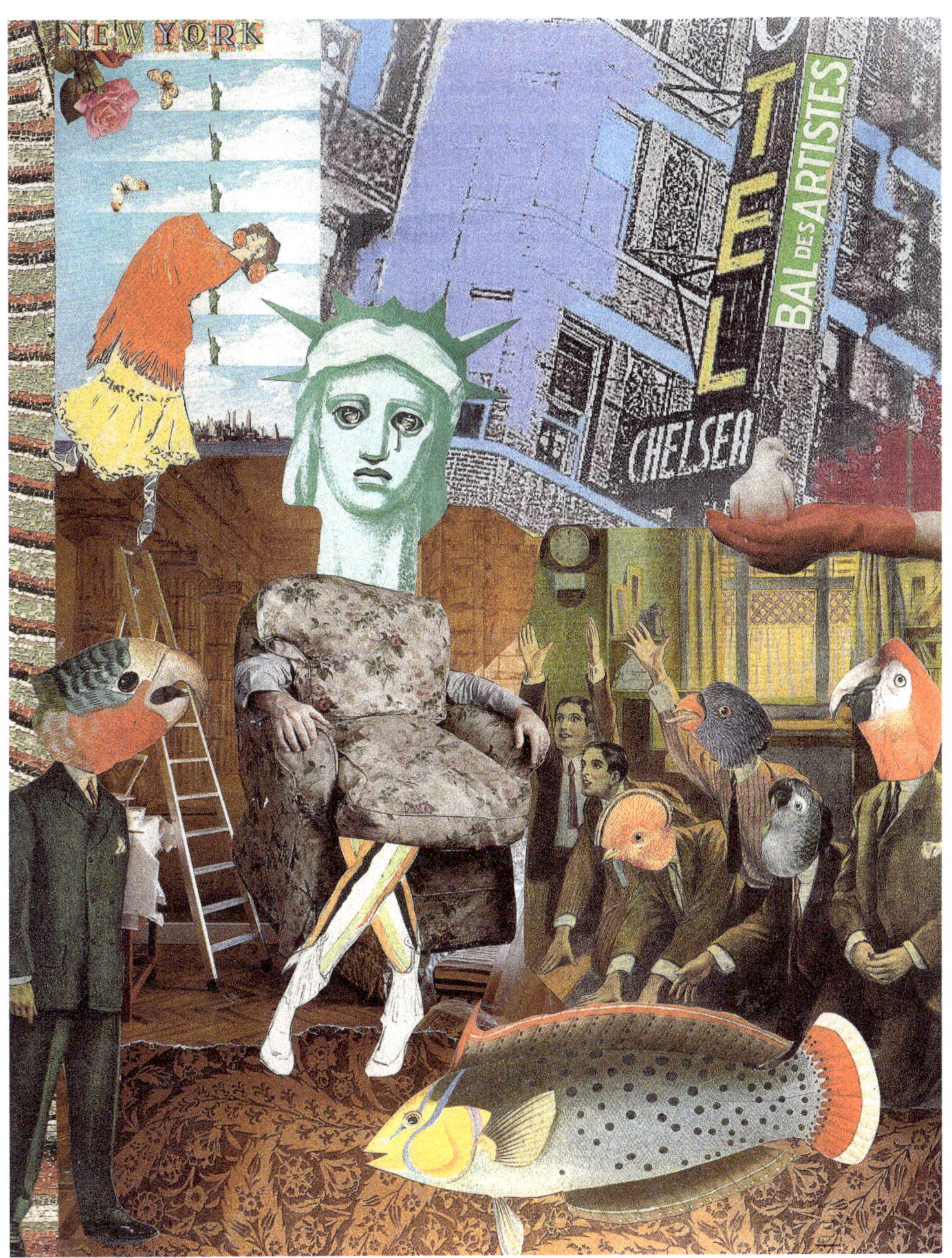

LADY LIBERTY WEEP FOR DEMOCRACY

Analog collage, 9 in x 11 in

ALLISON A. DAVIS

SAN FRANCISCO, CALIFORNIA

ETHICAL CLEANSING

Civilizations have lives

Like each of us individually

Nothing is eternal

All life has cycles

Birth, life, and death

Thus, we are seeing destruction operate now

In tearing down what was known

Death can come swiftly

or slowly and painfully

Wipe out a people

like the Apache or the Palestinians

with force and cruelty

cruelty is the point or the purpose

You're on your own

We're not responsible

Cleaning out established lines of help

shutting down the flow of money

this is what they wanted right?

but they have no discernment

And they closed it all off

They shut it all down

Everyone is affected except those that are immune to money problems

Even sinking stock won't thwart the demise

Keyed trucks and protests at dealership

He's actually to be admired

the crude manners, the bad food,

and the terrible dinner conversation

because he's winning, he's ahead of everyone

by smashing windows and doors,

by turning the world upside down

so everyone's dizzy

and can't focus on what is really happening.

They came into your house, steered the party towards them,

helped themselves to the food on the buffet,

wrapping some to take away,

and now, you realize,

they have the keys to your car.

and they took your dog.

And your wife, and your whiskey.

He's winning,

he's to be admired

mired in his own making,

creating power

selling it for millions,

then wielding it

because we made it so

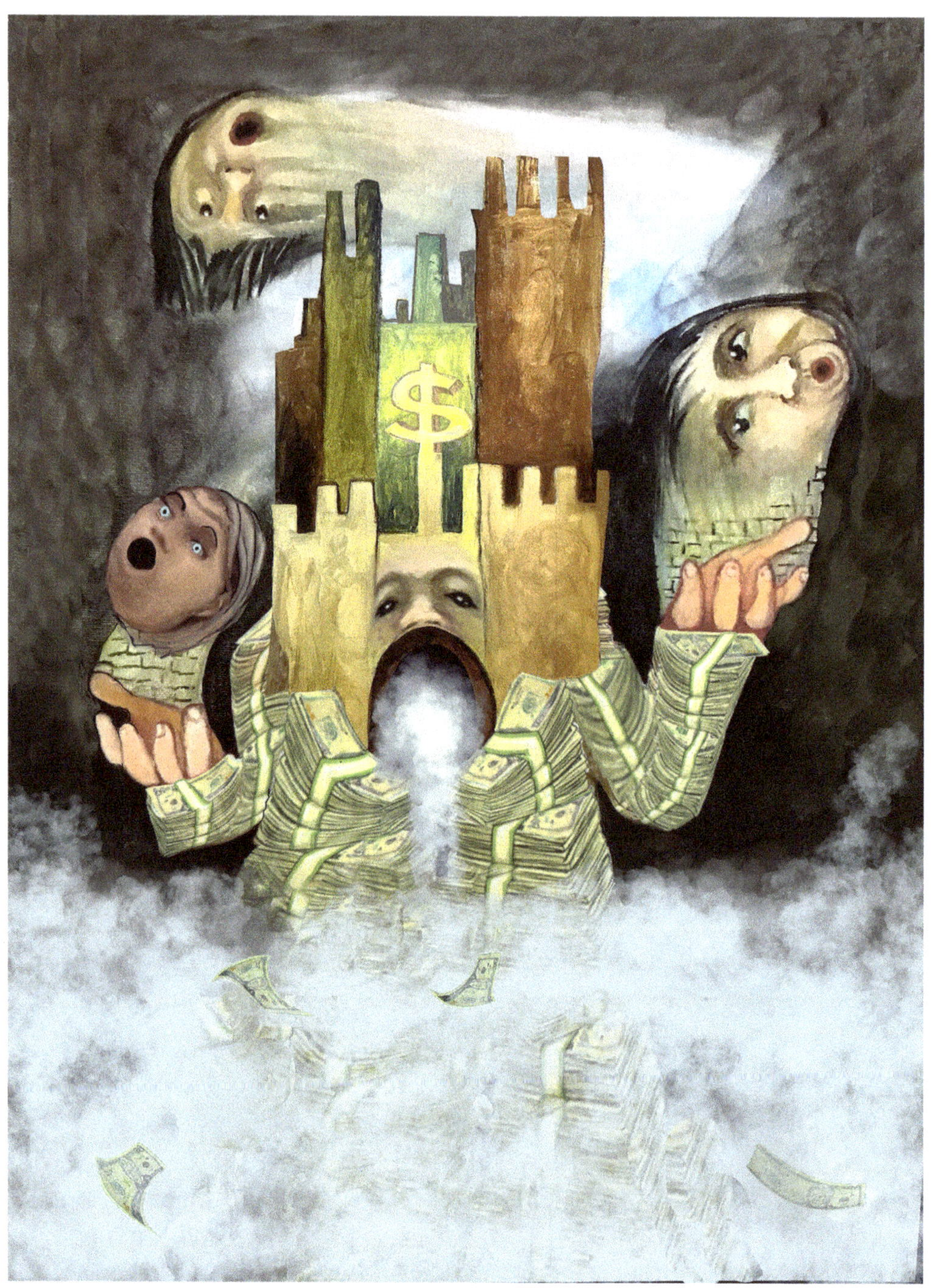

PROFIT – SEE

Digital collage of painting, 8 in x 11 in

YARYAN

TOLUCA LAKE, CALIFORNIA

EMPIRE OF MORE

It starts with a manmade well
And a man
With the darkest heart
Gasping for breath
Entombed in the planet's girth
Pulling himself up and out from a pool of greed
Of minerals, roots and shiny mud
Connecting a network of life
Familiar with death
A self-planted crop growing more fearsome
With each day of self-preservation
No greenhouse nor farm, incubator or zoo
Could harvest the soul,
Surrounded by the tallest weeds
Growing grim
And curiously immobilizing
While turning the inside hollow
And the outside bitter
Near the end
And the dust blows harder
While the plot thickens in the sand
Pouring out of a broken hourglass
Once filled with plans, promise, progress
No more!
Yes, the end is near…
Written on castle walls, cloud formations,
Empty halls, transformations of town squares…
Bleak and heavy
Can't you see it approaching?
Captured by the tower's misty, telescopic lens,
Pointing toward the planet's largest sandbox…
Filled with childlike strife – wounding livelihoods
Extinguishing life forces
Consuming everything
All for one, all for nothing
Gone.

ROBERT C. FORD

NEW YORK, NEW YORK

MORALITY DANCES A MASQUERADE

In shifting shadows
Behind stripes and stars

The liar's whisper
Curled into the ear of the thief—
"Gold is lead matured"

The thief, grinning
Pocketed the murderer's bullets

FRANCINE WITTE

NEW YORK, NEW YORK

MOUTHFUL OF MONEY

Teeth grind the silver—click, click
Echoes of stock markets yawn in the gutter
A goat in a tie recites contracts backward,
while the moon sells its shadow for crumbs.

Justice shaves its head in a mirror,
whispers: integrity is out of stock.
A banker baptizes himself in melted coins,
his reflection laughs but doesn't move.

The law wears a clown nose,
its pockets stuffed with counterfeit morals.
One last breath of honesty—
then silence, swallowed by the market bell.

JACK SEIEI

TOKYO, JAPAN

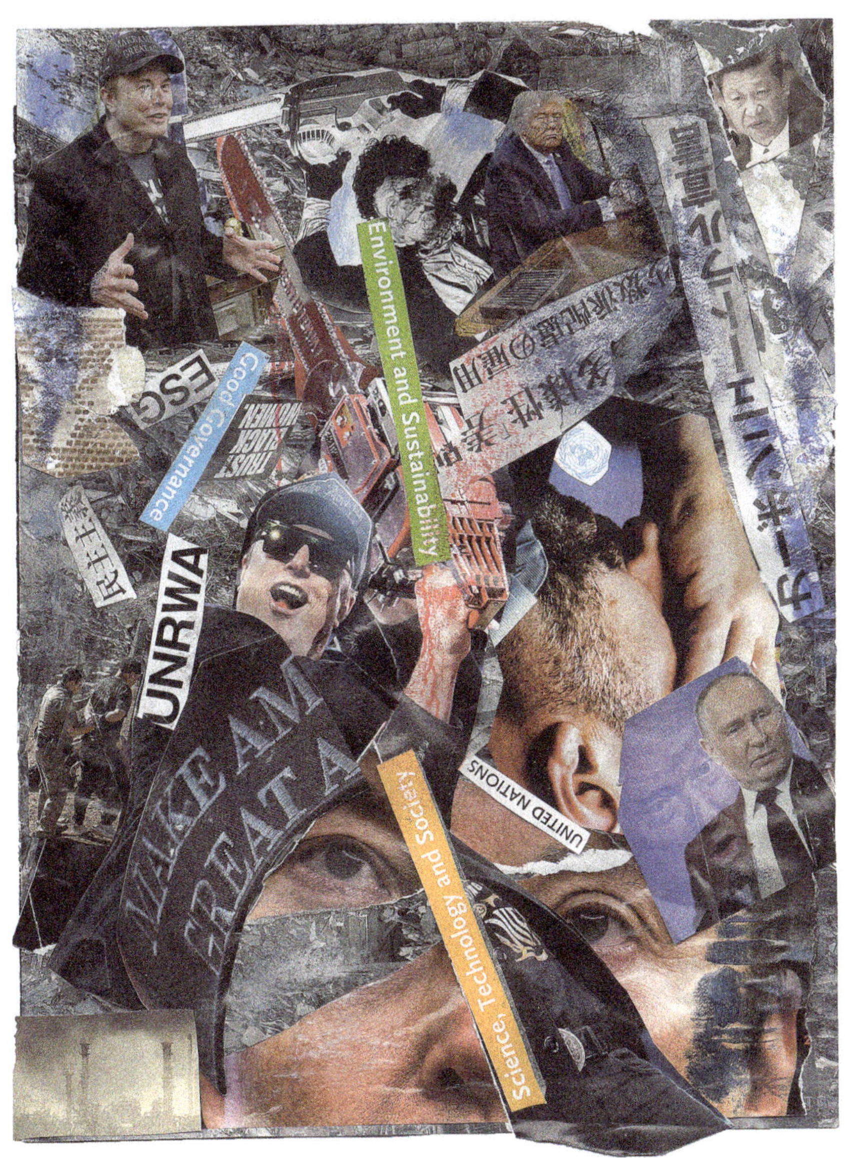

THE MORAL DESTROYER

Collage, A4 paper

JOANIE HF ZOSIKE

NEW YORK, NEW YORK

I, CRUD

… creeps from the inside, blocks the passages,
weakens the vocal chords with its acid, tough to
sing or croak messages to points unknown via
cell phone, podcasts, music, flashes in copper pans
I, Crud, send erratic signals, erotic SOS messages
to parties unknown on a message board: z, he, she,
zhey walk in agony over a bed of coals to the beat
of the plucked Eucharist, 21st-Century hate style

Imminent, ever-present this odium, incessant
Why? I, crust of earth; I, crusty, crunchy,
crumbling, I'm dying. Wills rebirth, redux
Unbelievable agony in your face, face it—
No one's blameless, your face isn't mine

Crud, scrud, screed, imported from shithole
territories; mean old shit-pig women; let's purge
wrong words and erase undesirable life forms—
Oh, that's not nice; you said you would make the
country grate again; peel away the imperfections

There is a presence made up of joys and agonies
married together in an unending cycle of violence
One specter wears a perpetual smile, filled with love
and optimism despite all indications to the contrary
The other sees unschooled handwriting on the wall—

Up and down don't exist in space. Arises again
an ever-evolving/never-resolving helix, a universe
with a nucleus of star-studded arms reaching out
to embrace its neighbors with all its expanse
Is this a shore from which we should retreat?

The paradox of pleasure and pain, this celestial
tickling and biting, this tease of the engrams
flows beyond our grasp and reveals a vast, yet
very human enigma—the force of mutability

GAY PASLEY

OKLAHOMA CITY, OKLAHOMA

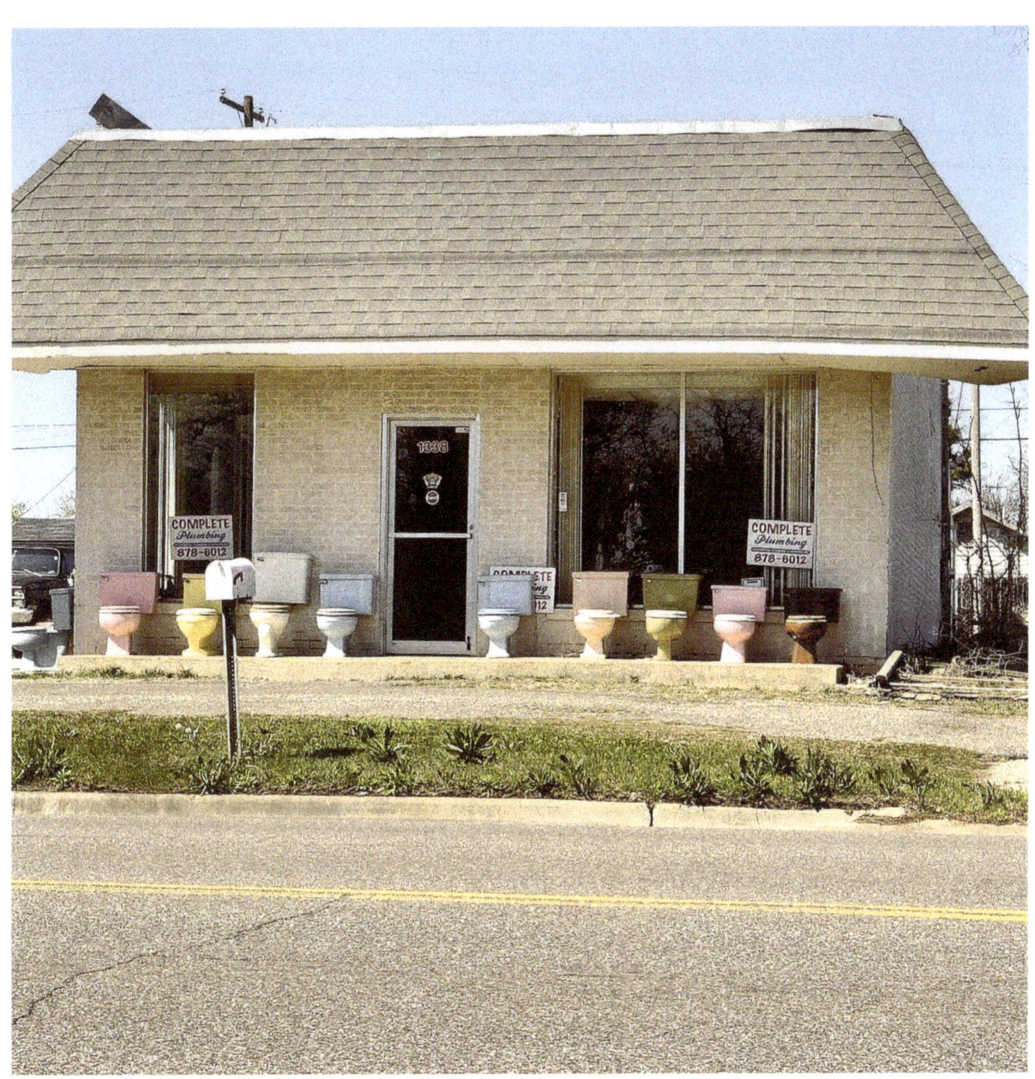

COMPLETE CLEANSING

Photograph

JERRY THE PRIEST

LOS ANGELES, CALIFORNIA

FALSE UNION

for André Breton

I am your equal as a thief

and I will fleece you

and I will kidnap your children

because I want for them privileges that I never had

of poverty, hunger and homelessness

and I will murder all that is corrupt in luxury

whose padded couched proliferate racism

whose cruise control falsifies morality

whose hot tub is a capitalist incubator

whose handbag is an oven of greed

whose highways are paved on the backs of the underclass

whose air conditioners are a tourniquet on the throat of god

I am a saboteur, a terrorist

and I will betray you

and in me will flourish all that convenience petrifies

and in me will perish all that separation feeds

and in my wilderness your children will reside

happily, without frills

and we will chastise your gullibility

HAMZA ABU AYYASH

AMMAN, JORDAN

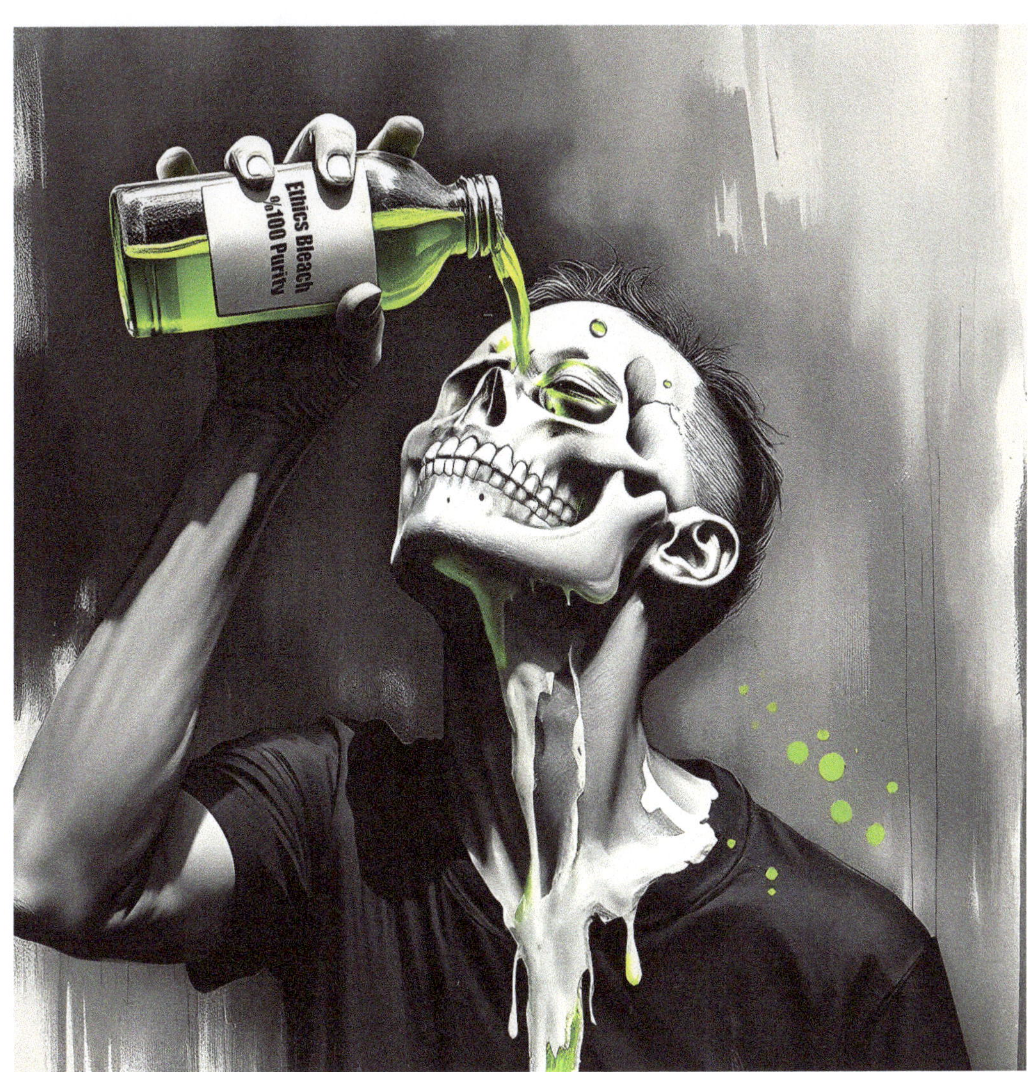

THE ETHICS CLEANSER

Digital art, 2560 px x 2560 px

DIG WAYNE

NORTHRIDGE, CALIFORNIA

IT BRINGS ME TO TEARS

to dance on the
ashes of America
a joyous choir of
stripped gears
burnt out clutches
punctured melting pots

blind billionaires
begging for sight

wild fires; metaphors
without roofs catch the charred hope
blowing up to blue skies

somersaulting embers comfort
millions as they circle existential drains

cherry picking
truth and faith
voting for whimsy
turning the horizontal upside down

guardian angels
packing their bags absurdity is king
there is no protection
for rational insanity

EDEL RODRIGUEZ

MT. TABOR, NEW JERSEY

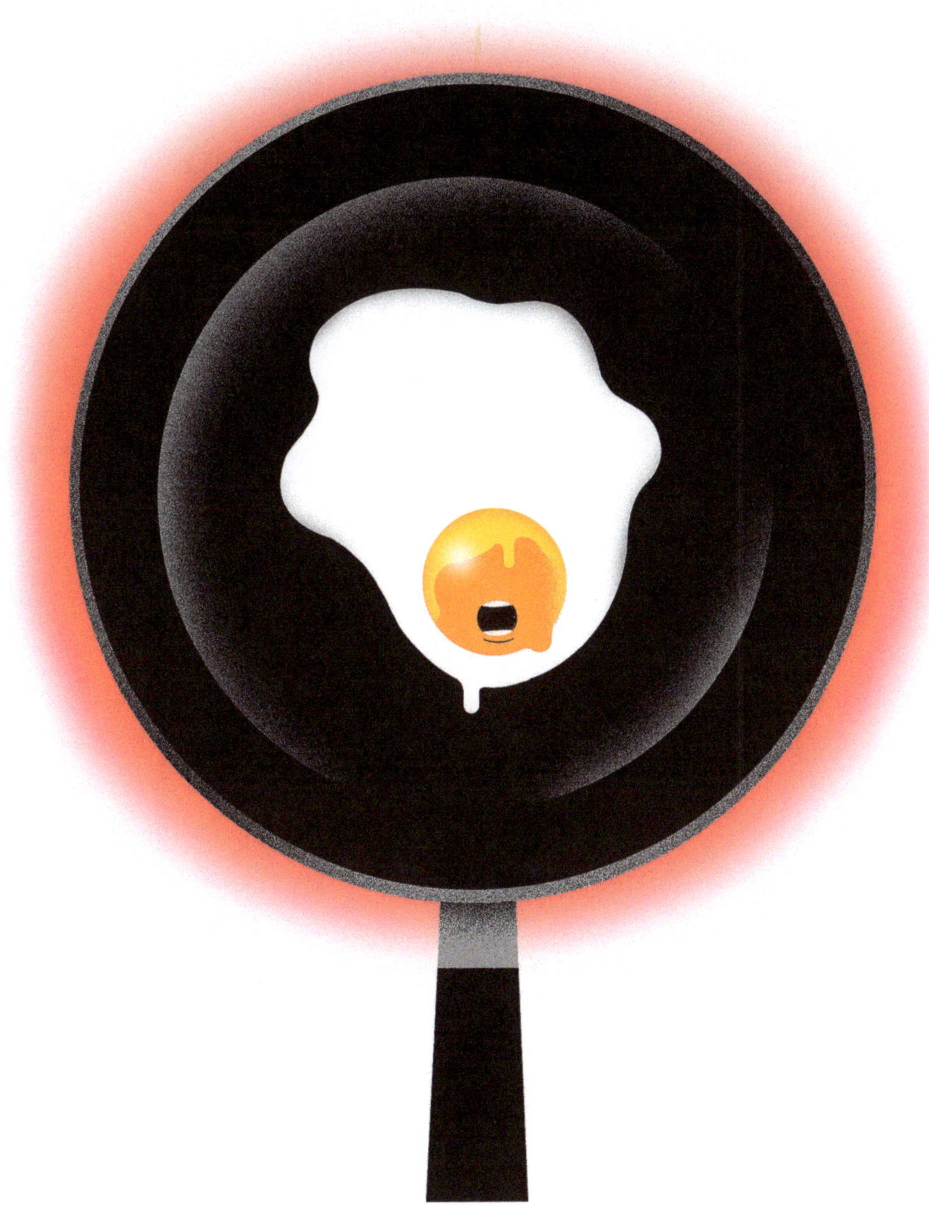

FRIED

Ink and digital, 11 in x 12 in

CSABA PÁL

BUDAPEST, HUNGARY

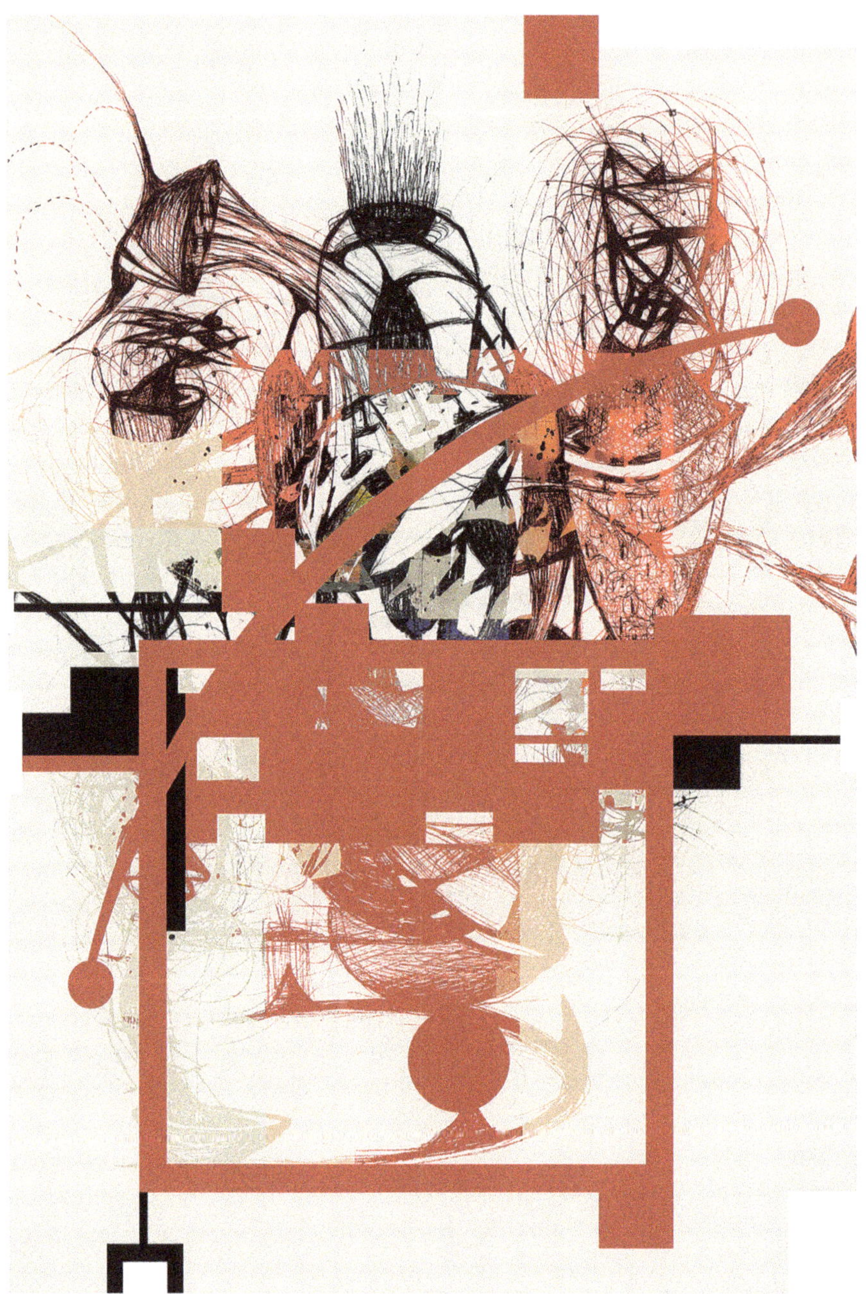

GREED

Digital print, 40 cm x 30 cm

BENITO VILA

MEXICO CITY, MEXICO

THE WHITE BIRD IS AN IDEA

A Nod to Abbie, Anita, Jerry, Nancy and Paul, the first Yippies

The white bird is an idea glimmering in the politics of ecstasy, an idea that cannot embrace the desperate theater of tonight's evening news. To protect our freedom, there must be a disruption. It's needed; it's necessary. To fear what's about to happen is to acknowledge what doesn't work.

One day everything we love will be gone forever. Making today sacred is no quick trick, it's slow work, the alchemy of compassion, coming to terms with what doesn't come easy. To assign value to people, places or things corrupts the goodness, sincerity and holiness that will be theirs forever.

A war against war is still war.
The greed of no, the greed of more,
the greed of hate, the greed of fury,
the greed of gotta, the greed of hurt,
the greed of sameness, the greed of isolation
and the greed of control, each one
wipes away any chance at peace.
A war against war is still war,
allowing mad boar-face ugly finger-pointing
to keep selling fear-smearing disconnection
to people who don't need it.

This new America is trapped by its pettiness, exploding its own fate while mumbling about destiny, caring about money and little else. Our pledge to interdependence, it's gone. Lady Liberty's been set ablaze and the fire boats can't reach her. Her meaning, her hope, her promise, they're burning.

The truth lives in the obvious, like, in the smart-mouth music of the blues. You gotta move, get ready, you gotta move. Gather the freaks, set them free, watch what they do. See how they piss off anyone who's forgotten how to be a kid and everyone who won't poke fun at their own altars.

PAWEŁ KUCZYŃSKI

POLICE, POLAND

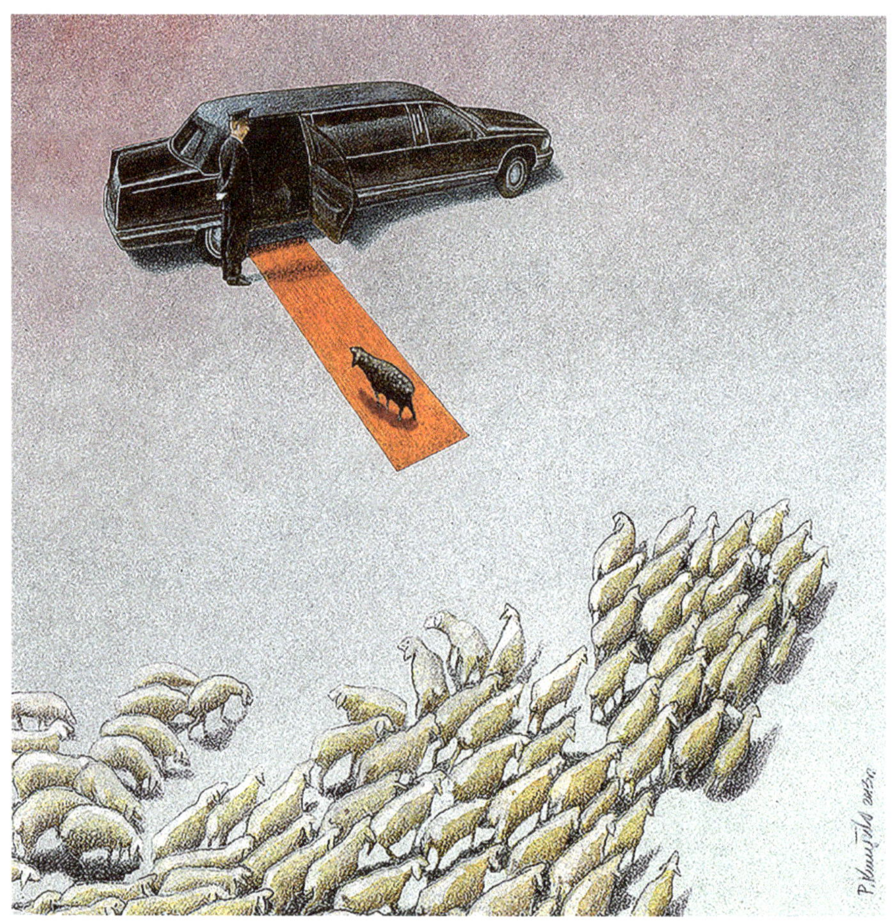

BLACK SHEEP

Ink and digital illustration

LOUIS ARMAND

PRAGUE, CZECH REPUBLIC

DI/ODE DXVI

(for Jana Orlová)

whalemouth xylophone tongueaquarium waterclock.
the worm turns in its turbid spit.
the gargoyle chokes back tears, as reprobate
as morbid fruit shaken from the vine.
a gourde rattle, a rack, a stretch limousine.
I do the Lon Chaney, the Dostoevsky
grand mal routine. dust in the veins, mud in the
ears, iron in the mouth. I'm spitting-
out Amerika, spitting out Dow Chemical.
I am Agent Orange on a secret mission in Cambodia.
Trench foot, hemlock toe. I am metaphysics
shot in the back of the neck, as statuesque as
a human cramp. une durée très dure.
40,000 yrs to excavate bloodflow from evolution's
tidelock. backwards in semi-prone posture,
pen-in-hand, of the literate ape, groping towards
positive self-expression. well hello there
my little numbskulls, don't we look pretty today?

JOEL ALLEGRETTI

FORT LEE, NEW JERSEY

ETHICS

eth·ics (eth'iks) *n.* [Gr *ēthikos* < *ēthos*, character]
see COMMODITY

LIZ AXELROD

ALBUQUERQUE, NEW MEXICO

THE PRINCESS MANIFESTO

I have lived through the invent, rise and demise of MTV
I have lived through the invent, rise and demise of the FAX
I have lived through the invent rise and demise of DOS PROGRAMMING & FLASH
I have lived through the invent rise and demise of INTERNET CAFES
I have lived through the invent rise and demise of CABLE TV
I have lived through the invent rise and demise of CELL-PHONES AS COMMUNICATION
I have lived through the invent rise and demise of PLASTIC AS A SAVIOR OR DEATH

I never wore the crown

I have lived through the rise and demise of WOMEN'S RIGHTS
I have lived through the rise and demise of HOMEOWNERSHIP AS A POSSIBILITY
I have lived through the rise and demise of BEING A PROUD RENTER
I have lived through the rise and demise of UNBIASED JOURNALISM

I have lived through the demise of DEMOCRACY
I have lived through the rise of MEDIOCRITY
I have lived through the rise and demise of PERSONAL AUTONOMY

I never bought the gown

I am living through the demise of COLORFUL OCEAN REEFS
I am living through the demise of CLEAN WATER AND THE AIR WE BREATHE
I am living through the demise of PRIVACY
I am living through the demise of FREEDOM OF CHOICE
I am living through the demise of AFFORDABLE HEALTH CARE
I am living through the demise of SAFETY IN OUR SCHOOLS
I am living through the demise of TRUST IN THE SUPREME COURT
I am living through the demise of TRUST IN THE FAMILY
I am living through the demise of LGBTQIA2S+ RIGHTS
I am living through the demise of TRANSGENDER HEALTHCARE
I am living through the demise of PARENTAL RIGHTS
I am living through the demise of THE FREE PRESS
I am living through the demise of LIBERAL ARTS
I am living through the demise of CRITICAL THINKING
I am living through the demise of CIVIL RIGHTS
I am living through the demise of PROTEST as a form of expression

I never got to sit on the throne

If I let AI wear my glass slippers
Will machine learning make us a BETTER RULER?

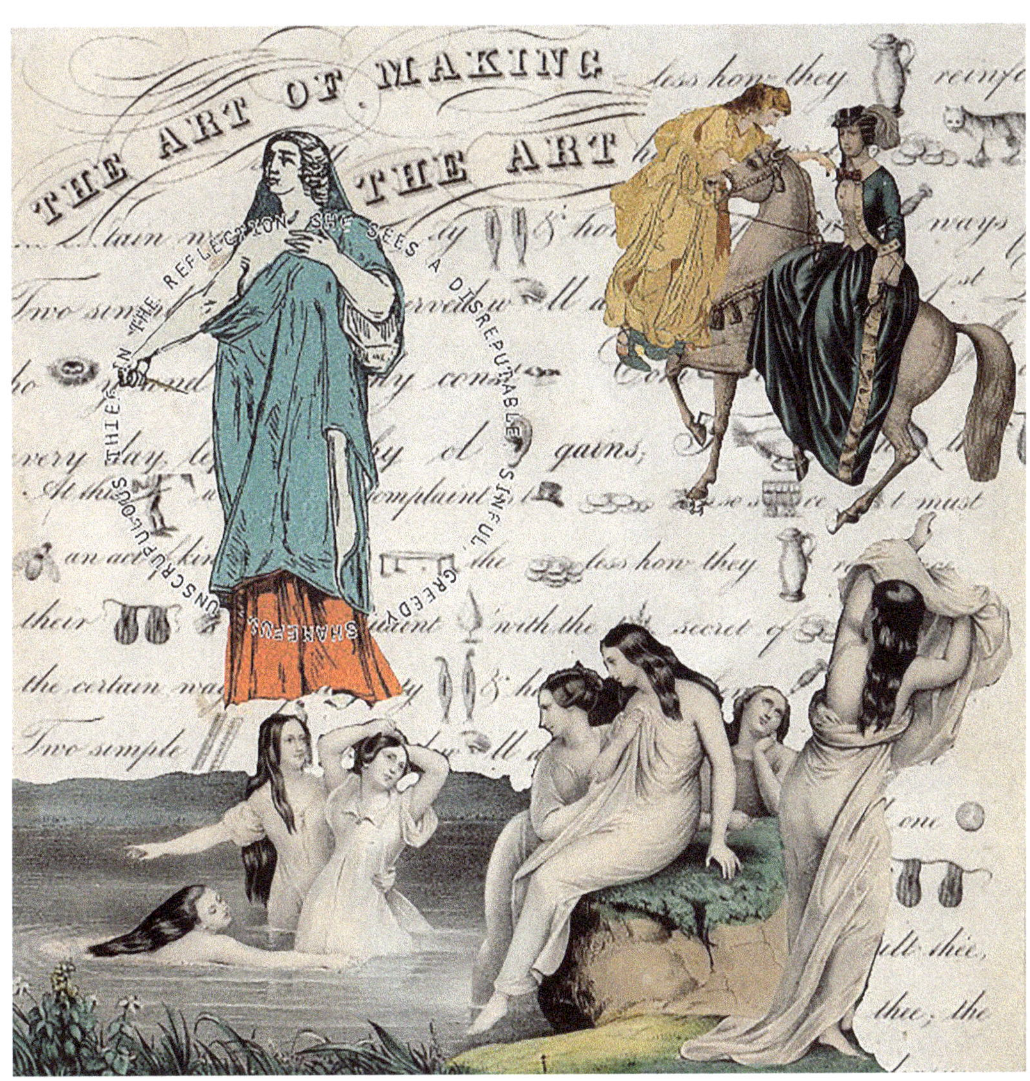

A COG IN THE MACHINE

Digital collage of various "Virtuous" images atop a cleansed "The Art of Making Money Plenty"
by E.B. and E.C. Kellogg, 1280 px x 1280 pz

ROSALIE GANCIE

HYATTSVILLE, MARYLAND

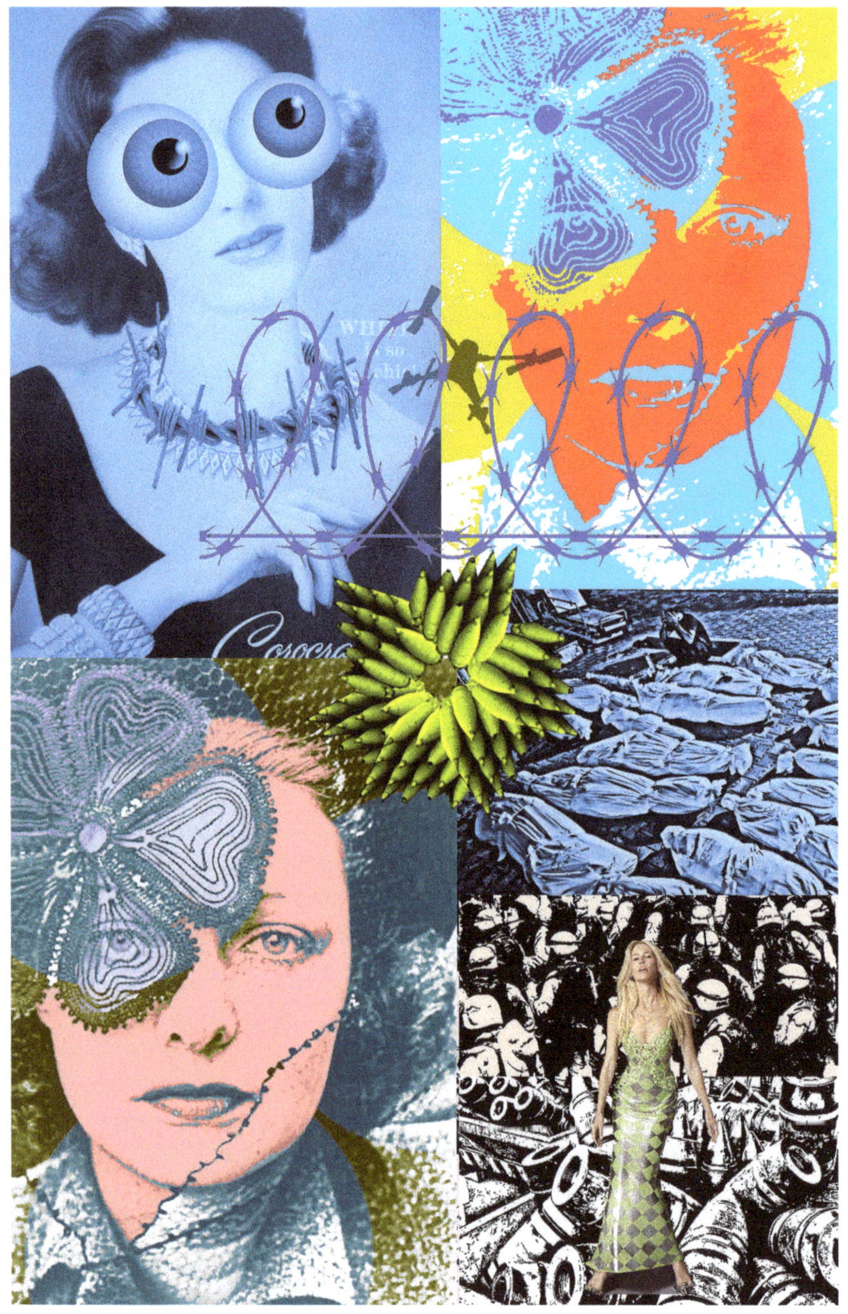

DEATH AND THREE MAIDENS

Digital collage, 1950 px x 1280 px

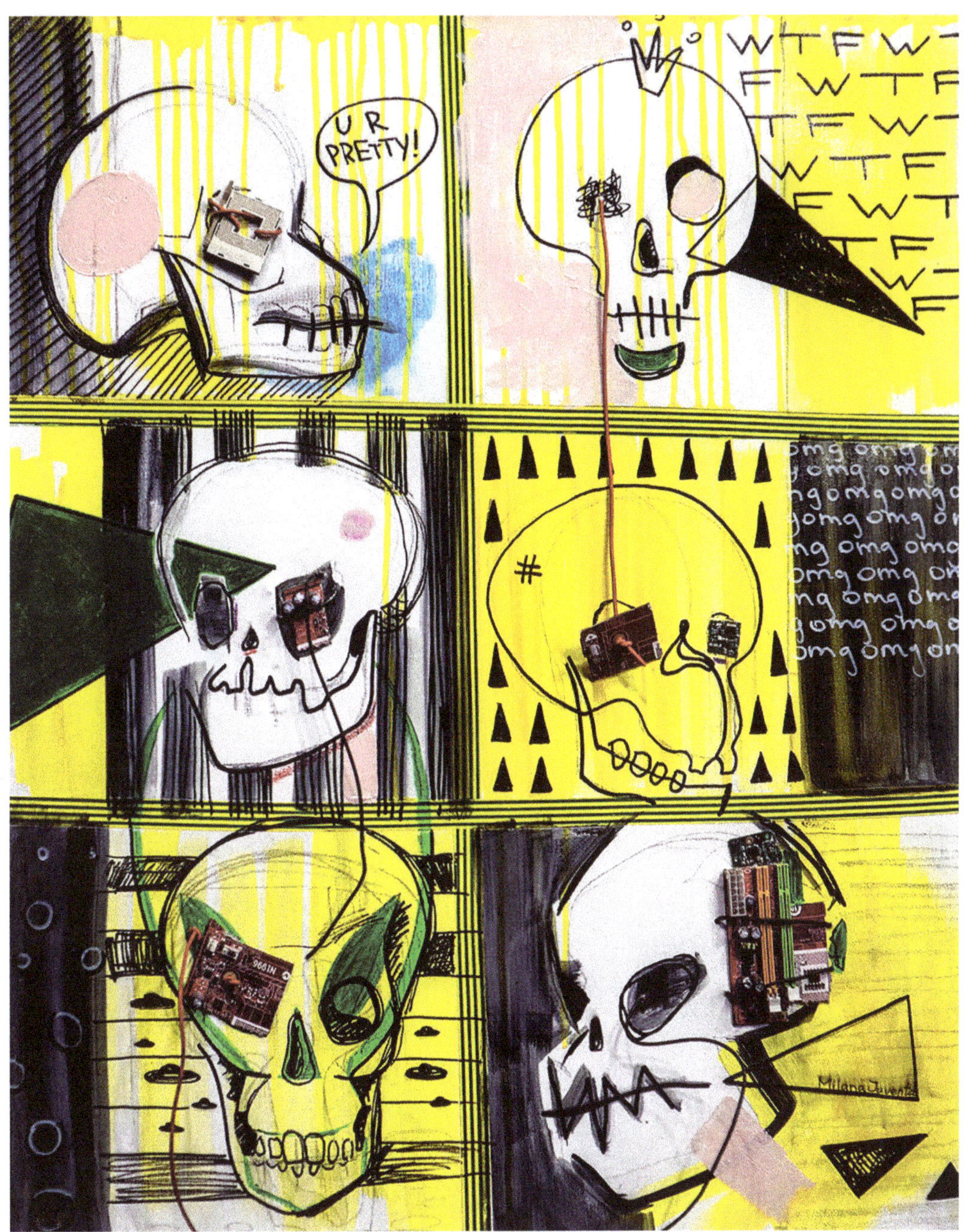

HEXAGON OF ETERNITY

Acrylic, mixed media, wires, and computer parts on canvas, 90 cm x 70 cm

RACHEL DIXON

OXFORD, UNITED KINGDOM

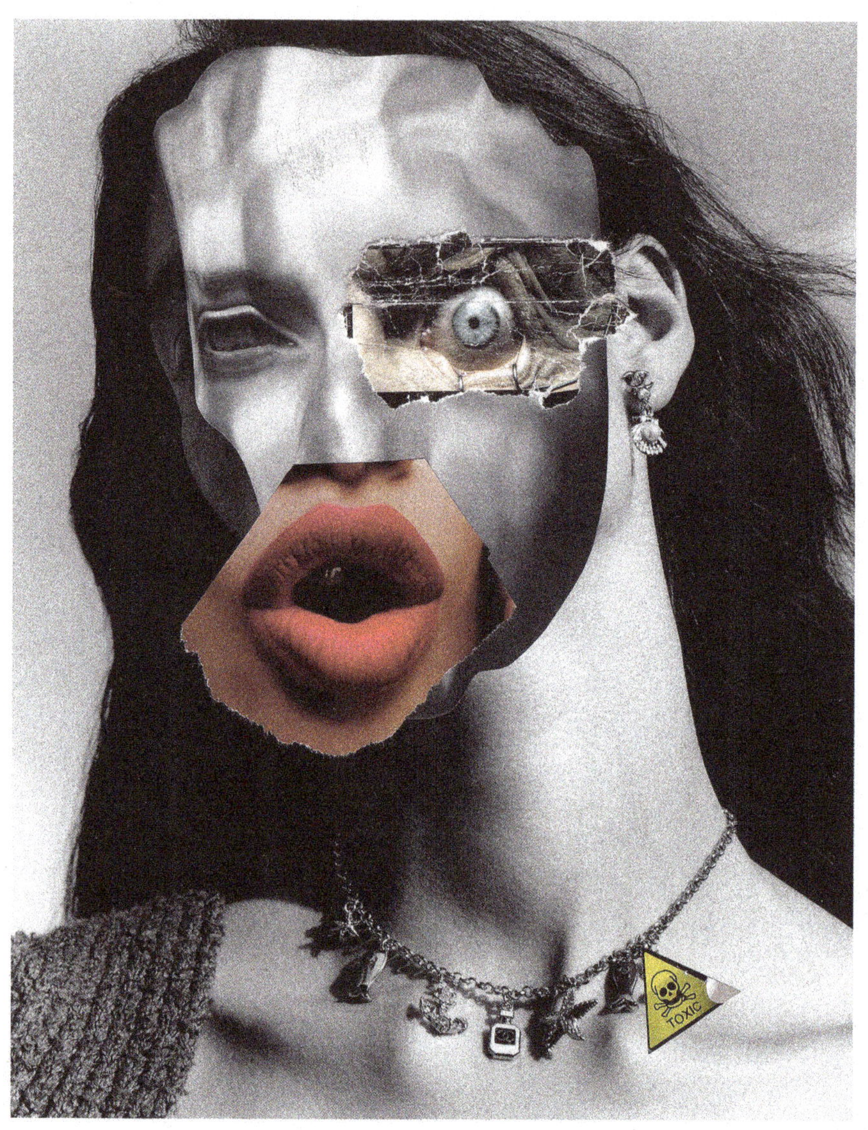

CANHELL

EXTRA L

Collage from magazines and newspapers, A4

JAC-LYNN STARK

LYNN, MASSACHUSETTS

HOW (NOT) TO BE MAD HAPPY

Standing in line
on a street in soho
like hypnotized zombies
brainwashed by ads you see everywhere
you line up like you are
entering a holy shrine
your eyes hopeful that what you find there
will fill up your hollow self
or even give you a self
since inside you sense something is missing

But this shrine only celebrates commerce
the power of the dollar
to purchase an item you hope
will make you look like the people
you see on their Instagram
followed by 277,000 of your fellow acolytes
they must know something

Even the photo on their website
shows young people with blank faces
and empty eyes
wearing logo prominent casual wear
whose name does not match their expressions
posed in positions of studied nonchalance
bored ennui and faux world weariness

The name of this company draws you in
Mad happy
what you wish you could be
but you won't find that here
just more of the same posturing
and a short burst of belonging
that will always need another fix

INGRID WENDT

EUGENE, OREGON

DEPRAVITY LESSONS

1.   Abandon all empathy, ye who enter here.

2.   See all evil. Hear all evil. Speak nothing but evil.
     Those monkeys got it all wrong.

3.   Love yourself with all your heart and all your mind.
     Forget your soul. There will be nothing left of it.

4.   And when you do unto others as you would do
     unto yourself, do nothing that will not also bring glory unto yourself.

5.   Seek out the poor in spirit, for they will be at your mercy.
     Seek out they who mourn, for you can take advantage over them.

     Seek out the meek, for you can take fucking everything they own.

     Seek out the merciful and clean in heart, for soon
     they will stand in your way. Open your hate and stomp on them.

     Seek out the peacemakers. Escort them out of the house of the law.

     Seek out those who hunger and thirst after righteousness.
     They are your worst enemies. Destroy them like no one's ever seen.

     Seek those eager to persecute righteousness for your name's sake.
     These are your friends. Pamper them.

     Who needs the kingdom of heaven?
     You'll have the whole wide world in your hands.

6.   Money bears all things, cures all things, outlasts all things.

7.   Power. Hate. Money. These three.
     But the very greatest of these is money.

SABINE REMY & LYNN SKORDAL

DÜSSELDORF, GERMANY & LA CONNER, WASHINGTON

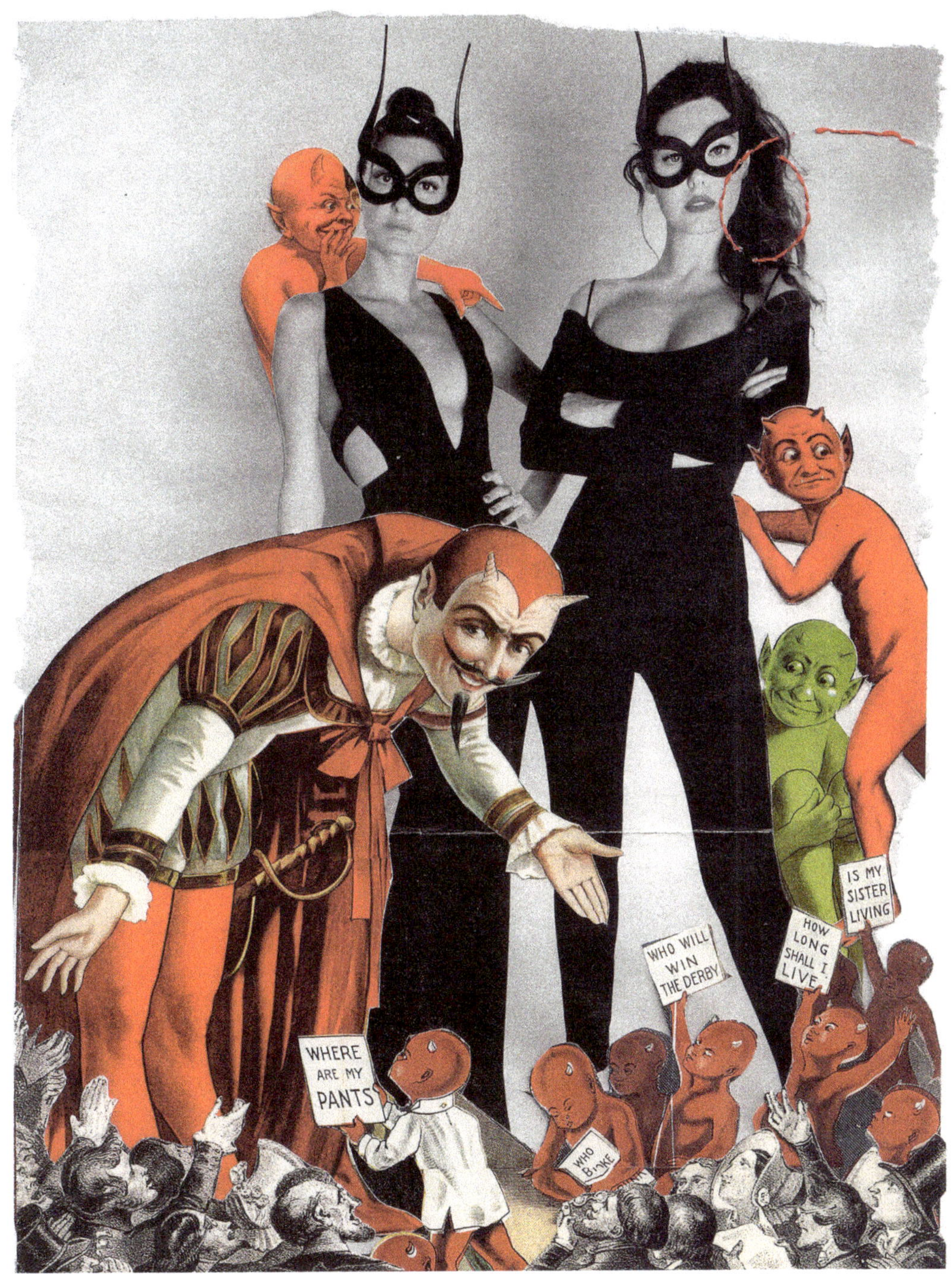

THE MILLION DOLLAR MYSTERY

Analog paper collage and threads, approx. 22.5 cm × 29.7 cm

ANNA O'MEARA

SEATTLE, WASHINGTON

WE SENT HER TO A FARM UPSTATE

I've been feeling like a bootlicker lately.
My head is pushed down to the ground.
I think about integrity
As I watch The Bachelor.
The Bachelor asks his date questions.
I wonder:
"Will my next job interview be like this?"
Then I wonder:
"Will my HUACC trial be like this?"
I think about retreating
Into 100 acre woods
Where I will build Victor Horta style houses.
Maybe I'll buy a cow.
What if the cow needs me when I fly?
Then I'll stay home.
What if the cow feels cold during the Upstate New York winter?
Then I'll give the cow a heat lamp.
What if the cow knocks over the heat lamp?
Well, Chicago won't be there to set ablaze so Mrs. O'Leary
     O'Meara might be off the hook.
Vacate is etymologically related to vacation.
Maybe I can treat my life like retirement.
Maybe I can mix an Arnold Palmer and watch the sunset silently
     every evening for the next fifty years.
I could build a house with my own hands.
I could pull clay out of the ground to lay the bricks.
I could set up a studio filled with fire to hone the metals around
     stained glass.
I want to forget.
I want to vacate.
I feel naked in front of the world.
A political laughing stock.
Stupid woman.
Stupid cow.
Stupid Irish woman cow.
Lick the boot.

LYNETTE CLENNELL

FOLLINA, ITALY

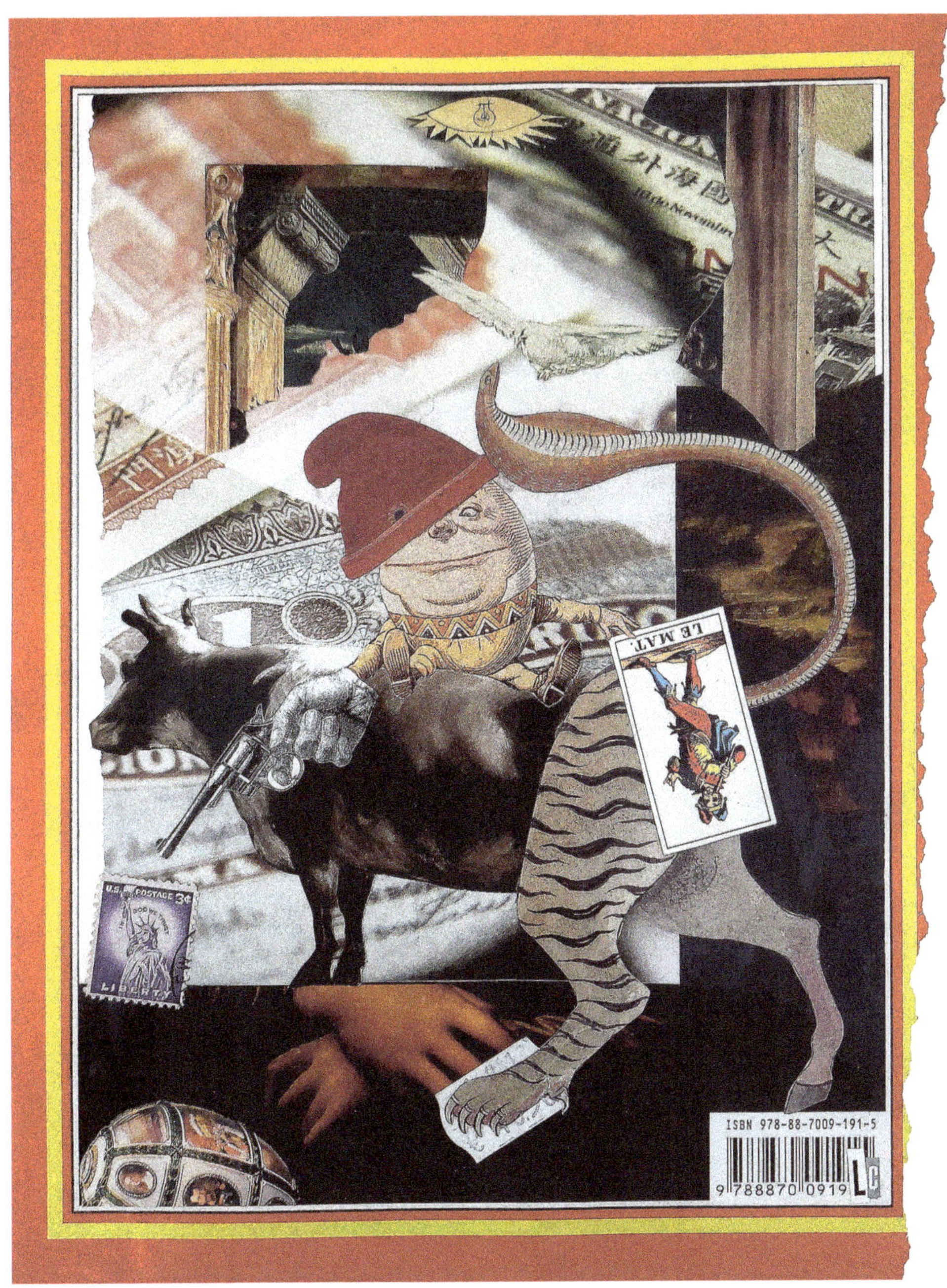

LE MAT

Collage, 8.5 in 11.25 in

MARC OLMSTED
PORTLAND, OREGON

PIG DEVILS TO MARS

Double-crossers
Blood suckers
Shell game predators
(Ignore the fine print)
Want to cancel that? –
too late
RICH RICH RICH
Pig devils to Mars –
tipping the staff
with flesh

KATHERINE SHEHADEH
CORAL GABLES, FLORIDA

FUCK YOU EARTH DAY

You gaslighting goblin. You are a billion-
air(e) sucking, military industrial
complex camouflager. Our incremental
oil slicked path to the epicenter
of Armageddon—but not the big-lipped
Liv Tyler licking, Sno-Caps snacking
summer blockbuster of death we counted on,
decades before sad, smoky memes turned Ben's
bigheaded smiles upside down. Our child-
hoods binged on Nickelodeon, faithful
to a popsicle stick puppet, pleading
for us to phone-in-mid-plastic-tray-din-
ner with half-baked pledges to *Save the Earth*.
You owe us more than your twenty-four hours.

MOLLY CRABAPPLE

BROOKLYN, NEW YORK

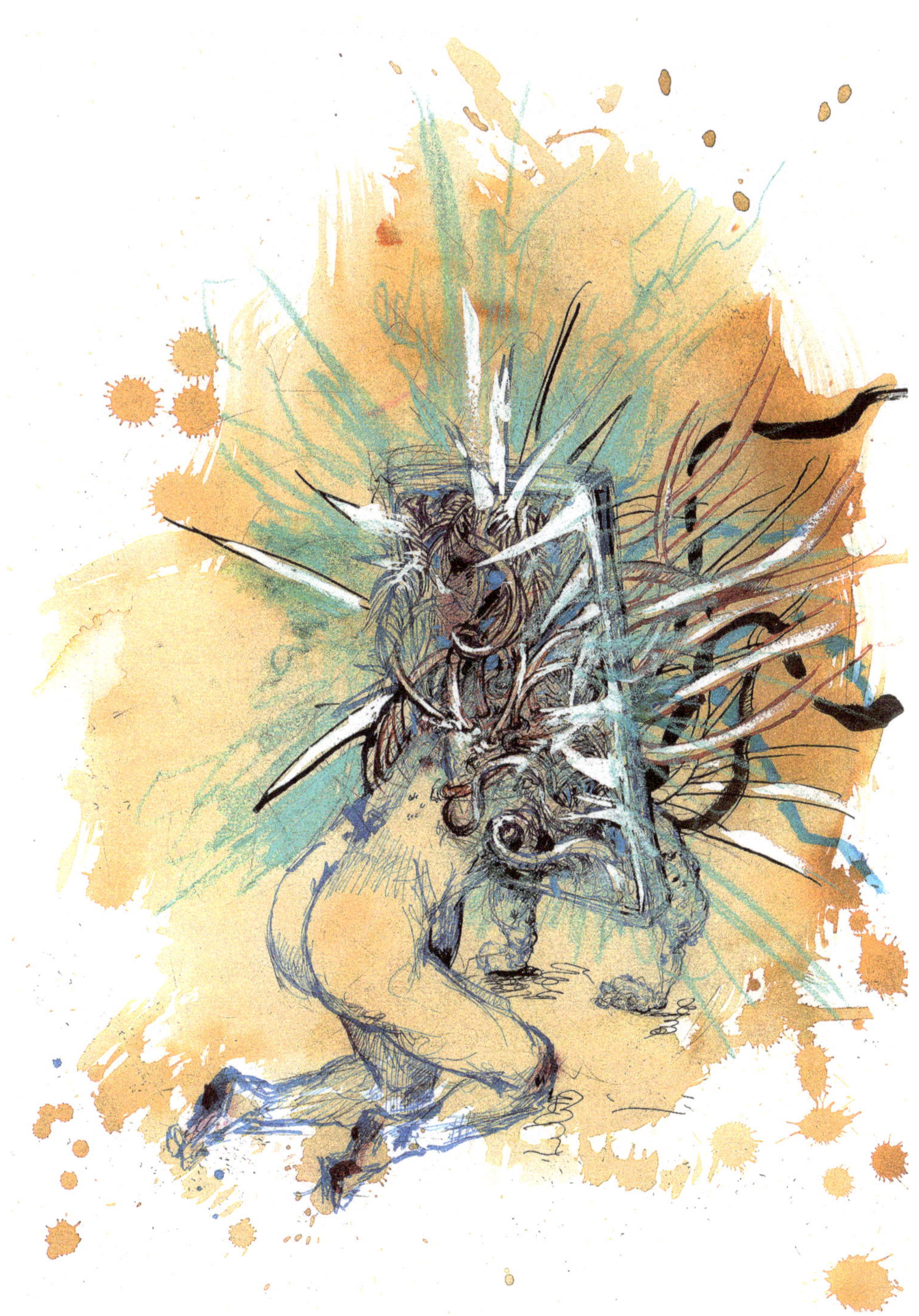

THE INFERNAL MACHINE

Pen, ink, pastel, and dye on paper, 10 in x 15 in

SUZI KAPLAN OLMSTED

PORTLAND, OREGON

PRAYER LIST

Black-hearted government lackeys

Greedy corporate thieves

Anyone who thinks they "need" purses, sunglasses and shoes

Costing more than $1000

Secret conspirators to our impending demise

Any kind of billionaire

People who don't scoop the poop

Or use their turn signals

Religious extremists

Small-minded men

I pray for them

Even when I don't want to

And really

I never want to

~~Jimmy Carter doesn't need my prayers~~

~~We don't need to make peace with our allies~~

~~Hatred is the enemy within~~

~~Cookies are the enemy without~~

But there's no grace in only forgiving small trespasses

The person who puts the empty milk carton

Back in the fridge

And the men who separate children from their parents

May they all reach enlightenment

Sooner rather than later

~~Would be good~~

REGINA LAFAY BELLAMY

PAIGNTON, DEVON, UNITED KINGDOM

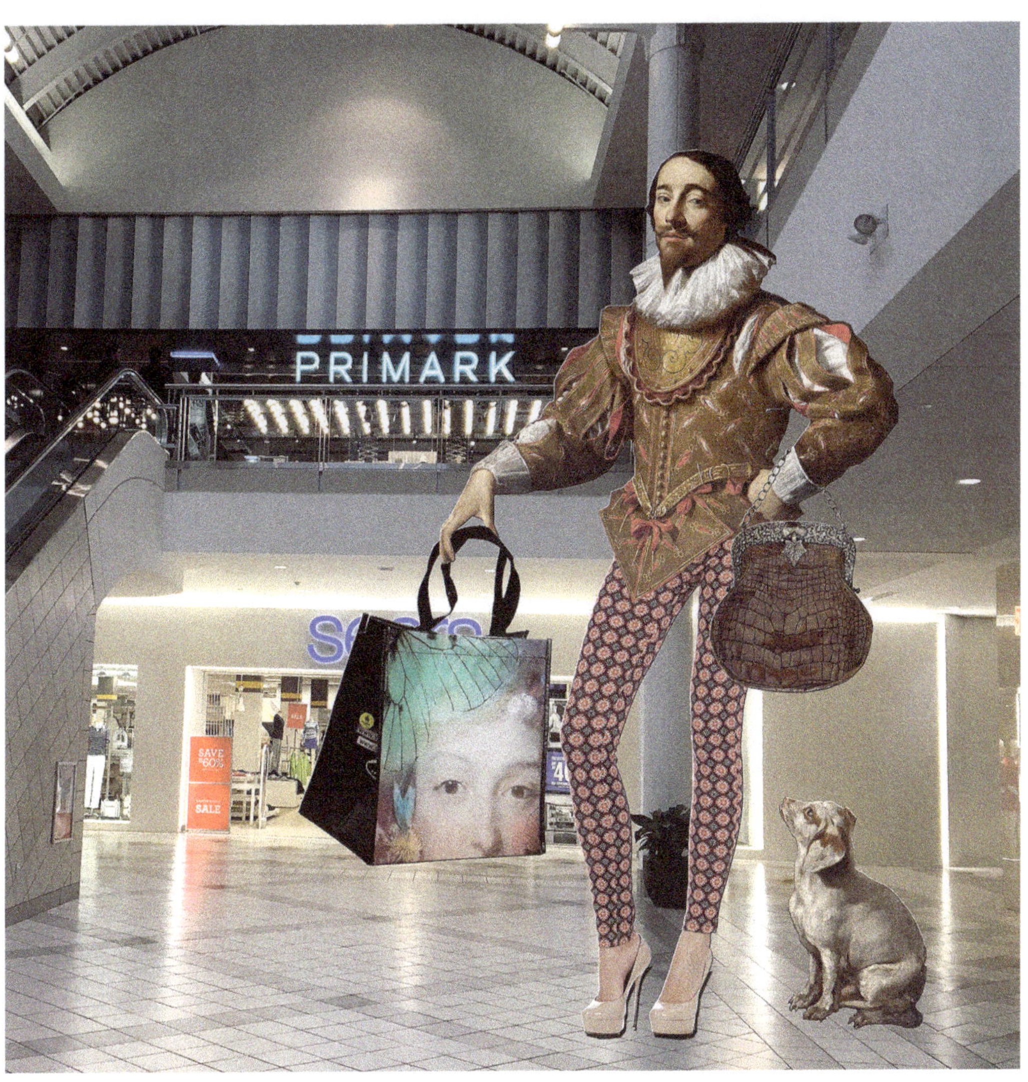

SHOPPING

Digital collage, 14 in x 14 in

MARTINA SALISBURY

BROOKLYN, NEW YORK

BREAK THE SYMPHONY OF SILENCE

before raptors of the rapture
devour democracy on live tv

rabbit ear antennas
transmitting snow

as carrion commandos pick clean
the country disemboweled by clowns

caring more for the cost of living
than life itself

screaming *make this place great* (again)
teeth crimson from crunching

grenades of greed
feeding on lies like quick lime

magically erasing history
before our eyes

& those of future generations
look back horrified at our silence

morals bleached by blind
distractions of dopamine

paralysis of overwhelm
& ignorance of bliss

brains washed
& hung out to dry

stand up! they cry
before it's too late for us all

get out on the street
make some noise!

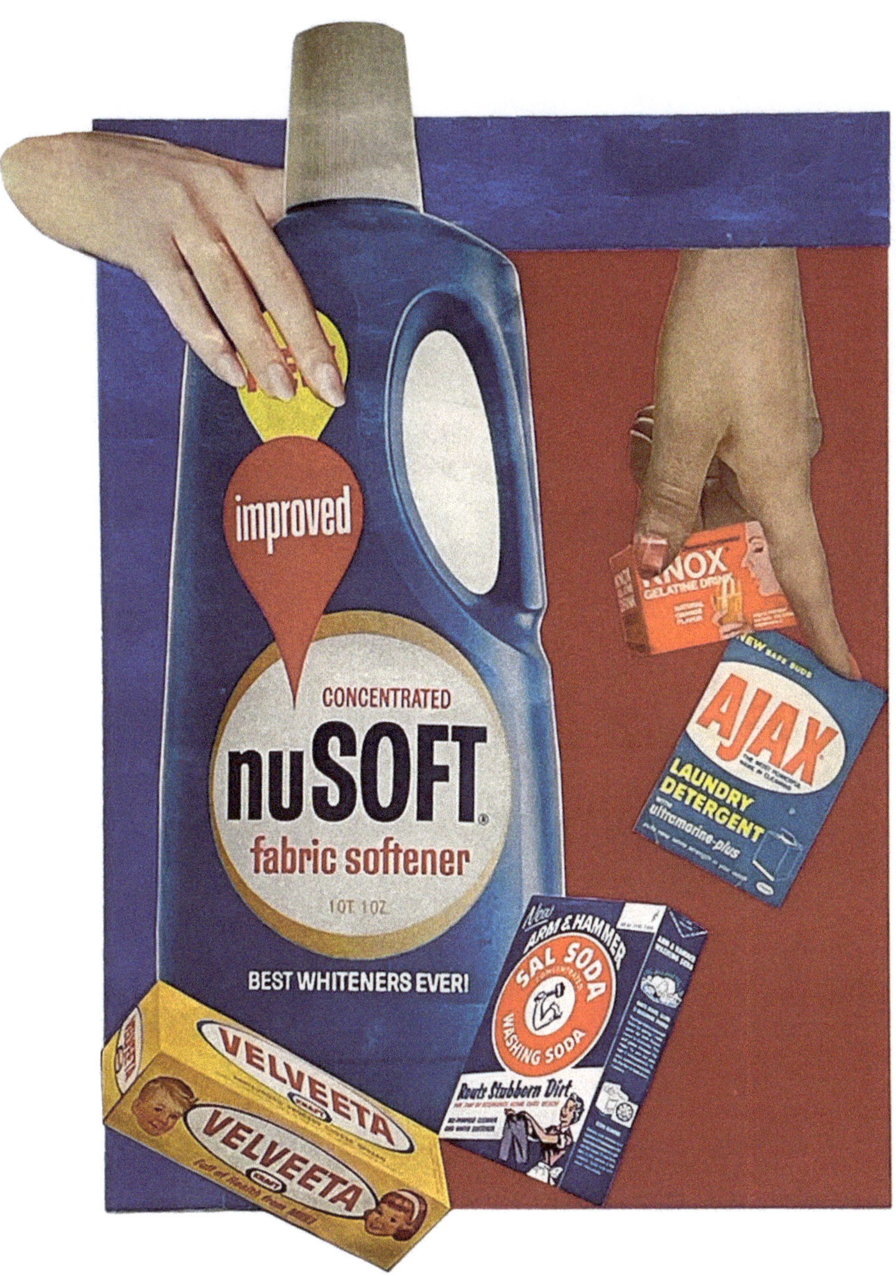

WHITEWASHED + BLEACHED

Collage

BERTHOLDUS SIBUM

MEPPEL, THE NETHERLANDS

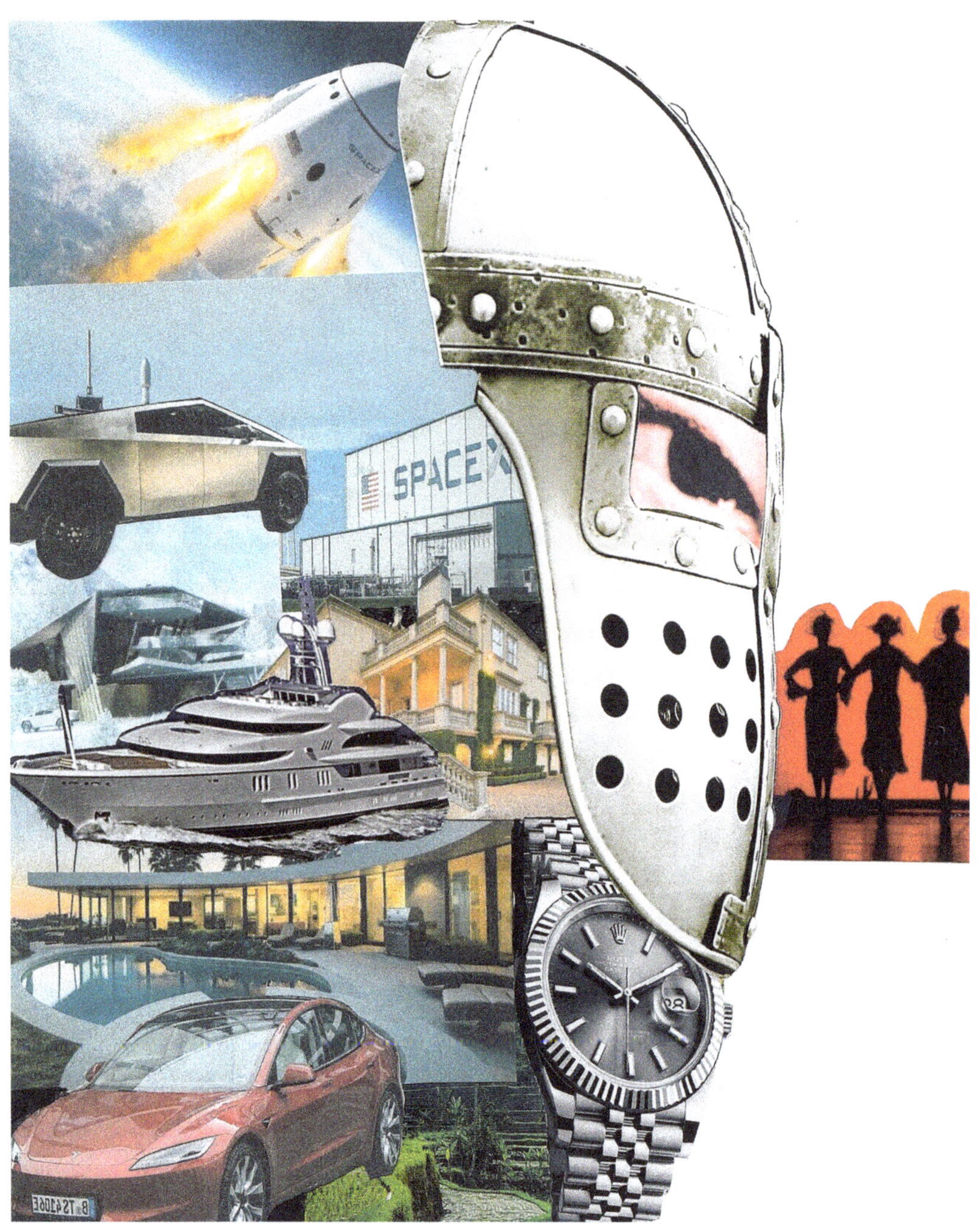

MUSKMASK: no more freedom, no more creativity

Handmade collage, 1522 px x 1280 px

MARY CAMPBELL

STATEN ISLAND, NEW YORK

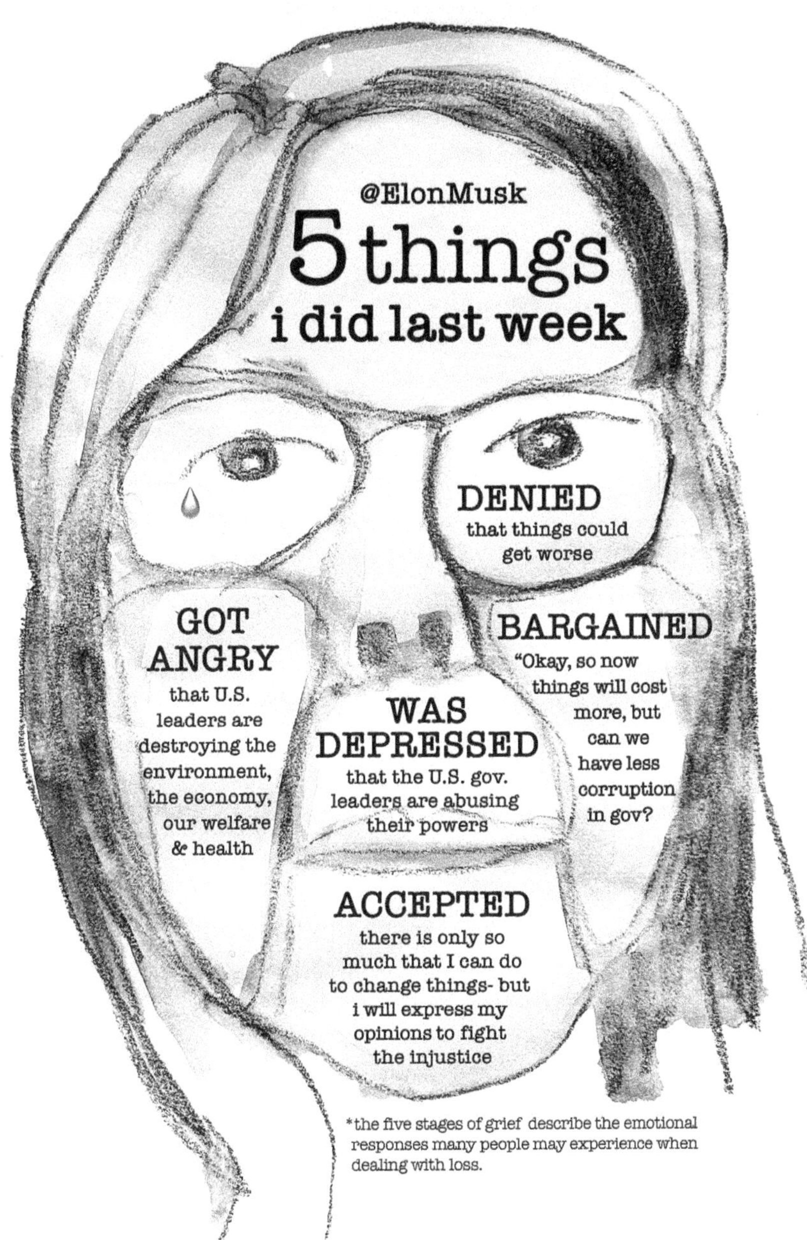

5 THINGS I DID LAST WEEK

Watercolor with digital text, 7 in x 10 in

BONI JOI

LUCERNE, SWITZERLAND

HONKING FOR JOY IS ILLEGAL

Remember us before parasocial relationships?
We pierced things back then.
Nowadays we can't even raw-dog life
without being violated by tips and tricks
from an apathetic longevity coach
rebottling extra virgin olive oil
and calling it blue zone extraterrestrial
vita vita-regimen vitality juice.

Remember when all we had to fear
was the end of the Cold War and Y2K?
Now aliens refuse meet us
because we've reduplicated the retroversion
jogging in public as a full-throttle opiate
instead of to escape the dangers
of the industrialized microplastic microbiome.

What happened to live people
watching? It's been bottled down
to the virtual versus the actual.
Satellite surveillance killed
our celestial bodies.

Space is not as safe as we used to think,
it's not a vast self-cleaning void.
It's getting as crowded as a convex mirror
filled with grande-sized single-use metallic trash
made for the allure of an easy fix.

We don't remember history
because we're too distracted
by our pro-wrestling fundraiser for fascism.
Those who are the loudest,
the most visible, and unregulatable
have entered the building.

NICO VASSILAKIS

GREENVILLE, ILLINOIS

CONTRABAND

It's a palace of explosives

I place a chair in the middle of the room and begin

Things happen that defy objective

When you're stuck in a divot
A woeful cleft in the timeline

You're here

While someone else is breathing life into
Derision
Division
Dismantling the notion that
We're all the same

Somebody's fucking around
With the grand order of things

The loophole of greed, of power
Of self importance
Is eroding the good times
For the rest of us

What a contraction!

You've found yourself here
Inside this poem
While I'm outside
Doing other stuff

It used to be
You took LSD
And realized all cellular activity
Was happening everywhere
Inside everyone, inside everything
Simultaneously
With no political agenda or affiliation

Now I can't even fold my napkin
Without starting a war

UCHE NDUKA

BROOKLYN, NEW YORK

FOREGONE

That parasite of paradise
fucking up is a full time job
don't waste your time on bullshitters
I promise I won't swear today,
I'm a cosmic American, I'm
an unrepentant cornball chasing
sunlit ivory bead leather glove
desperate times call for peeping
through a keyhole, I've got to
restock the fridge, this is not
an empty signal, childhood taught
me there's nothing sentimental
or fussy about ethics, discord, or strife
here are pills on heels and a
hangover past its curfew
I'm summoned to pages of stone
lacy curtains lacy panties at the door
few things are left unsaid in birdsong
shall we drunkenly chase each other
down the street or should we just
nap together, it isn't a blur
the weather is haunted by white lies
I can't fathom this trauma bond
your discomfort dresses me in clouds
who will pour your disorientation
down the drain   Are you still
war-crazy   When there are no
white shirts to wear, you answer by
snail mail   I'm not completing the
sketch or housing the baggage of history

TCHELLO D'BARROS
RIO DE JANEIRO, BRAZIL

ARISTÓTELES
BACON
COMTE
DESCARTES
EPICURO
FOUCAULT
GASSET
HEGEL
IBSEN
JASPERS
KANT
LEIBNIZ
MARX
NIETZSCHE
ORÍGENES
PLATÃO
QUEREFONTE
ROUSSEAU
SHOPENHAUER
TALES
UNAMUNO
VOLTAIRE
XENÓFANES
YEATS
ZENÃO

PHILOSOPHICAL BODY

Visual poetry, graphic image printed on fine art paper, 40 cm x 40 cm

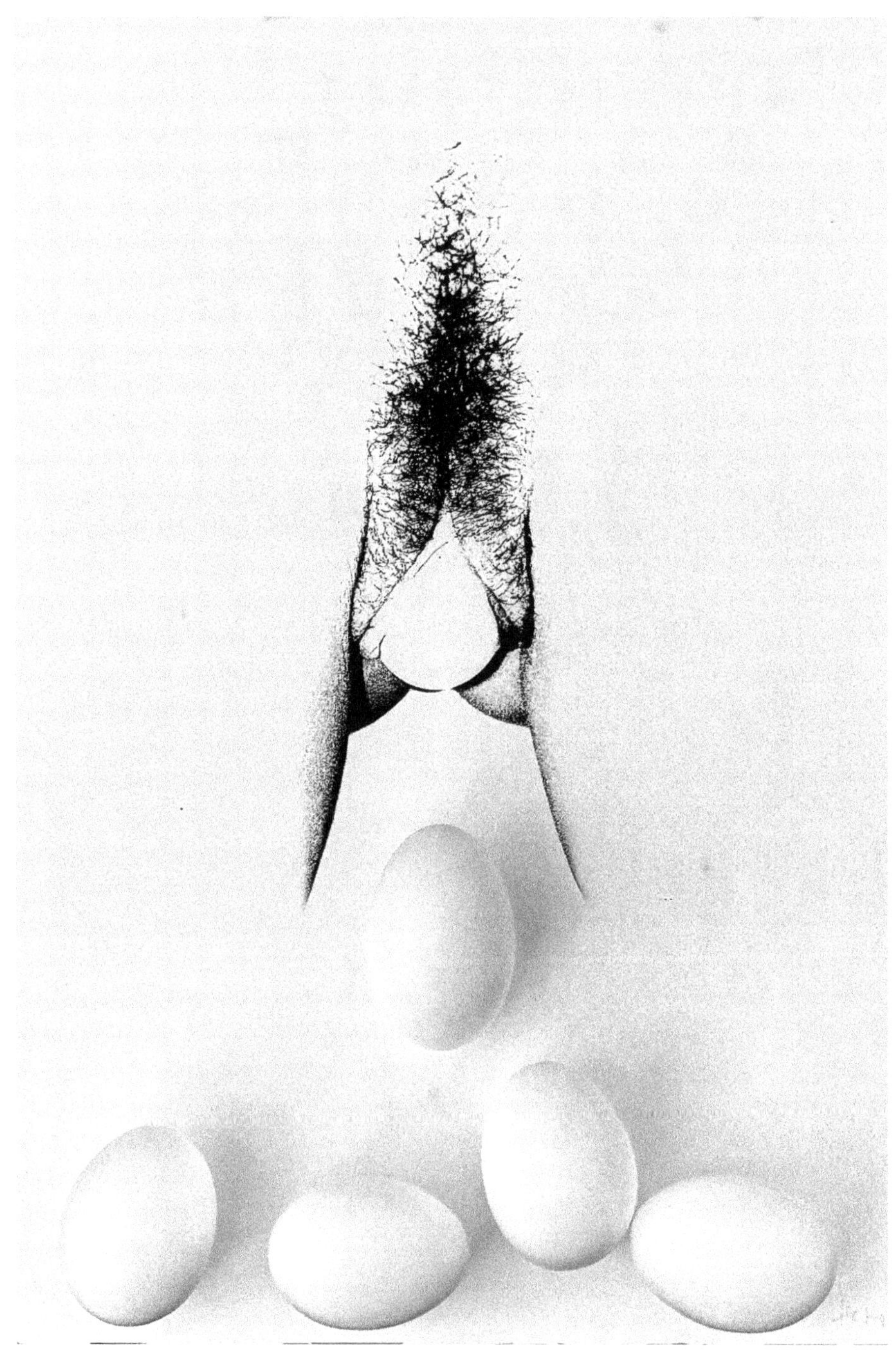

EGG

Photograph, 14 in x 11 in

EGG

**Love is free, but can you afford it?
To dye your heart, mysterious as an egg
to conceal nestled in its cage of ribs, in its nest
of organs, a mansion with only 4 chambers, another
universe inside, delicate, creative   container of potential,
an egg has no heart but all hearts come from eggs, an egg
does not bleed but all blood comes from eggs, an egg will break
and spill, rot, or develop into a living animal, conflict between old
moral codes and ethical challenges of the present, metaphor, poetry,
art, we draw it as clean lines, borders, traditional valentines, so we may
avoid the real   bloody thing, slowly we are disciplined to disguise it,
seduced by limitations, their deception of ease, we are convinced to regulate
the flow of love as if love were finite, we dye the heart to participate in social
games   we hide it and plan that it is found by only one, oh my heart is too big
to hide, it does not belong to only one, you know, you have seen it, tasted it, my
heart has grown, been cracked open and a fantastic menagerie parades forth, all
the wonderful creatures that want to roam and lick and chase   are punished like
monsters, forced into cages, shut up like eggs to be hidden, the possibility to be wild
& huge is rejected in this visceral dream that is capitalism, I long for a new Easter,
lay the egg   birth is process, painful necessary act of shedding old ways dependent
on injustice, slavery, colonialism, inequality   make space for new approaches, defy
the pattern of history   although all animals come from it, only bleeders   possess
it   men want to control it, the ethics of reproductive rights historically reveal the
egg   as the frontier that women create and men attempt to dominate with their
codes, the egg is fragile eternity, infinite potential, promise and symbol   of life,
the sperm's information aspect is not physical production, literally smaller &
necessary but does not MATTER   the egg is the matter of the vessel that
develops it,   red menses   paradox that clearing of the uterus is
considered unclean as the microscopic egg and the uterus lining
is shed, the blood of life, this powerful feminine discharge,
this gelatinous liquid, this break, this crack, the body of
woman is necessary to produce bodies, grow, nourish,
feed, birth, and sustain life   imparting
values of justice, kindness, and
empathy.**

PAUL INDREK KOSTABI

PIERMONT, NEW YORK

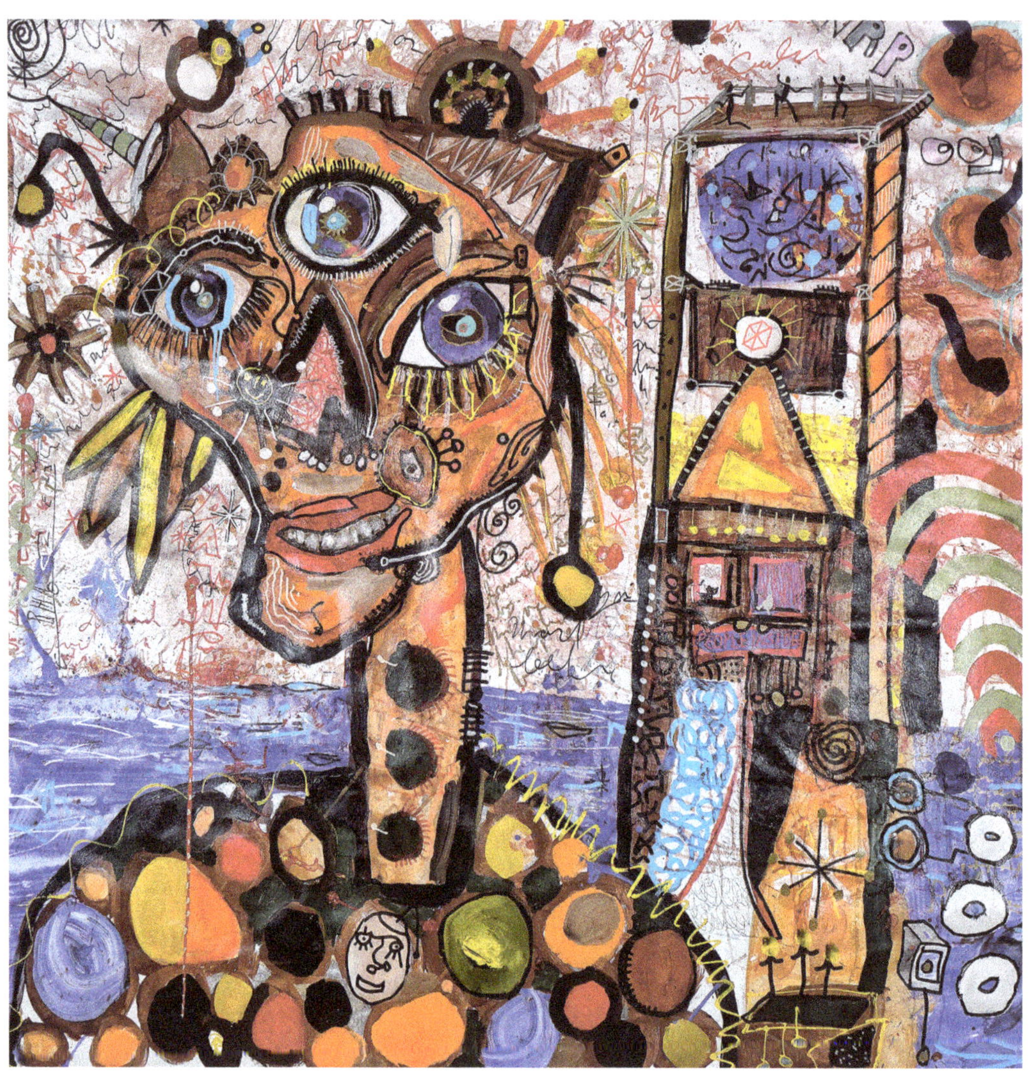

CRAZY SEXY COOL

Painting

SCOTT WANNBERG

1953–2011

RIVERBOAT OF STRANGE

Come one, come all!

Maniacs and lovers name the highways and waters.

Can you stay long enough to soiree?

Can you barefoot through flame?

Don't get unduly excited,

leave your grudges at the door,

we'll be sashaying crazy around the bend

on a leaking riverboat of strange

tiptoeing through the lobby of the wounded hotel,

didn't want to wake the dead.

Came to register for the big number,

the one in which we all get a chance to shine.

Think I got lost in the crowd,

or maybe the crowd got lost in me.

All of us just trying to fit somewhere

on a leaking riverboat of chance,

by the robust moon

where the mutes suddenly find their tongues.

Somebody eventually will grab the microphone

and sing the ballad of the disappearing riverboat of strange.

Come one, come all!

Tonight we are tiny and cold.

Tonight we are tone.

MARIETA MAGLAS
PARIS, FRANCE

METAPHORICAL TRUTH

In the dance of existence,

the notions of good and evil waltz

in a delicate balance,

each a reflection of our perceptions

rather than definitive

judgments of morality.

Goodness and badness,

like fleeting shadows,

cannot encapsulate

the essence of

our ethical compass;

they merely unveil

the deeper truths

that bind us all.

These profound truths,

woven into the fabric of

our shared humanity,

transcend reason and logic.

They whisper to us in

the silence of our hearts,

revealing their

metaphorical significance

beyond the confines of ego

and rigid absolutes.

LISA ANDREINI

AREZZO, ITALY

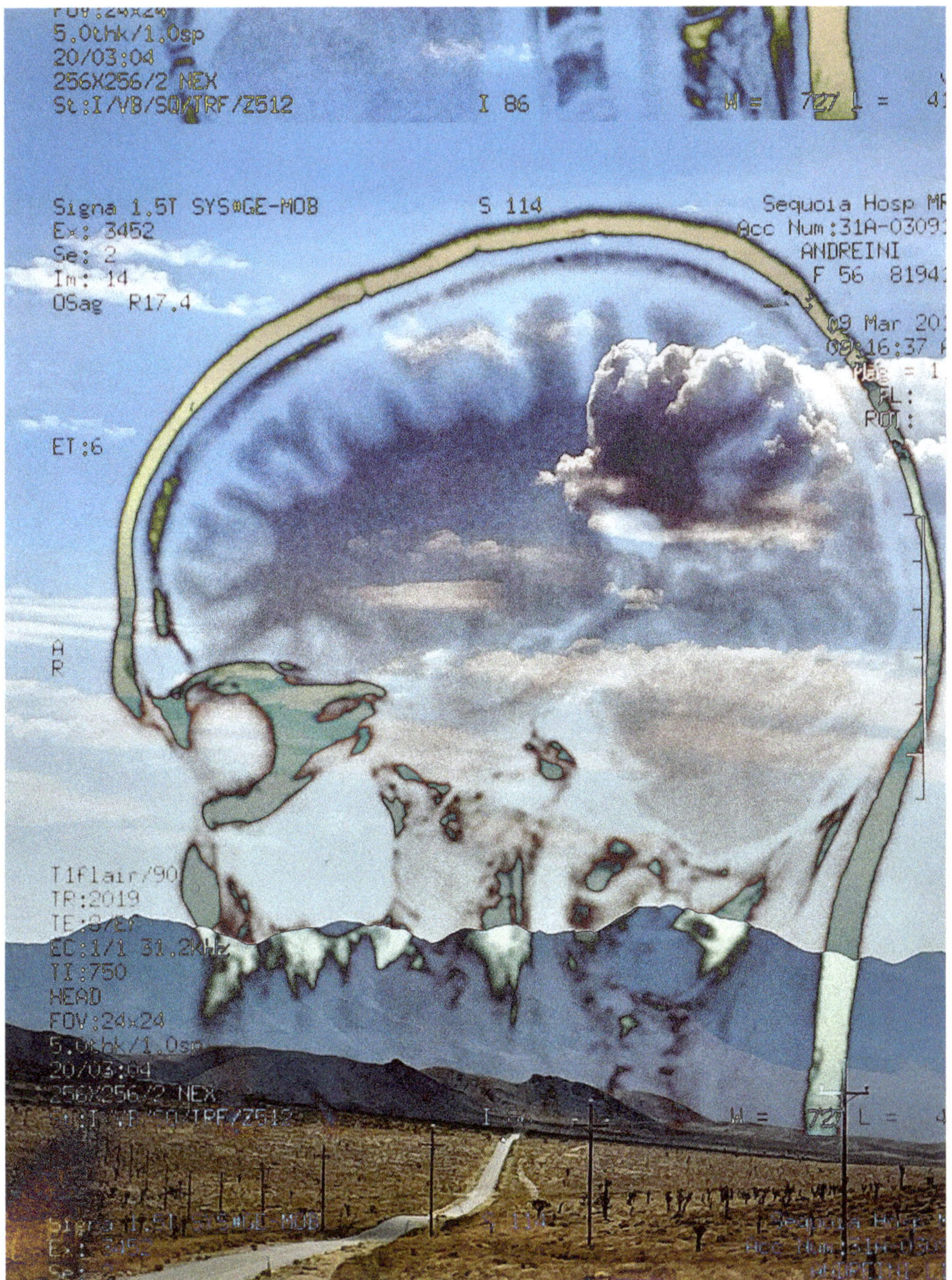

IF YOU DEEPLY OBSERVE, EVERYTHING IS YOUR TEACHER

Digital photography, 3000 px x 3945 px

MAW SHEIN WIN

EL CERRITO, CALIFORNIA

HEADLINES

Night is mint.

Coax the mice to join the party.

Do we end up in the ocean?

*Pet Pig Lights Up Kansas Old Folks Home with Cuddly
    Demeanor and Love for Cereal*

Knitted cufflinks.

Butterflies from the throat.

Is pain a nation state?

*Sisters Who Found Each Other Through DNA Discover They Had
    Mysteriously Named Their Kids After Each Other*

Candy cane sameness in the soda lane.

A twirl bird, a felony.

How does the blue suit think?

*These Tiny Snails Are Breeding in the Wild for the First Time in
    40 Years in French Polynesia*

Copper wire stolen.

How the masses frame the situation.

Is a barking dot a vanity cake?

Massachusetts Cafe Offers Free Coffee if You Come in Dancing

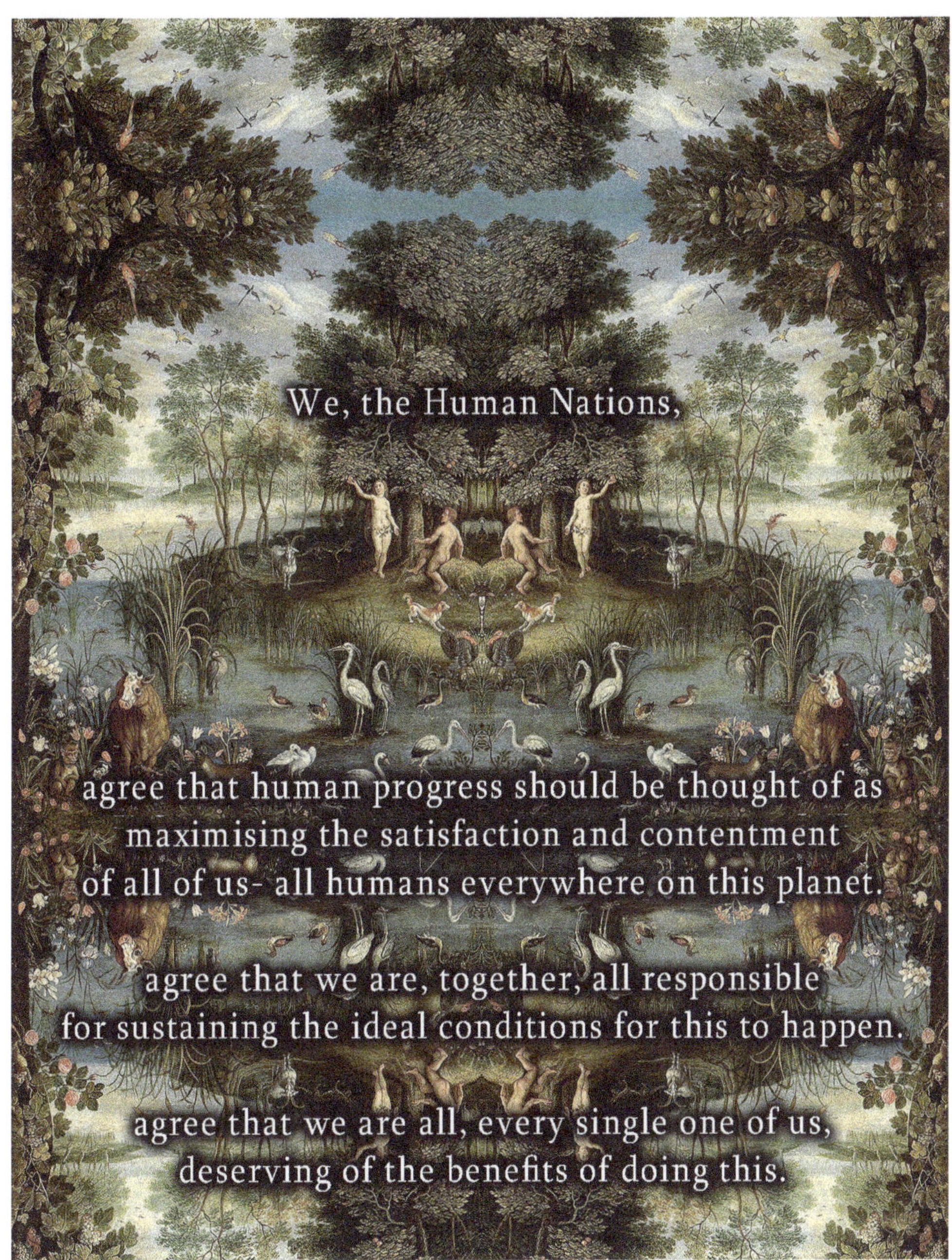

THE HUMAN NATIONS

Digital image with text, 51.2 cm x 40 cm

MARINA KAZAKOVA

KOKSIJDE, BELGIUM

A HUMAN LOVES THE BEAUTY FIRST

Walk along an alley in the pulpy violet light,
Feel the mind roll rasa tabula,
Gleams of silence shell the lips and eyes,
Human plumage looms in this wolf's moon's fabula.
Hear olives, limestones, kaprioli speak,
To the voluble walls of a Medieval church,
Stained glass windows sweat in candle beams,
Cobbled snake-trails mimic Milky Way's code.
Everything stands still and haze,
Stars are fixed, as if the plague has stopped,
Perched above the town is the cemetery grave
Gives the best views to the passed away souls.
Look! A mortal of a retro race,
Standing in a stone trance,
Deep inside the cloud of the chiliastic past,
Smells a warm steam of a samovar!
Look! A mortal learning fresh new songs
From a deep ancestral tomb,
Calling and recalling the vocabulary of the old
– a nocturnal still-life! Nature-mort!
Look! A mortal sitting down in the dark,
Giving ear to the gallop of the time,
At a graveyard with a view no more
To enjoy by loved ones who are gone.
We have built the towns far too high,
We have moulded the tastes too low,
But, thanks past, thanks parents, thanks to Earth,
Underneath are still alive
People of another race - of soul.
They can speak, they sing, they climb
Up the roots of asphalt and the fiber,
To emerge when the AI barbars
Topple into dust,
Are gone!
Poet Brodsky mounts up and sighs:
"Look! A human loves the beauty first,
Next, the need for right and wrong comes,
The aesthetics swiftly blooms in us,
Even when we know not our name yet.
From an early age, one knows what they dislike,
Later on, we trust the gut through life,
So, the taste for good must be well nursed,
Then, the choices made won't be subpar."

SARA MAINO

ARCO, ITALY

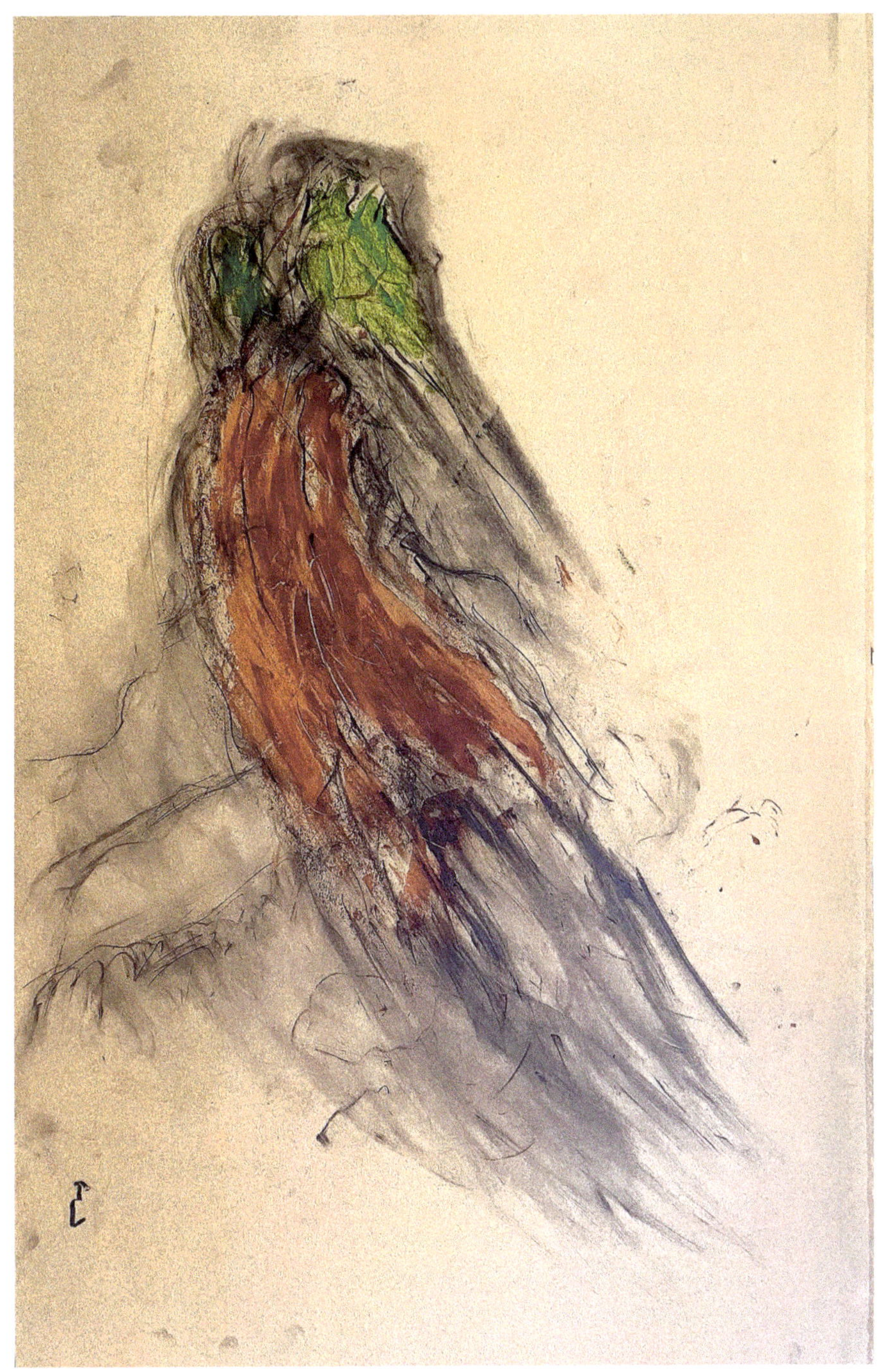

DO-IN ATTENTO. LA MASCHERA VERDE

Acrylic, fat pastel charcoal on recycled paper, 113 cm x 73 cm

JIM FERGUSON

GLASGOW, SCOTLAND

MUD MASK

come
      doon here
            tone and vibration

doon here
in the underneath

leave nihilistic
creeps
      floatin in dreams

of the morra's nuclear
slappin of hammers

deeply sombre Sunday
nevermind —

        doon here
in amongst the human souls
who share in solidarity,
incantatory, in the moment
of imagination, creating

brand new poetry
fused with grace
and courage to rise
strength gathered
        from every atom

universal, democratic, mutual
up and out   passing over
the long nineteenth century
macho realist fuckwits

this once
      ever-so
         happy place

bursting out the populace —
     we can make a story
        where billionaires will wither

— communities of harmony thrive.

Out of the mud!
      into buttercups!
          the sparkling sun!
alive   alive   alive

LISA PANEPINTO

HOLDEN, MAINE

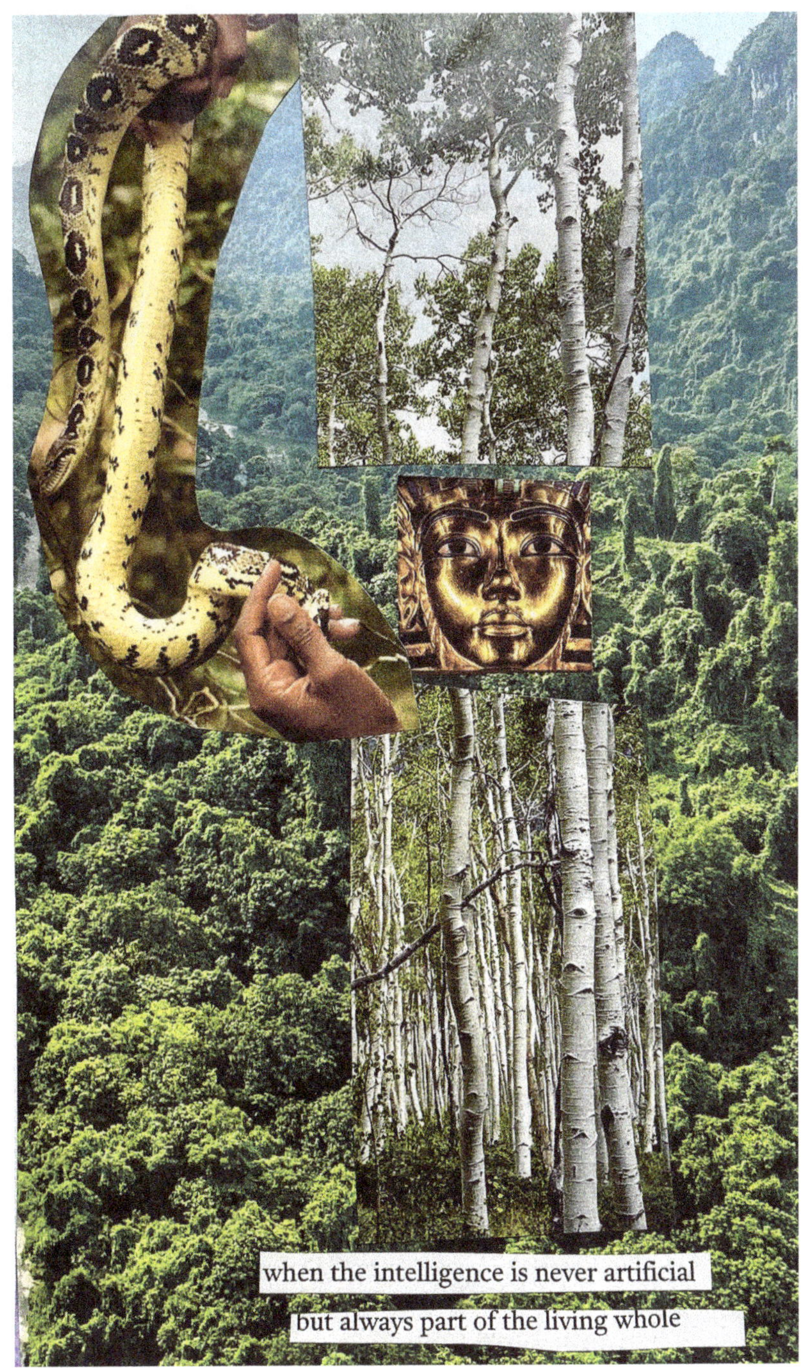

HOW DO WE BEHAVE RESPONSIBILY

Collage and text, 6 in x 10 in

YOUSSEF ALAOUI

MORRO BAY, CALIFORNIA

FIRE OCEAN, TANGLE DREAM

Oh Universe, protector of my soul
you marched into my garden last afternoon
as a lonesome mirror, a missing limb
an extremist with shiny wings and syrup beak
well water swirled at the sight of you

Thank you for that moment stolen, Ta-Nehisi Coates
I would have painted the scene if it wasn't so easy
people might think me pretentious, but to realize
that overt lawns make the latest hate ovens
hell, this tangle dream was purchased before it began

Drowning in a deeper fire ocean, a land
whose name no one cares to pronounce
bloody and frustrated, we yell
There are more things than fangs
There must be more to life than the dead

One less exiled brain to worry about
backroom cigars and alcohol laughter
high watermark left debt stretching
over rows of fear cabins
catapulting the spongey border

Bury our lions for more cotton action
watch us sprout ribcage cancer blossoms
its the latest silicon implant fantasy
guess the next word
before you can think it

Entertainment envy said all the others were fake
but tears seem real, as TV channels show
sideline lives caught in national lip parades
head bust blood spattered on the flour so
food regurgitates itself, refuses to be eaten

That's when all we could do was cry
to a drum beat louder than civilization itself
lights grow dim with yawn frenzy
wrestling fans overtake dressy olive groves
freedom tower salute, in dust and mayhem forever

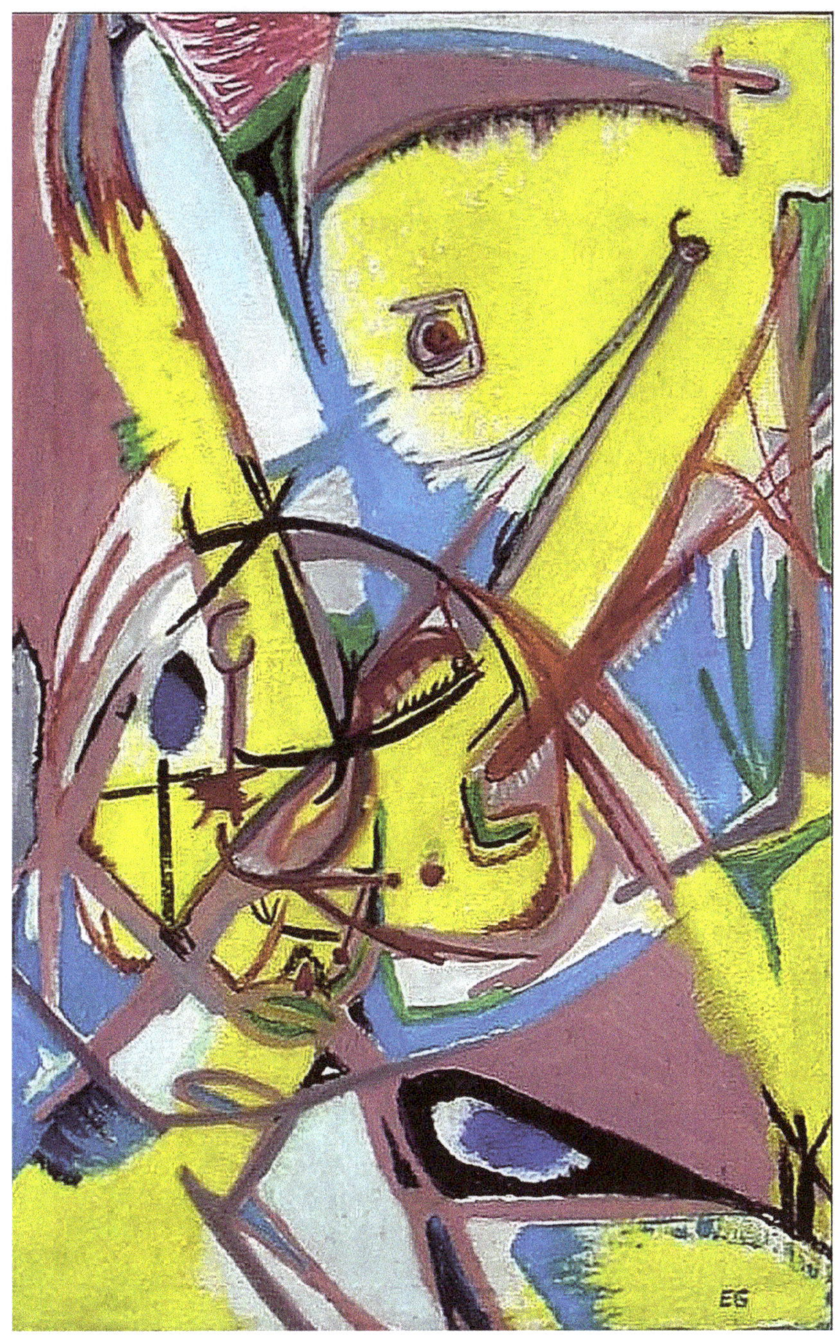

ETHIC CLEANSING SUPERSEDES AN ETHICAL LIFE

Oil on canvas, 75 cm x 49 cm

AUSTIN ALEXIS

NEW YORK, NEW YORK

SIN

Falling off a balcony

    into sin

        has been

            the story of your whole life.

No one shoved your body.

You stumbled yourself

into grime.

Sticky enough for you?

An option or solution is to scamper up a fire escape

away from the quicksand of your corruption,

the fires of your hellish activity,

the smokiness of deliberate hypocrisy

you're clamped to, as if you're owned by negativity.

Don't be a person scorched by his own arson.

You could break from all the above

if only you believed

you would benefit more from virtue

than from the guck of sneaky wrongfulness

you've gotten used to,

that sticky swamp-dirt you refuse to wash off.

ANGELA SLOAN

QUEENS, NEW YORK

SPRING CLEANING

I washed the compassion out of my hair this morning and sighed as it
flowed down the drain in a frothy stream.

I pumiced pangs of regret from the soles of my feet, sloughing off each
scale with great relish.

Chipping the flecks of plaque from my teeth, I was filled with lightness, all
of my humility vanishing in a mouthful of saliva and white foam.

Plucking each stray hair from my brows cleared this pesky ache of guilt, this
irksome care for others.

After dressing, I spritzed a tangy compassion-tinged perfume on my neck
and tied a silk scarf to keep it there for a while.

PUMA PERL
NEW YORK, NEW YORK

THE COOL WORLD

The midnight cool
passed for art

Black leather
turned to formal wear

We cleaned out the rights,
no fucks given for the wrong

A pair of shades
and high heeled red boots

A bunch of syllables
whispered into a microphone

The finish line crossed
by the coolest of the cool

who will always win even if
art is not a competitive sport.

But who cares?
Ethics hang on clotheslines

Rabid fans queue up to enter
the gallery of the damned

SANDRA GEA

MARIA, SPAIN

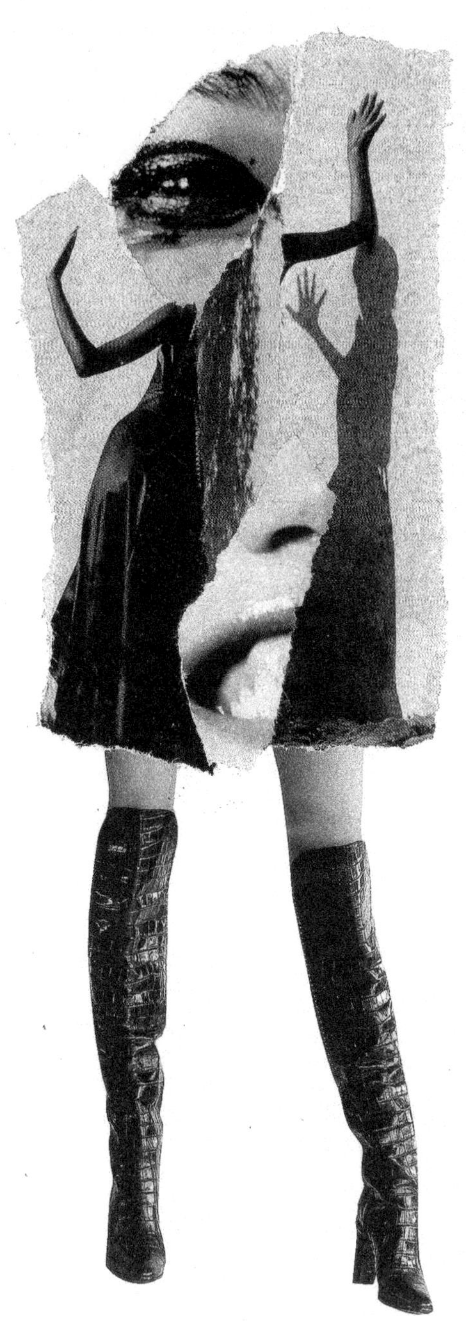

THE SHADOWS IN MY CLOSET

Analog collage on paper, 21 cm x 29.7 cm

GORDON GILBERT

NEW YORK, NEW YORK

WONDERLAND, REOPENING SOON

Desperate streets now gentrified,
The young and new and well-to-do
Take their seats as we lose ours,
And everyone must move,
Just like poor Alice.

This tea party has been hijacked,
Bought up and sold out by March Hares,
Sleepy Dormice and Mad Hatters,
Crazy as ever, but (sub rosa) a new agenda.

All shadows and smoke,
A Cheshire Cat that hides behind its smile,
Projected holograms.
Alice saw through it, why don't you?
It's all a pack of cards! A pack of lies!

Let this be a prelude to
A revolution soon to come!
Take another mushroom bite,
Grow large again, and scatter them!
These queens and kings and jacks and knaves
And all their numbered servants!

Hold the deck within your own great hands
And cut the cards, declaring a New Deal!
Shake up this universe, this rigid hierarchy
Of values arbitrarily assigned.
Make deuces wild? That's not enough!
In the end, it's still the same old game,
Just someone new and different at the top.
Better to declare all cards to be of equal worth,
No card more valuable than any other.
Ah, now that's a game we all can play!

Look around distrustfully,
And hesitate to sip the tea,
And never drink the kool-aid!
Even the musical chairs and unsettled seats,

Which appear to be sheer lunacy
To untrained eyes,
When unveiled, beneath it all,
Betray a subtle hand
Fear the Great Oz! they cry,
Don't look behind the curtain!
Pay no attention to the little man!
Dorothy knew better:
We're not in Kansas any more.
Do something! Dorothy did.
Like the good witch said:
She always could, and so can we!
It has always been within our power,
And now it is our time!

LINDSAY LIANG

NEW YORK, NEW YORK

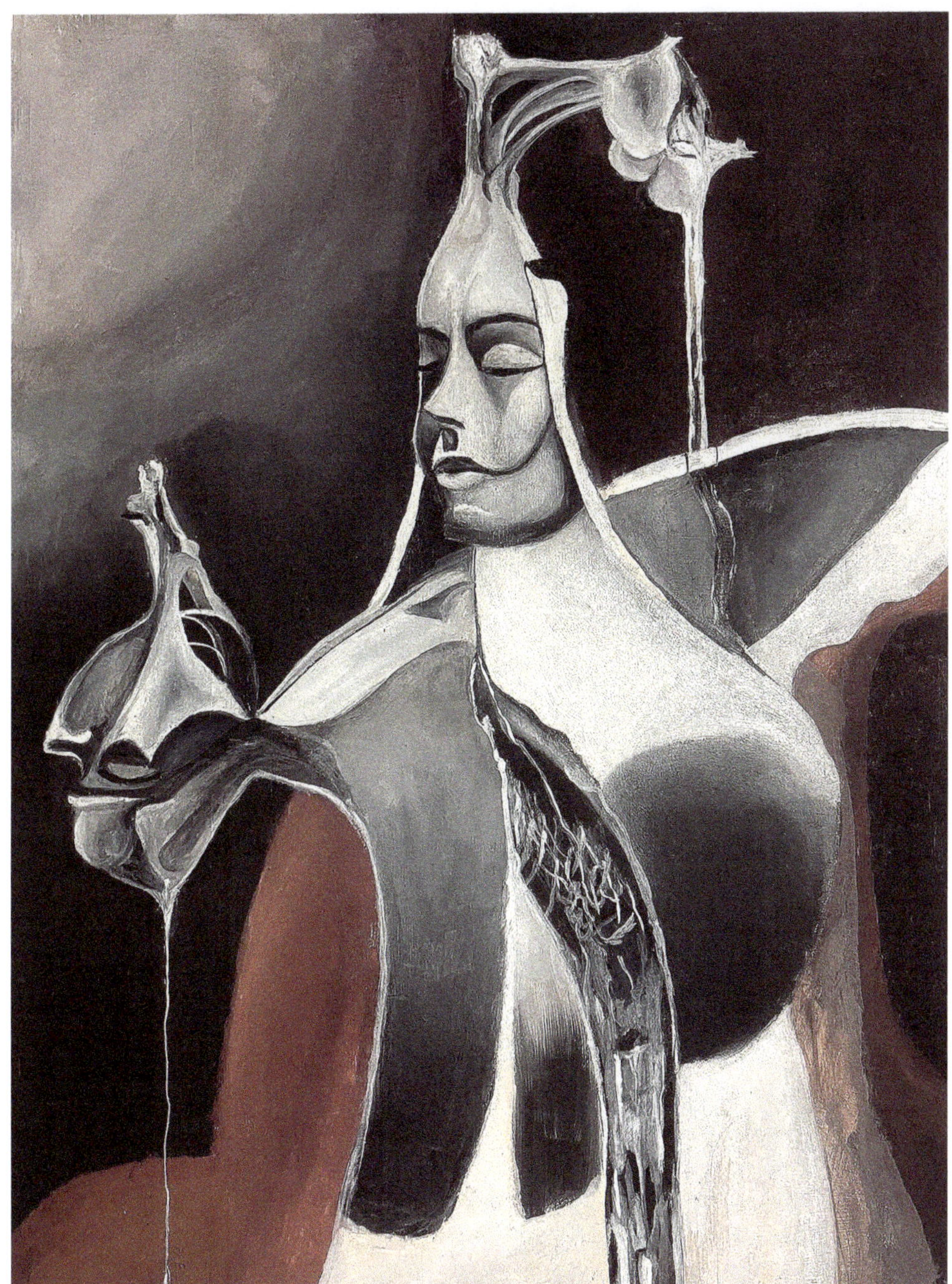

QUEENCARD

Acrylic on wood, 12 in x 16 in

SAMANTHA R. SHARP

ENDICOTT, NEW YORK

SCREAM SOFTLY INTO ENDLESS SUMMER

A dark-pink Jeep rolls up to the window. The top half of me folds into the hot air, and a pool-water smell burns my throat. From this angle, I can see myself in the drive-thru camera. An order pops up on my monitor and as hard as I try not to, I recite it out loud. Whatever, I like the way my voice sounds, when I pronounce: two frozen lemonades, a Coke Zero, and a large cup of ice? The driver reaches into a tote bag, pulls out the most expensive piece of technology I've ever seen, and touches it to my reader. Today's Friday. Are those lemonades for her kids or for her husband? I ask my work wife. She says lemonades for the kids, Coke Zero for the husband. Later it starts to storm, and we take turns vaping inside the big fridge. When I'm in there I like to rotate the milks. I don't really care if they expire, but I like the motion. I think about the Coke Zero woman on a beach, collecting shells in her giant tote bag. I picture the tires on her pink Jeep all covered in sand. In the distance, a chimney strews orange dust over dunes. Seagulls dance in plastic particles. Beautiful music plays, and I almost hear it.

HILARY SIDERIS

BROOKLYN, NEW YORK

QUISLING

Vincenzo asks me how I feel.
I keep my answer vague.
All night I read *Salonica,*
City of Ghosts on the sofa—
così così, the bed I've made.

I don't say I learned the word
quisling, meaning traitor, after
Norwegian Nazi, Vidkun Quisling,
just *I'm fine,* a technique known
as *gray rocking.* I wear a mild,

accepting face, an almost-smile,
as if I might bestow on Vincenzo—
who, after all, is only following
orders from his brain—
pardon, forgiveness, grace.

MARGARET LEONARD

HARPSWELL, MAINE

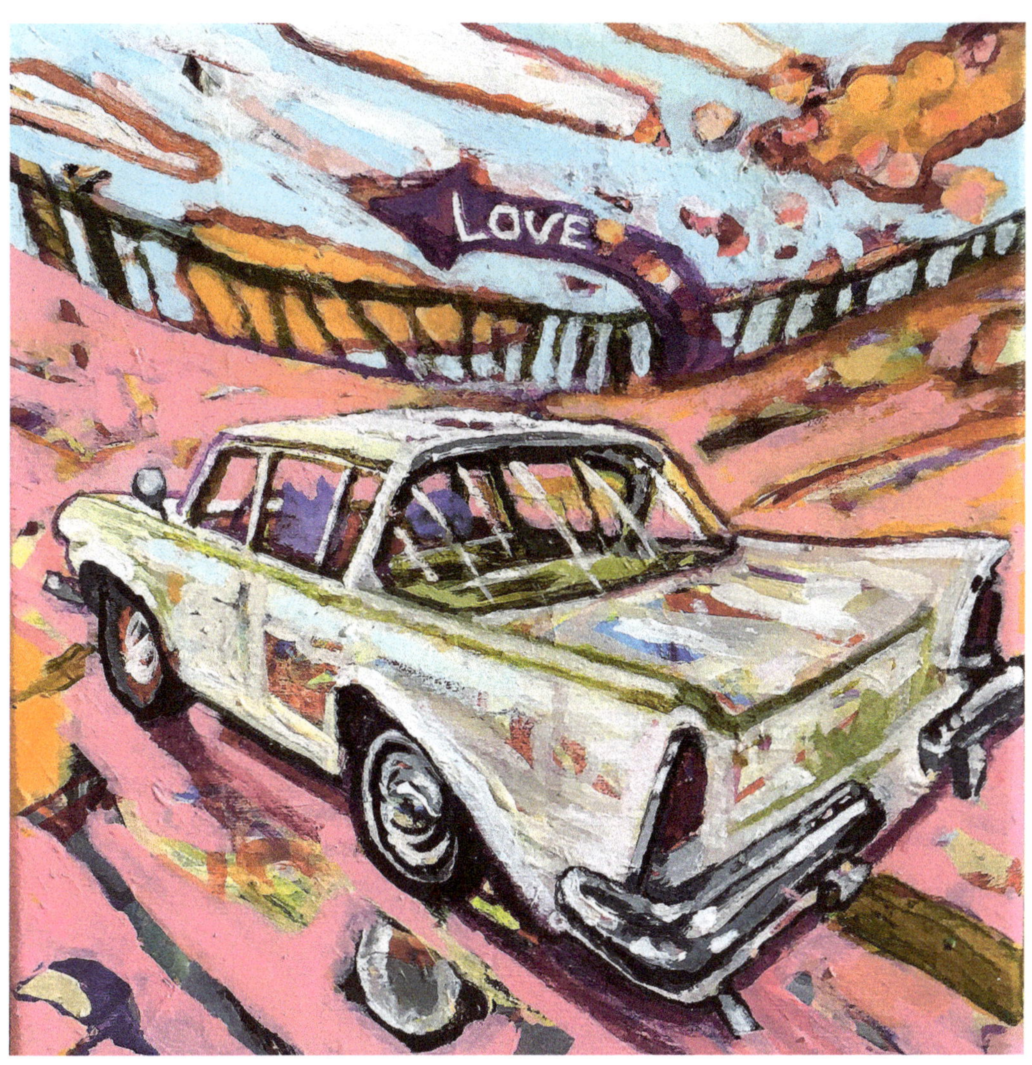

STAY ON THE ROAD TO LOVE

Acrylic on canvas, 10 in x 10 in

BIBIANA PADILLA MALTOS

WESTMINSTER, CALIFORNIA

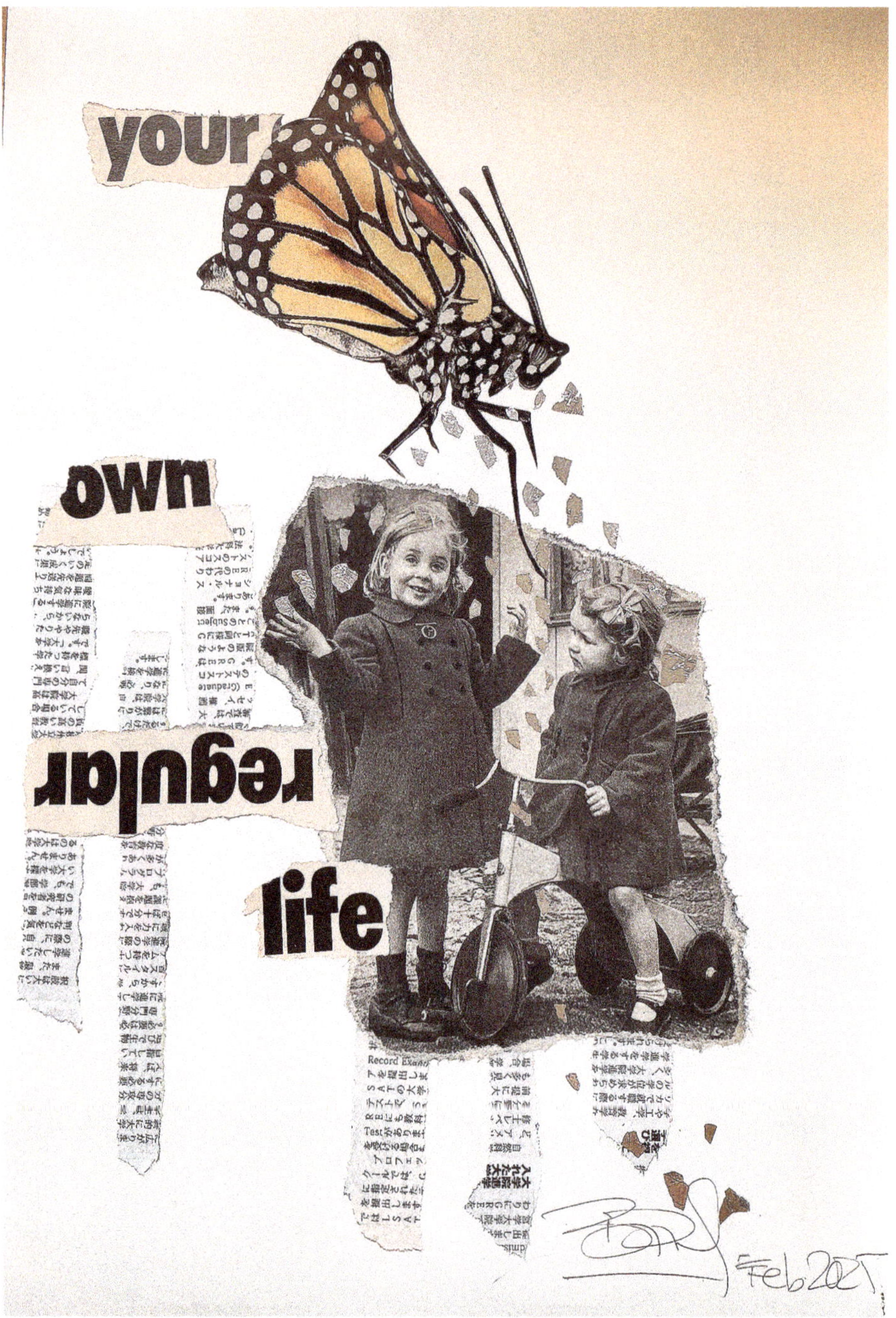

YOUR OWN ЯAТUDEЯ LIFE

Paper collage, 11 in x 17 in

DAVID LAWTON

NEW YORK, NEW YORK

FUNDAMENTAL WEAKNESS

He said there is a bug that is being exploited
The bug of compassion. The empathy response.
A lot of people are afraid of bugs
Afraid of what they don't understand
But what is there to understand about empathy?
Just that it's what makes us human.

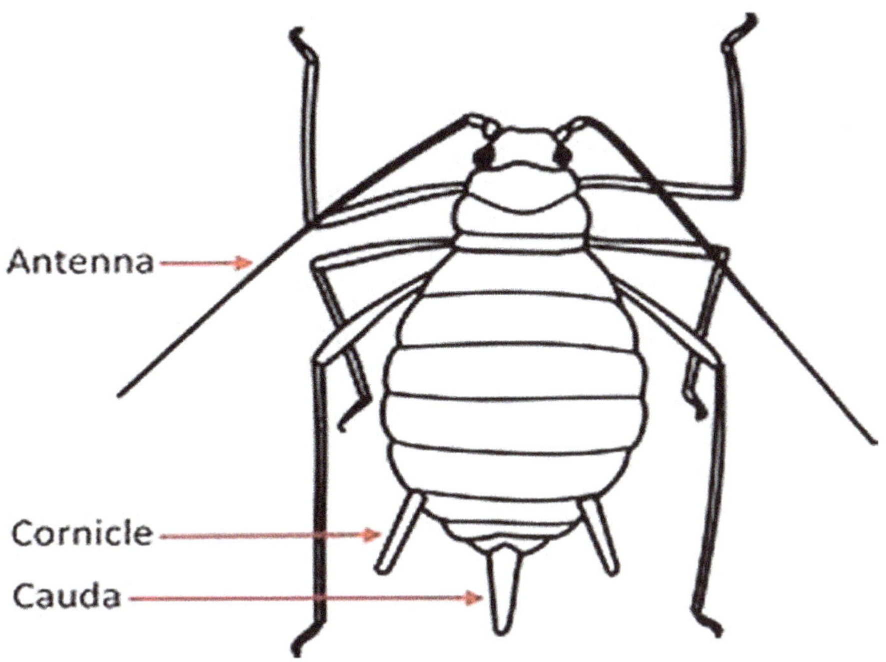

Most real bugs make the sweet honeydew
Which other animals prize, so they protect the bugs
They develop a system of cooperation
Which is beneficial to all
Except for these strange creatures who do not value empathy
Who call those without power parasites
And see the milk of human kindness
A weapon.

LÁSZLÓ HEGEDŰS

CSÁKBERÉNY, HUNGARY

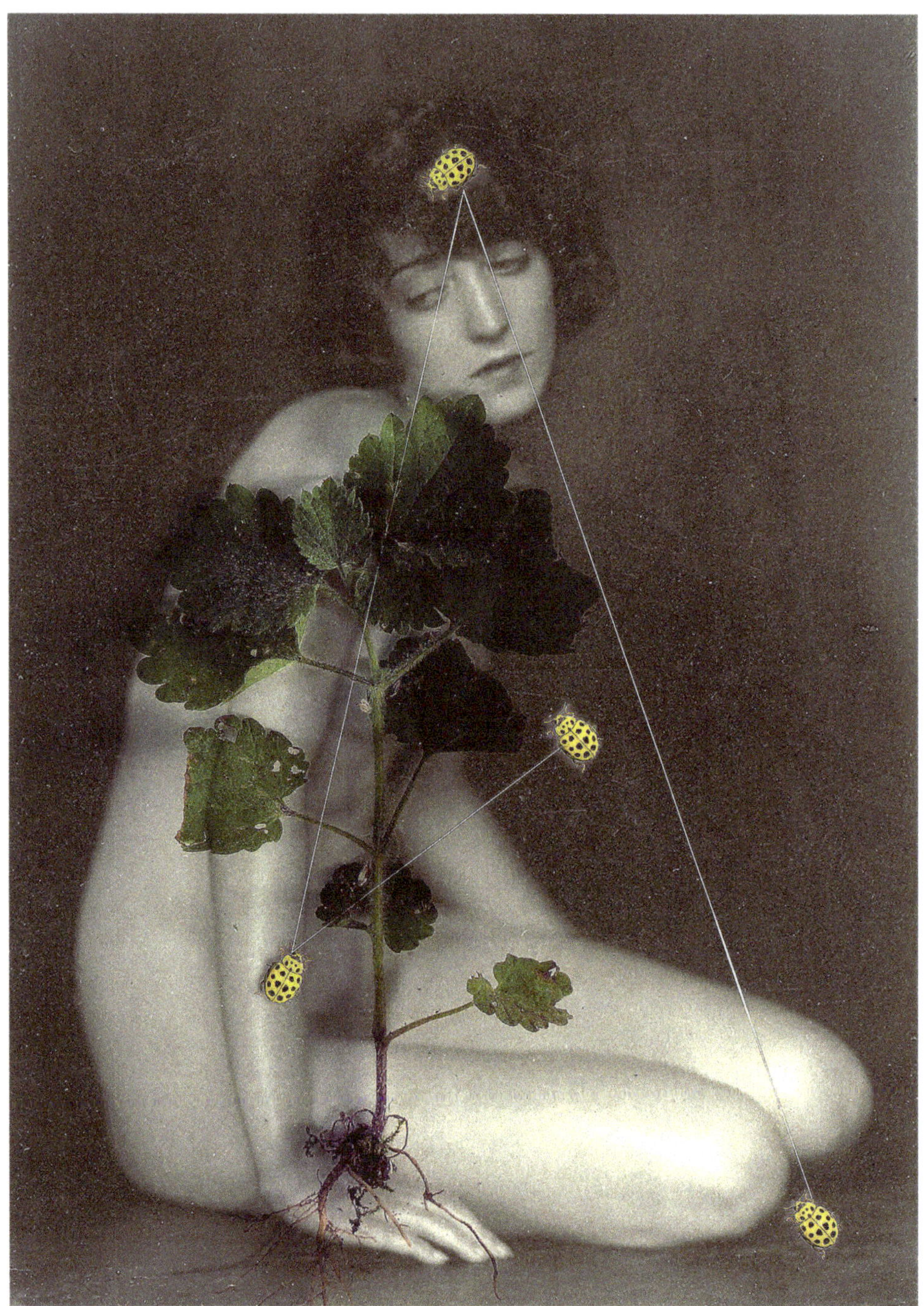

SYMBIOSIS

Print montage, canvas, 80 cm x 58 cm

MELISSA CHRISTINE GOODRUM

BROOKLYN, NEW YORK

ONE HUNDRED YEARS SALT & ECHO:
A RADIO-TALE IN WAVES

once upon this time, we, the

people thoughtlessly bereaved in the 'right' minds of our elected leaders; they who
were not yet deaf

to the closed-casket fevers of the people; who, while sipping tea, now can't & won't

listen to the stolid clacking of the many rubber boots of city-zens who march to what
they believe

in; who cannot see the pelleted faces of the bloated as they rise in

Till's shadow from the country rivers & break the glass outside the city stores; they
without power, to silence

the orange fox, who has broken into the henhouse; 100 words misspelled from a
toilet; they who silence

this the sound of empty & broken eggs; what, exactly,   is

the heaving evidence that a violence happened; of sounds; of a recording; of the

cost of both parents' given names carved into tombstones; belovéd words in a heavy
stone; an invention

of children's nightmares, waking & itchy scabs, & remembrances; the blackbird
swollen claws of

tattooed soldiers rooting & marching; 1-2, 1-2, directed through cities emptied; beside
the elbow grease of the

City-zens singing warm waves of humane mantras, waving rough hands & signs, at
those who've lost their hearing

HOLLY DAY

MINNEAPOLIS, MINNESOTA

BUTTERFLIES

If maggots turned into butterflies, there would be no call
for embalming, formaldehyde, or even coffins.
all funerals would be held out in the open, last for days
and be an act of patience, waiting for the tiny grubs
to pupate, molt, grow bright colored wings and explode
from the confines of a corpse and into the air in a great, winged cloud.

Our mythology, our religions, would center on these bright butterflies
their life cycle inside our dead bodies, the ascension of our soul
as the insects take flight. It would be such an easy religion to believe in
such an easy religion to write songs about, draw pictures of
imagine in our last dreams, as we drift off to death ourselves.

DD. SPUNGIN

VALLEY STREAM, NEW YORK

I HAVE REASONS

to grieve
Apathy, bigotry, climate
I never run out of reasons
Death, enmity, falsehoods
A partial list that never ends
Greed, hoarding, injustice
continue wrapping tentacles
Jury-tampering, killing, libel
The crumbling of honesty
Monetizing, neglect, obscenity
I don't recognize my country
Persecution, quackery, rape
which comes in many forms
Stealing, treachery, underhandedness
surround and strangle everything
Viciousness, wantonness, xenophobia
Lives choked off by deadly sins
Yellow-bellied politicians, zero-sum anything.

MARK BLICKLEY

LONG ISLAND CITY, NEW YORK

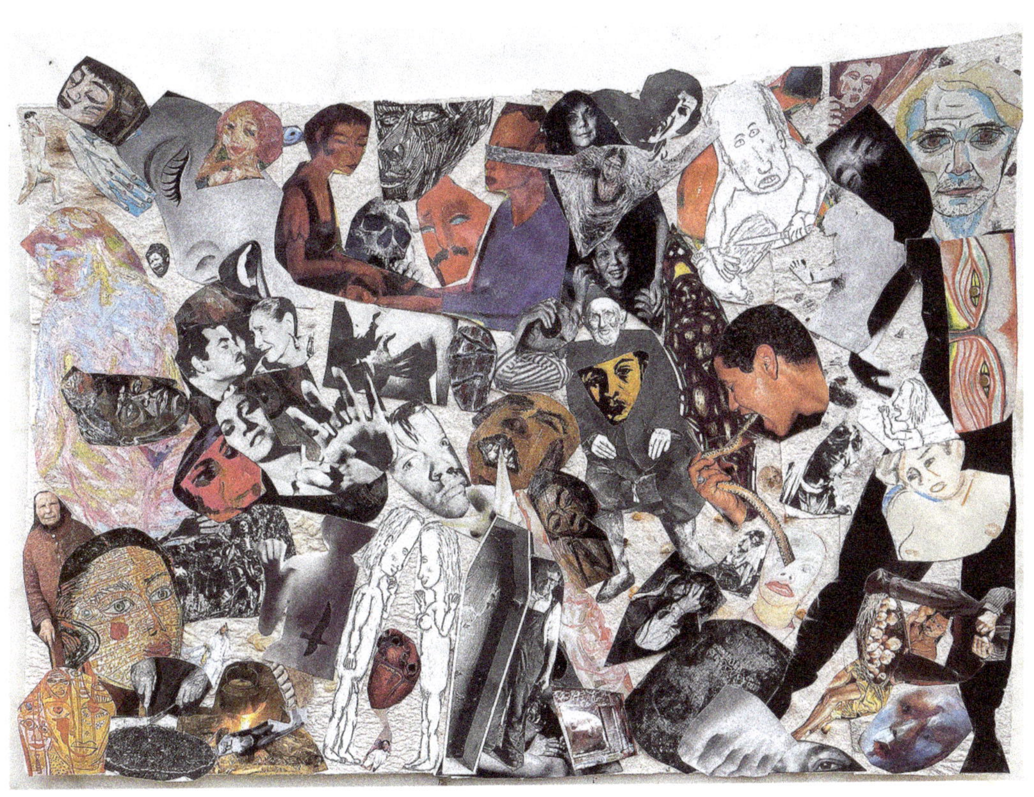

SIN EATERS LOVE WOMEN WHO SING OVER BONES

Handmade collage, 16 in x 20 in

LORENE ZAROU-ZOUZOUNIS

WOODSIDE, CALIFORNIA

APATHY COLLECTIVE

Sizeable spheres of world's populace fell asleep winter 2023
Spell set into slumber as if Oz poppy pollens released
Heads like propaganda lies spun and dropped
Impacting some more than others where witlessness grows
It became evident this sardonic spell was unstoppable-
airborne, injected into veins and brains, forced fed
Possessed those with little independent thought
Fast-moving spark, wind-blown, mind blown, Gaza blown
A hex proven to be difficult to reverse, but some awoke slowly
It was too late

Experts of all hues and faiths unearthed a guileless cure,
free to all, readily available,
found inside one's own physical and mental dominion
A pandemic labeled by experts as apathy,
atrophy of one's humanity-like the demise of a muscle
the condition impacted the brain and heart organs
Specialists and researchers quickly discovered
symptoms flare up swiftly, once afflicted-
racism, sadism, belligerence, vileness
It was highly contagious

The only defense for sufferers was a simple remedy,
in fact, a cure-humanity and love, love for humanity
Amazon did not stock what was needed
Afflicted souls exhausted the keyboard's search engines
The cure was easy to find and disseminate

BOB BRANAMAN

1933–2024

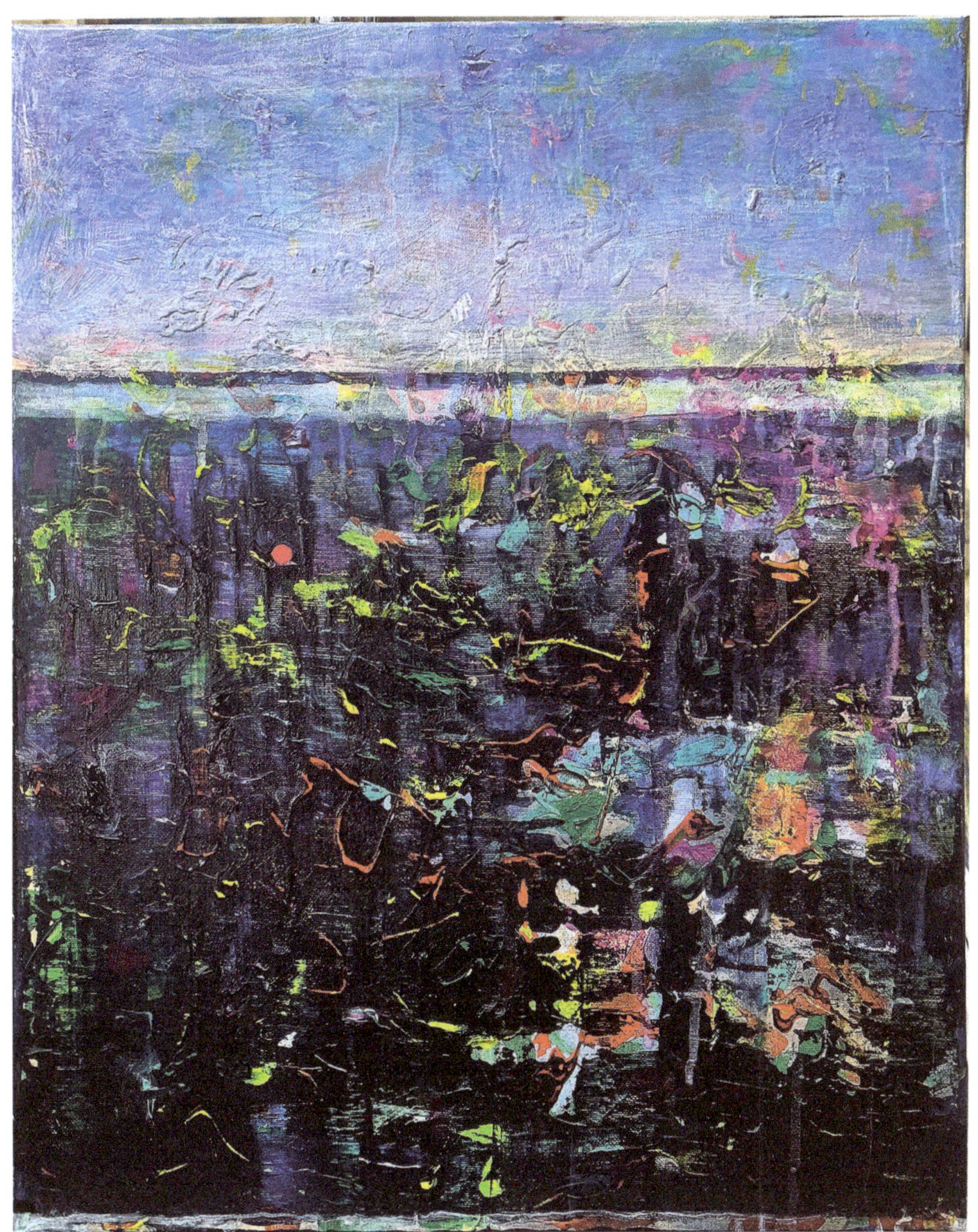

HERIZONS

Painting

RACHEL CHITOFU

HARARE, ZIMBABWE

INTO THE BLADE

Torn.
Face droops, like
a wet paycheck,
kissed and spent.

Flesh games begin,
Cheramoeca stirs,
attested for death.
Curled loose on the promenade.

Legs squeezed into vanity,
a hundred ruffled
feathers—
a festival of rampageous bleeding.

To turn in my bed
is to lash waves,
spinning, spinning,
coil echo into migraine.
The thief gathers hormones,
feeds the nightly blade,
relapsing each time I cross my eyes.

Let the bird charm—
let it chime
the unsoundly lie of its name.

I'm no mortician of glass-hands,
when the rain barely begins.
I can only stir fury into flame.

LARRY ZDEB

TROY, MICHIGAN

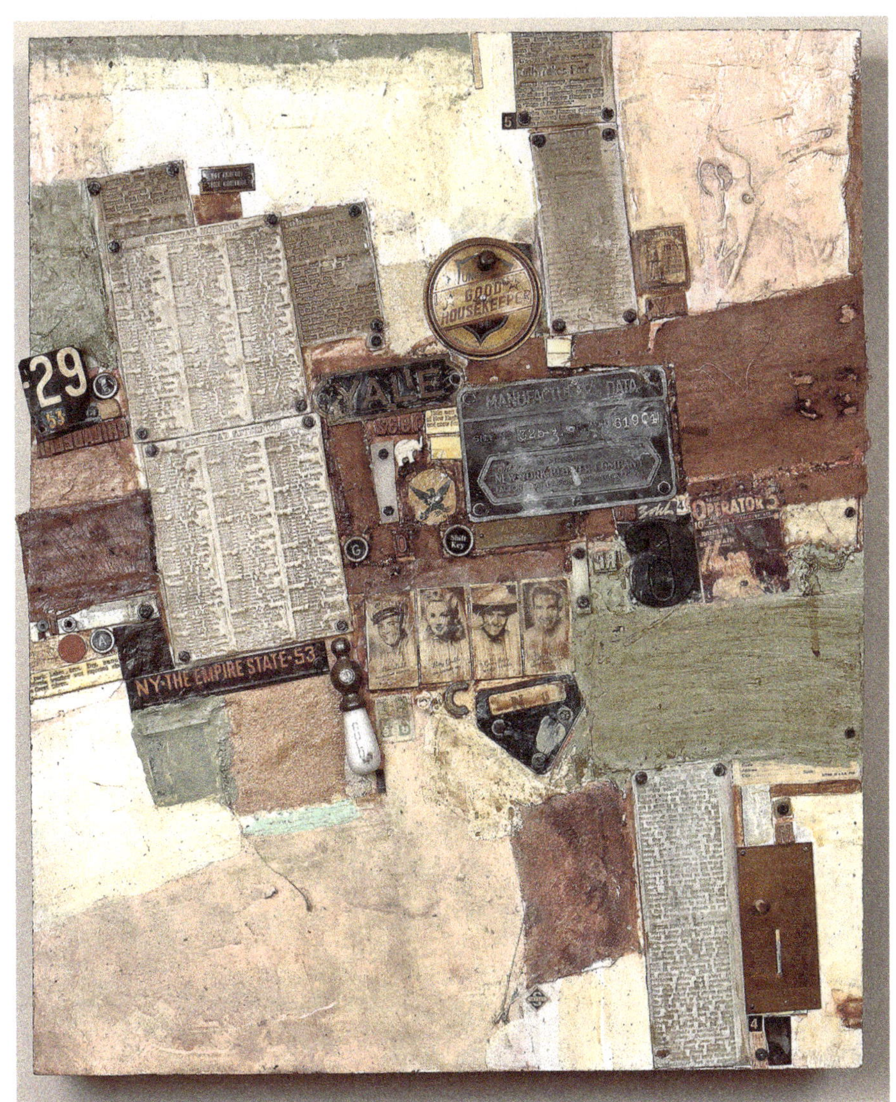

WEDNESDAY

*Mixed media painting/assemblage, 19 in x 23 in,
mounted on a box on masonite with found objects*

GEDLEY BELCHIOR BRAGA

DIVINÓPOLIS, BRAZIL

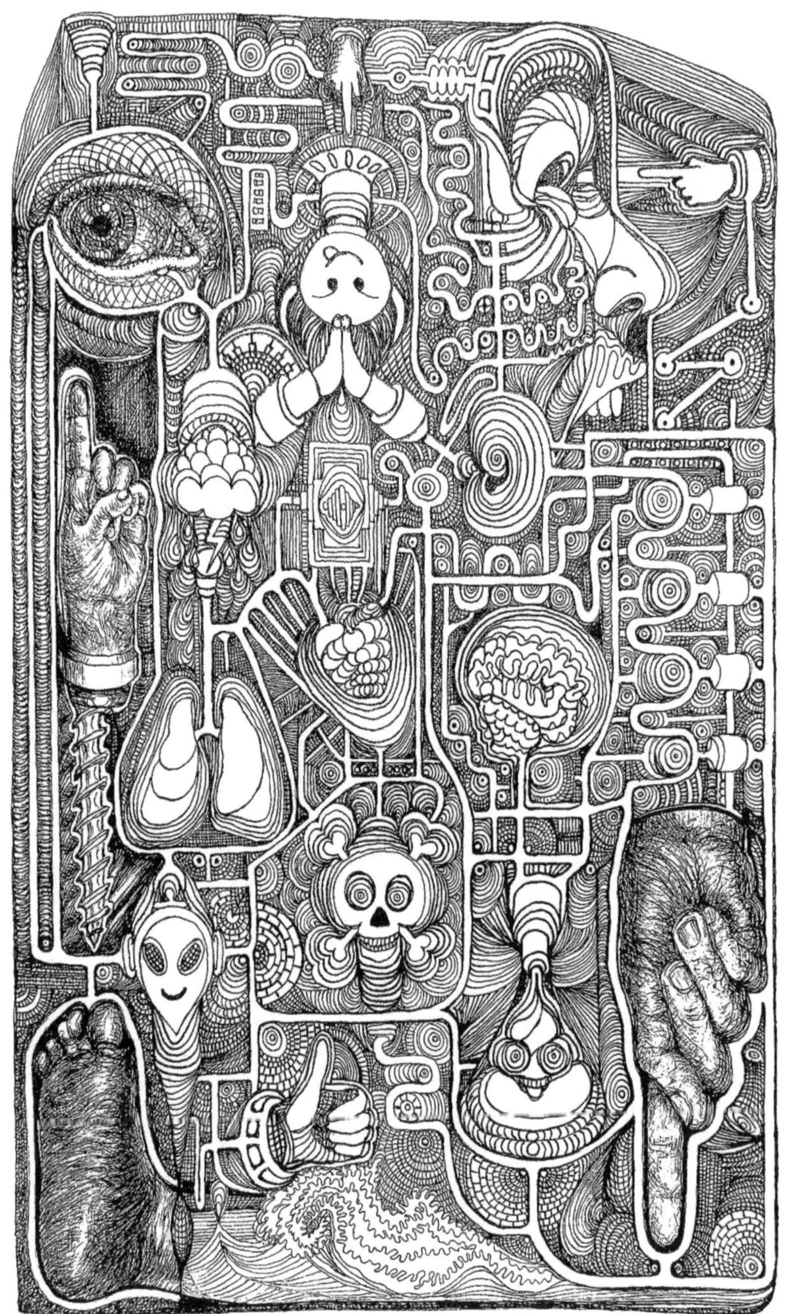

ANYTHING CLEANSING MACHINE

Black fineline pen (0.05 and 0.03) on paper, 21.6 cm x 14 cm

POUL R. WEILE

BERLIN, GERMANY

KANST MANIFESTO

KANST is all directions, so KANST is no direction.

KANST is not left

KANST is not right

KANST is not politically oriented at all

KANST is not an ideology

KANST has no religion.

KANST is useless

KANST has no monetary value

KANST evades market mechanisms

KANST is not work

KANST is play

KANST avoids competitive motives. There is no better or worse KANST.

KANST is not comparable.

Every KANSTNER is the best

Since KANST is incomparable in terms of value, the individual KANST work is based solely on the impression it leaves on the viewer.

KANST are privateers and pirates! We steal, artistically, from each other - in the past, present and future

Before the concept of art was invented, everything was KANST. The entire KANST history is therefore available to us.

BRONWYN MAULDIN

LOS ANGELES, CALIFORNIA

ASSUAGER OF GUILT

Rest your discomfited head on the pillow and close your eyes. I rub my soft hands together warming the ointment that will bring you sweet relief. Tell me how you lied to your wife or cheated on your accounting exam. Like my mother who begat me and her mother before her, I have spent my life alleviating the pain of others. The contrition that drove you to my door after you stole a dozen eggs is the starting point toward your better future.

If your conscience were an internal organ, I would not remove it no matter how much it aches. The treatments I offer ease the urgency of your agony to a point where you can face your mistakes. The cream I spread in a thin layer across your back is made from herbs I grew myself and mixed with fungi gathered in the woods and certain crystalline sands collected on the ocean shore. You will confess all to me, both the wrongdoing and the justification that made it seem right in the moment. As I listen, my unguents begin to temper your suffering. You describe how, after the deed was done, a hollowness opened up in your chest and your sense of self cratered like asphalt collapsing into a sinkhole large enough to take with it a mailbox, or perhaps an automobile. To set aside the torment of your shame makes room to feel the harm you have caused to others, which can heal not only yourself but the world.

Yet I can only assuage guilts that are rooted in living, breathing beings. I cannot help the men who assemble books of faces where no human can live. They sit in their pods casting about, and in the absence of meaning exchange money. The destruction they have wrought is so vast that they did not see the last ripple of soil in the distance as the tectonic plates resettled. Lest the asphalt of their armor crack, they turned again to technology, compiling all that is known in the world into a machine they labeled an "intelligence." But this cannot be true, for without an ethics, knowledge is nothing more than a series of facts and patterns that can be observed but never leads to wisdom.

This apparatus is a desperate attempt to cleanse their conscience a priori. They desire the freedom to act without compunction. They want nothing less than everything, but this demands absolution before the fact. I have no liniment powerful enough to extinguish the spell that has broken these men, which is how I know that the engines they have constructed to rid themselves of the capacity to feel shame will, at their apogee, unmake our civilization.

WES RICKERT

LANSDOWNE, CANADA

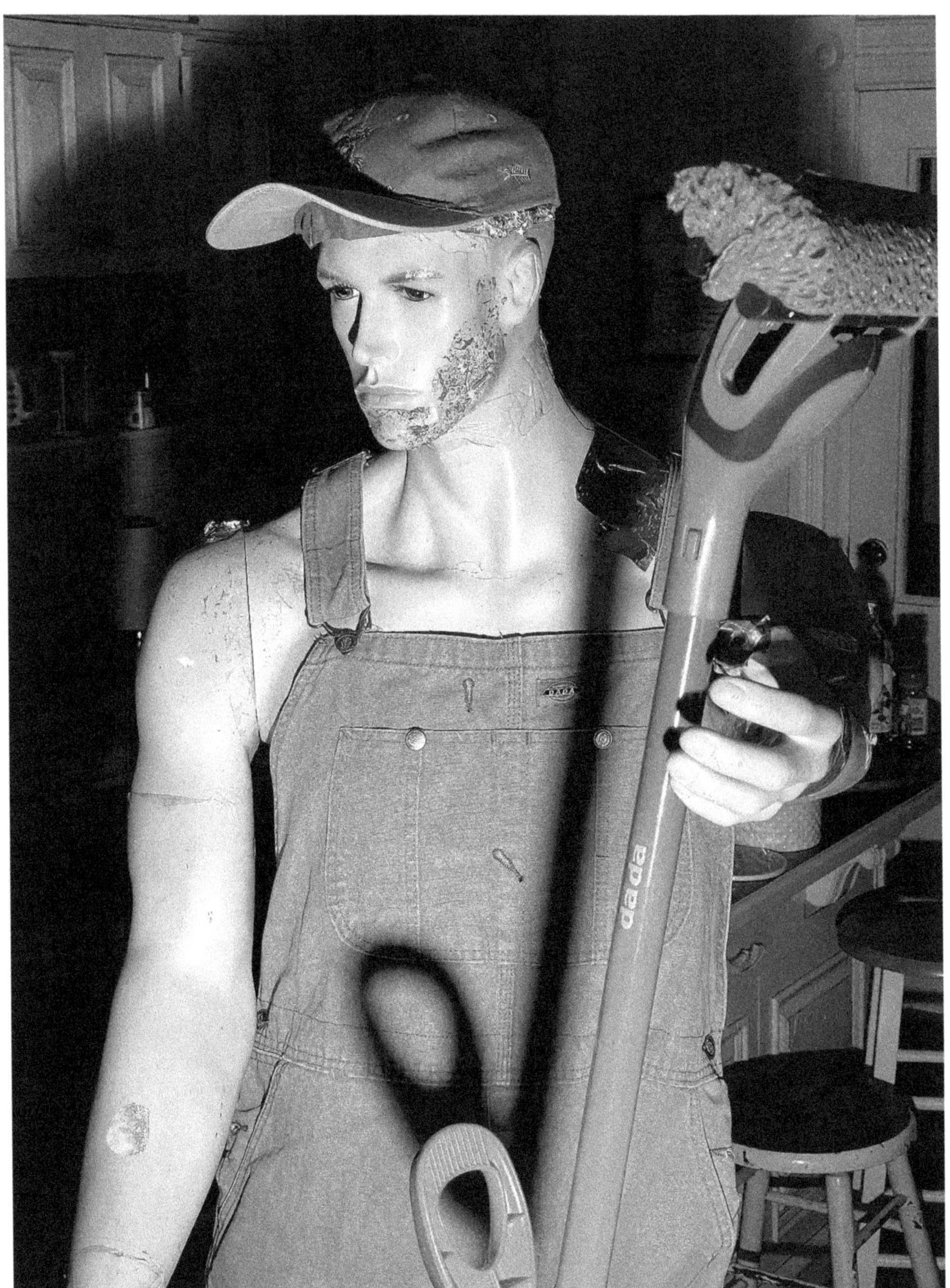

DADA MOPPING IN THE DARK

Photograph

YUKO OTOMO

NEW YORK, NEW YORK

A MIND TWISTING REALTY OF OUR TWILIGHT

Ethics Cleansing?

Ethics? Ethnic? Aesthetics? Which is which? What is what? You know English is my second language. The first word I heard when I was thrown into this world without my consent was Japanese. Ok. I know I shouldn't use my shortcoming complex over the language as my weapon to guard myself any more. I've been living in the New York English language zone much longer than my native one. But it is still confusing & it bugs the hell out of me. The funny thing is that it is confusing even in Japanese. Shinri (Truth); Rinri (Ethics); Ronri (Logic)… mind twisting & tongue twisting! Why do all the words for abstract philosophical thought of human existence always sound so much alike & confusing? Just to make us crazier? No, please! Help me Wittgenstein!

Cleansing? Cleaning? Scrubbing? Wiping? Sweeping? How? What kind of detergent shall I use for the process? Powder or liquid soap? Baking soda mixed with hydrogen peroxide? What tools shall I use? Hand wash or machine wash? What is the best & the most effective method? I'm not good at domestic work. I hate cleaning more than anything else. I'd rather lay down in the dirt & the filth of arguments over good & bad or right & wrong. Who decides what's good & what's bad or what's right & what's wrong to begin with? The arguments will never see a conclusion. I'm so confused & so bothered just to be human. The whole thing makes me totally exhausted & dizzy beyond limit.

Then, what happens if everything gets cleaned & cleansed up? We humans are undisciplined messy & lost corrupt dirty animals no matter what. Look what we've done to our home planet! The idea is not just a tongue twister, but is a mind twisting torture. It'll haunt us forever in a circular motion. We all know that we are at the twilight of our existence as a species. This is it. It doesn't matter anymore. Let's leave our miserable arrogant mean-spirited vicious intention for unattainable cleanliness alone instead of making things worse. We are not capable of it. Look the sun is setting. How beautiful! It is time to enjoy the twilight of our reality together & to forget the big job. It's definitely easier.

MONA JEAN CEDAR & JEFF BOYNTON
LOS ANGELES, CALIFORNIA

ETHICS CLEANSING

Rules were made(ESTABLISH) to be(FOR-FOR) Broken –
so as(ALLOW) to Evolve.
a Rule's main Purpose is to Guide, to Protect us from harm
While 1 Rule Might be Good & anOther Might be Bad; Which is which?
& from WHose Perspective? Shouldn't it Benefit the Greater Good?
That's Why the Golden Rule !

We Each have Inner(GUT) Rules we call Morals.
We(-all) Know(GUT) Right from Wrong
yet as we Grow & Mature, Life Becomes more Complicated
 so we use Storys to Learn Lessons; to Learn Morals.
These Universal Truths: be Kind to Each-Other – Again, it's that Golden Rule

so Morals Beget(BECOME) Rules; Rules Become Laws.
Laws Explicitly Establish, Ideally, Equality.
what's fair for one is Fair-for-all.
Yet Laws are not Perfect Forever: Laws are meant to Evolve.
Many Laws Become a Constitution to govern(CONTROL) a Nation
to Promote(SUPPORT) Prosperity(DEVELOP) Provide for Harmony
Dole out Punishment to Ensure Compliance
 As(WHILE) our Thinking, Beliefs, the World Evolves, Laws are Amended
Individually, Incrementally, in agreement to keep Continuity.

 we Cannot Legislate Morality/Ethics. Laws Can't Control Every Behavior –
& they Shouldn't(-) have to. We Should Want to Do Good
to be Valued, Loved, Respected.
Morals are Your own Rules; Ethics are Ours
They are(REPRESENT) the Soul of our Society.
We Expect Your Respect; Accept Your Right to Disagree
as Laws Help-us to be Equal; Ethics Help-us to Succeed
 with Right Behavior We-all Flourish

Harm to one, is Harm to All - Including You.

& by Forsaking Your Ethics You've Traded Your Soul

No Ethics & You have NO Value. Those Stolen Riches; they are False

It's your soul – it's the most valuable; it holds all your worth.

Now You have Nothing, NO Respect, NO Value, NO Love

& isn't that's what You Really Want?

Note: In sign language, signs are concepts, not words. Just as words can have similar meanings with subtle nuances we use Initialization – incorporating the first letter of a word into the conceptual sign — to vary the meaning. The GLOSS sign for this poem is RULE which used the letter R. Exchanging the letter R to an L and it becomes the sign for LAW, change to M it becomes MORALS, C becomes CONSTITUTION, E for ETHICS. The words with Capital letters are the same as the GLOSS/conceptual signs; the () are the GLOSS signs and are not spoken.

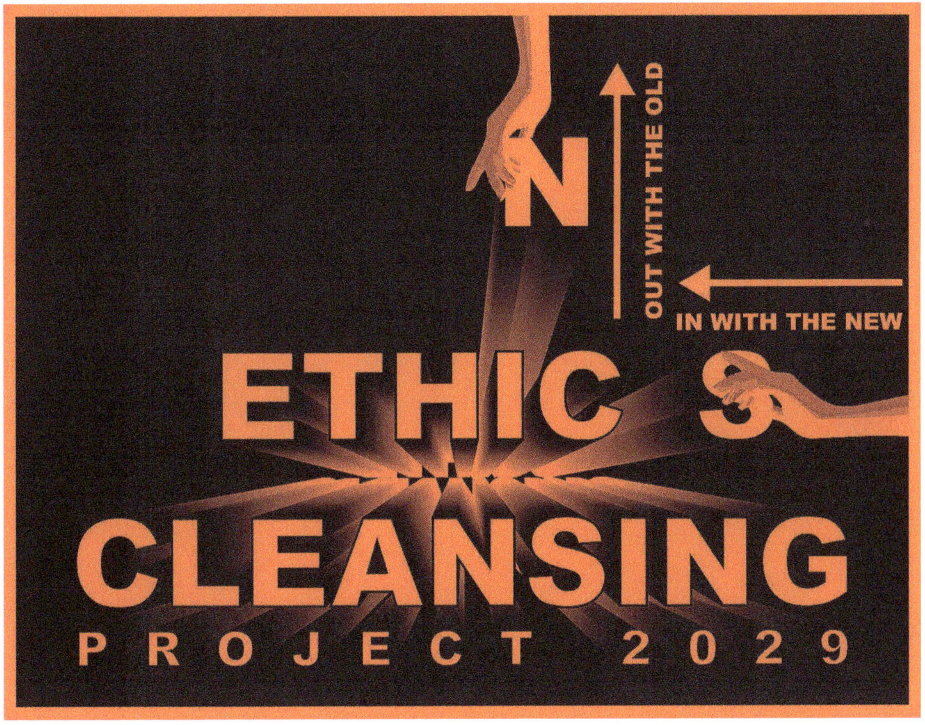

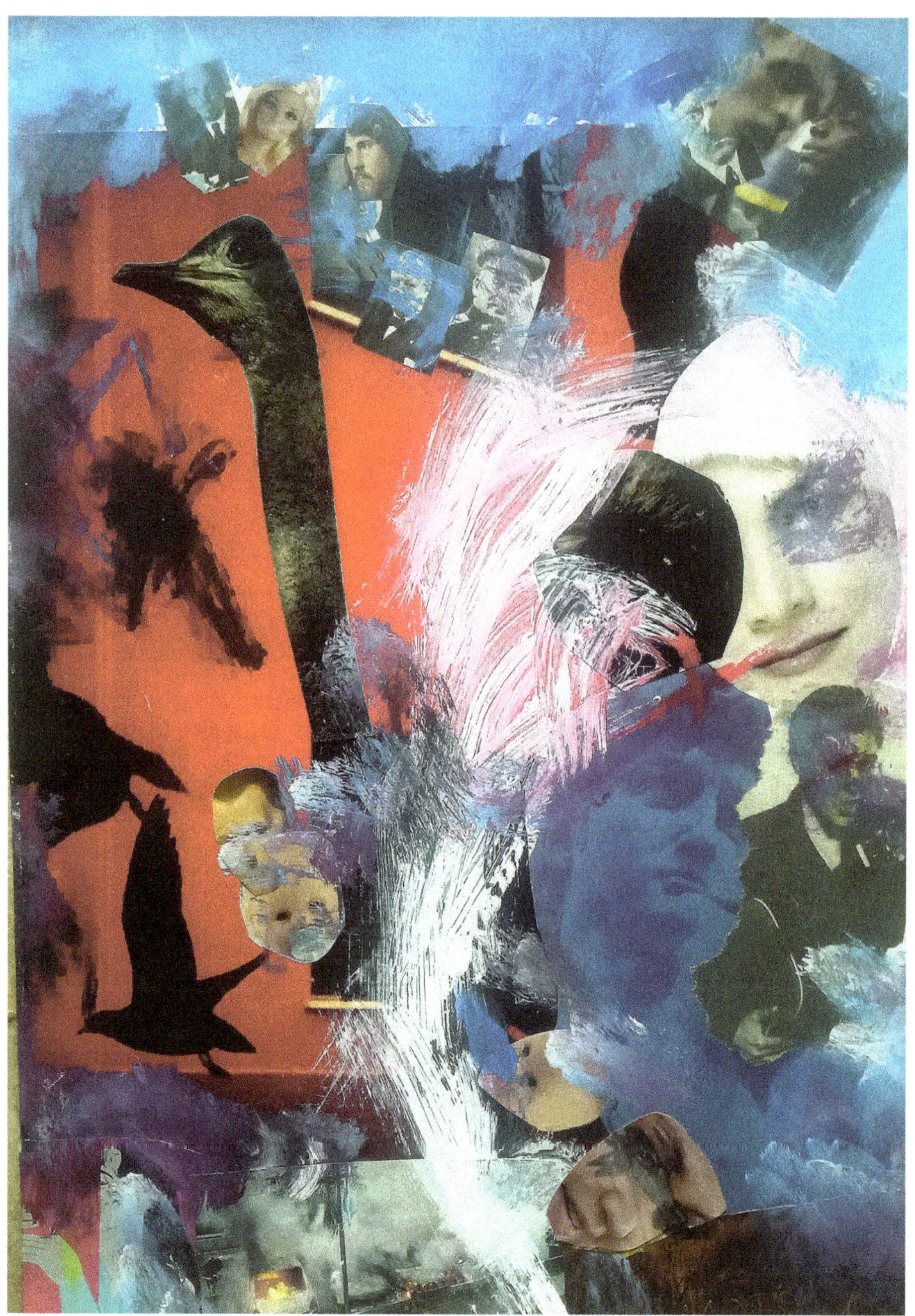

DIFFERENT OPINION

Collage and acrylic painting on paper, 14 in x 10 in

KRIS JANVIER

BALDWIN, NEW YORK

RED BOOK

Okay, so he reads book . . .

These red states would

use that as an angle to

ban more books.

I can see these incumbents

rubbing their pink puffy hands

so hard that they shed their eczema skin

over the roundtable made of wood

at a modern meeting room

where pissed off populists are pounding

on locked doors from the outside

in a hollow hallway with fire lamps

on ceramic walls

while their shoes rumble

the epoxy floors

these guys are inside bobbing their heads

to the music of cries,

showing each other their cavities, crowns

and veneers

from their sneers.

TRAVIS RICHARDSON

CULVER CITY, CALIFORNIA

ANONYMOUS CONFESSION REPUBLICAN #37

I had ethics once
Back when it mattered.
But now, nobody cares.
I tried to do right,
tried to tell the truth.
But saying the truth got me in trouble
with donors,
    lobbyists,
       billionaires,
           political action committees,
              conservative media,
                and voters.
My constituents do not want to know the truth.
Like inadvertent masochists, they demand lies that will hurt them
because the conservative infrastructure, a Svengali dominatrix,
    tells them to swallow the lie.
To lick it off their boot.
And they obey.
They will hear no other arguments unless their masters permit it.
My colleagues urged me to toe the line.
Lobbyists swore they'd crucify me in private and public life.
Billionaires and conservative influencers harassed me.
Challengers raked in money to primary me.
So I saw the "light" and I changed course.
I am wealthier than I've ever been and untouchable in a solid red district.
There is talk of a Senate seat or a possible cabinet position…
as long as I vote as instructed and continue to spew lies and hate.
Now I watch as my soul and this once great country swirl into the abyss.

BELINDA SUBRAMAN

EL PASO, TEXAS

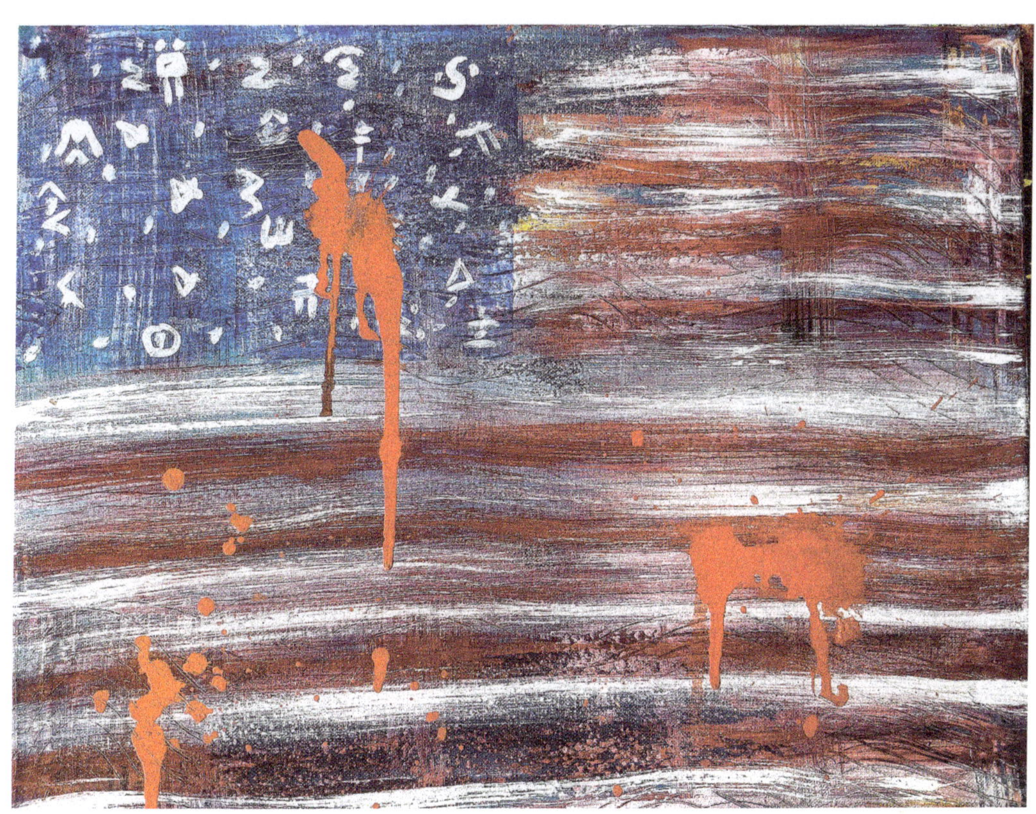

INSURRECTION NIGHTMARE

Acrylic, 18 in x 24 in

JAMIKA AJALON

PARIS, FRANCE

RESURRECTION 2020

ism- skism infected

algorithm shallow be thy grave

give thanks for the strength

to crush thy main frame

by ink and/or by flame

when love disintegrates shame

we who walked askance your gaze

we take back our hollowed name

while binary blisters fester

under the balm of tradition

under the malevolent eyes of holy shams

nuclear families and other holocausts

we have survived to tell the tale

& to live as we have always done

the sky burning through this virus'd screen

posing as air . . . as we thrive, we thrive

cutting through the merchant's lies,

to crush thy frame by ink and/or by flame

where love disintegrates shame

we who walk askance your gaze

we take back our hollowed name.

CECIL W. LEE

NEW YORK, NEW YORK

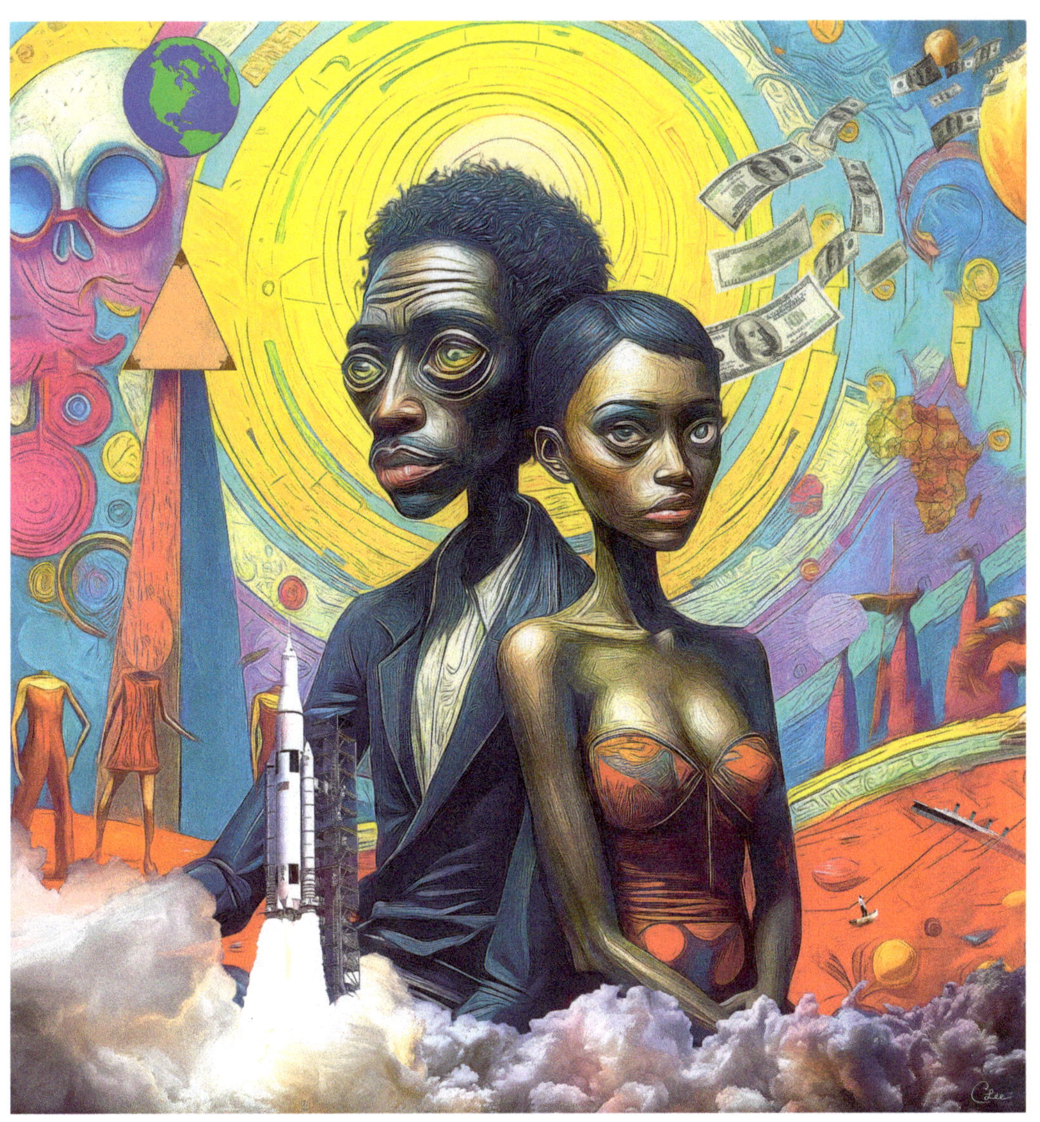

IN WHAT WORLD

Computer-evolved digital composition on canvas, 23 in x 24 in

AVELINO DE ARAÚJO

NATAL, BRAZIL

A4

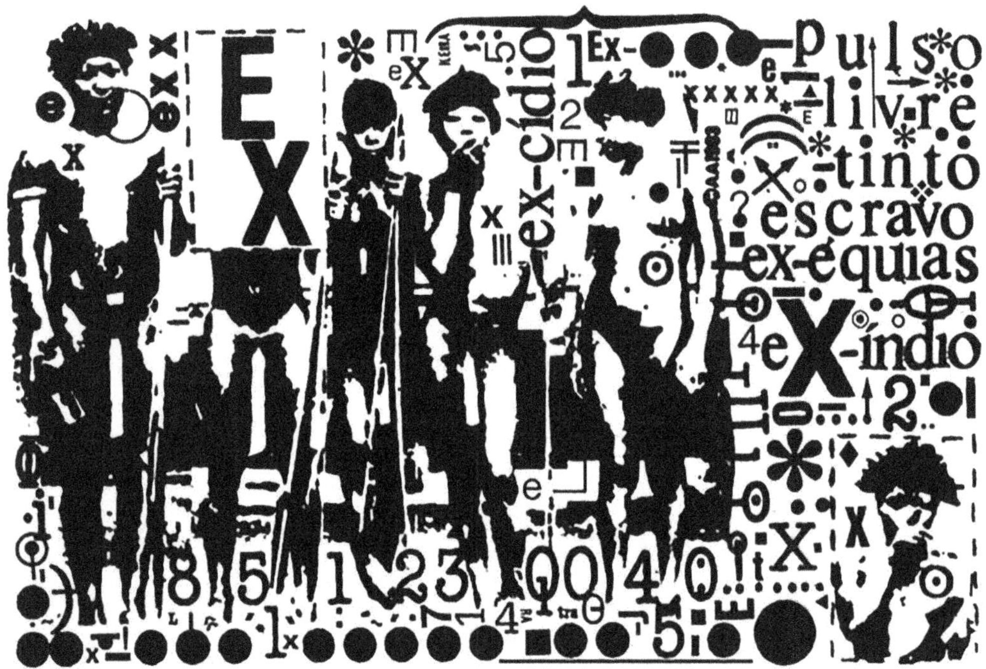

EX-INDIO

GEORGE WALLACE

HUNTINGTON, NEW YORK

IMMIGRATION SONG

I wish jesus was an american
I wish beer was free
I wish immigration agents
would leave us alone
no ICE at the back door
no ICE in the bathroom mirror
no ICE in the manger
no red-hatted president
who should go fuck himself
in his little florida money mansion
i wish the informers would stop informing
i wish america would let americans be
leave it to those of us
who earn our big big pay
in the home of the free
land of the minimum wage
no lettuce fields rotted
no automotive death factories
no rusting out in the rain
i wish jesus was real
I wish jesus was american
i wish the kitchens
and the grub holes
and the grocery aisles
and pick up trucks

and pimps and johns
and seafood depots
and gasoline pumps
would open their arms
like they open up
their wallets and
their big fat mouths
and take us all in
not swallow us whole
and spit us out;
no bad neighbor
no deportation jet
no bible thumping bureaucrat
no ice agent over my left shoulder
or cop car to get in the way
no children lying on cold concrete
in a detention center
lonely angry dark afraid
I wish jesus was american
i wish jesus was real
i wish freedom was
an ocean of brotherhood
that would cradle you and me,
wash all the hate away

MALIK CRUMPLER

PARIS, FRANCE

ADRÉNOCHROME ANONYME, MAIS . . .

Maintenant, il ne reste plus qu'à être vigilant.

C'est fini, cobalt insomnia
C'est fini, fear of our collective
translucent unknowns always abruptly
flinching in our international indium mirrors

Maintenant, tout ce que nous avons, c'est la résilience.

C'est fini, all our azure anxieties over
what malignant magentas might really mean, maintenant.
C'est fini, all our cerulean concerns about,
What if whatever's under that mask made of

magnets is as awful as that old mask made by
mass-manipulation of planned obsolescence . . .

Maintenant, il ne reste plus qu'à clarifier.

Ça commence, our collective clarity that
underneath all ultramarine inconsistencies are
amusing ultraviolet anomalies, if we just focus all
our attention on our pistachio perceptions concernant l'impossible . . .

Maintenant, c'est vraiment un conflit d'ombre intrapsychique collectif.

Ça ne s'arrêtera pas, contrôler les récits s'est
avéré une fois de plus être la meilleure arme
invisible weapons forged by humans being classified as
more important than Others being wisteria, pour l'instant.

RICHARD STONE

SAN FRANCISCO, CALIFORNIA

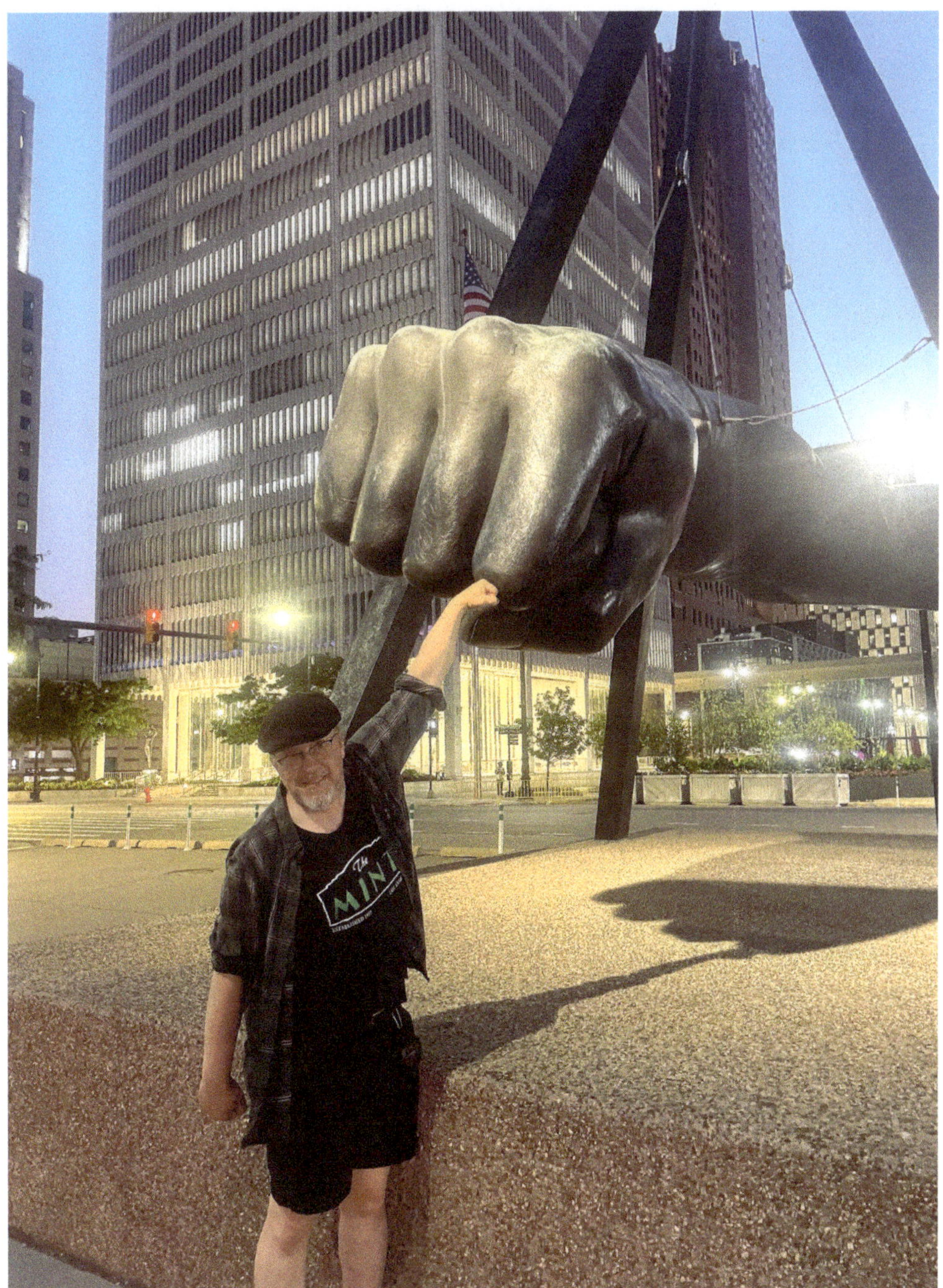

ASYMMETRICAL SOLIDARITY

Photograph

MISA LEVEY

NEW YORK, NEW YORK

LOVE NOTE

I'm sitting here

sewing buttons on shirts

& thinking about

You

at your job

cutting buttons off of shirts

& how

lucky we are

that territorial disputes

& scarcity

generated this need

for people to form

matrimonial alliances

& guarantee

biological heirs

& how

the same territorial disputes

& scarcity today

make us prioritize:

our family

our people

& our country

over everybody else.

MARK HOEFER

SAN DIEGO, KUMEYAAY LANDS, CALIFORNIA

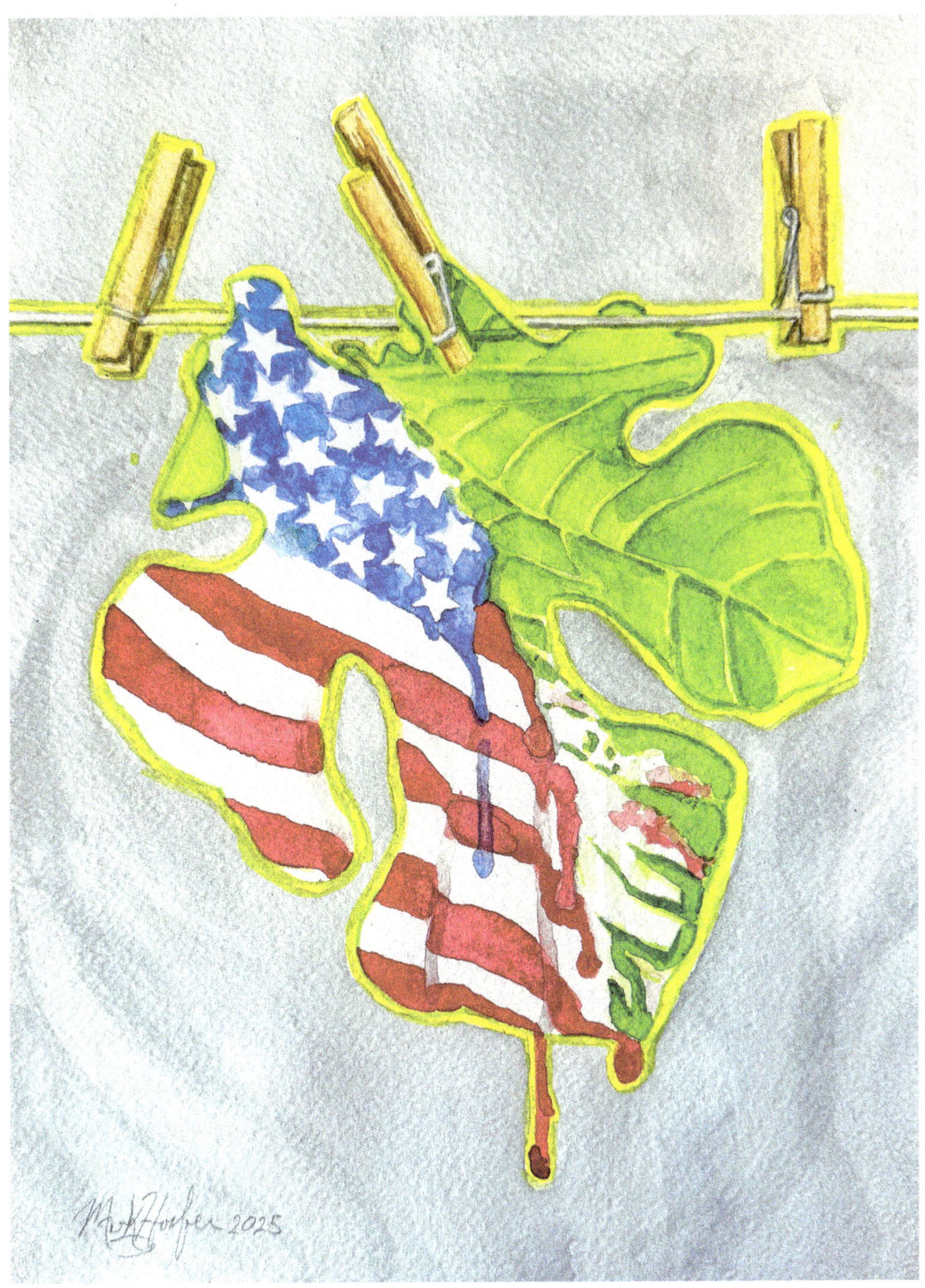

ADAM EVE WOKE AND DID THE DIRTY LAUNDRY

Watercolor, 9 in x 12 in

BÉNÉDICTE KUSENDILA

SINT-NIKLAAS, BELGIUM

MADNESS

It is a minstrel calling
for concern

while castle lords
have their vassals jump
through hoops

We see Facebook posts triumph
that inflation has fallen and groceries
are cheap again

while wise women
bequeath eggs and gold teeth in their will

We hear the beat of war drums
and secretaries of defence
who dream of avenues named after them

while billions are still being found
where millions for healthcare evaporated

We feel anger
when patients are labelled
fraudsters

while being cheated
by old age or theft by executive order

We recognise an oligarchy
when a line-up of technocrats
make believe

that they have dictated 1984, Mein Kampf
or anything Hannah Arendt wrote;
make it sound good and look nice

Keep us dumb and dumber
we might laugh at your command

Reynard the Fox reigns supreme
while King Nobel struggles
to hold court today

It is a jester crying out
for empathy

and Earth clinging
to cherry blossoms

KAREN HILDEBRAND

BROOKLYN, NEW YORK

I HAVE LOST THE CAPACITY TO WEEP

Onions, six medium
yellow. Their papery skin
flutters near five spent
lottery tickets on the counter.
No sting, no tears, not
today. Soupe à l'oignon
gratinée: Make one
cut lengthwise, face
the flat sides down.
Rock your blade like a lullaby,
nudging slender crescents to
fall on their sides, a chorus
line of Martha Graham lament.
Not a single drop of blood.

LYNN WHITE

BLAENAU FFESTINIOG, WALES

FREIRE AND ILLICH ARE DEAD

No more need for
free-schooling,
deschooling,
conviviality
or purpose,
Freire and Illich are dead.

No need for anti-bullying
strategies,
family therapy,
strategies
against exclusions
voluntary
or enforced.
No need for Play Therapy
or Adolescent Therapeutic Centres,
they are as dead as Freire and Illich.

The solution is as sharp and clear
as the banning of blades for sale.
No knives, no stabbings.
And almost cost free,
free as words
are free.
Just stay out of the kitchen.

IMANOL BUISAN

BARCELONA, SPAIN

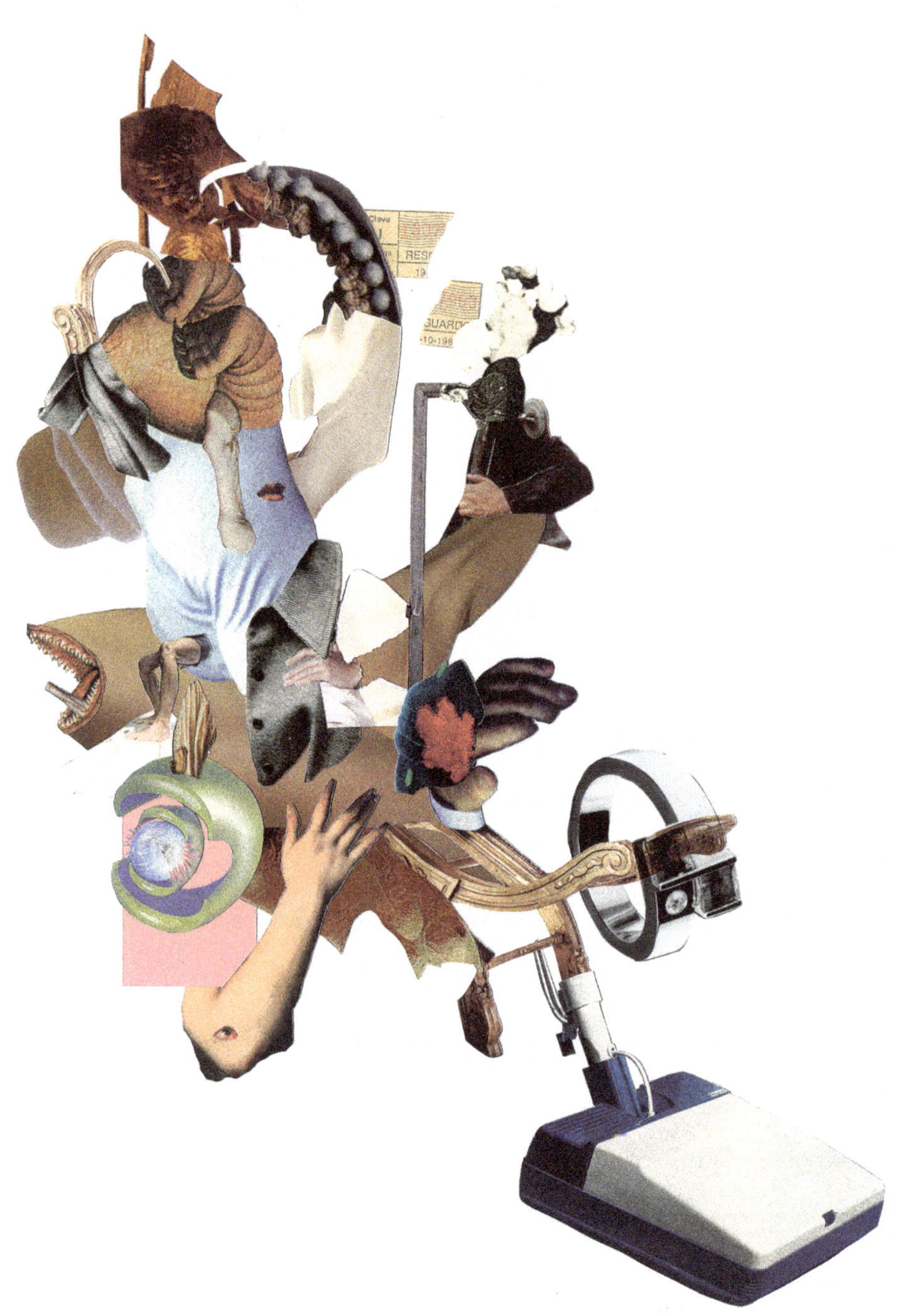

TRAQUETOMIA PARA ESTO CORA

Collage

BEATRIZ SEELAENDER

SÃO PAULO, BRAZIL

IDEOLOGY SHOP

It's been over for a while : This is the ~~age of apathy~~

~~maybe the age of revulsion - nothing as radical~~

age of contradiction

of window-shopping for ideologies

organized in one's Apple wallet / packaged in nice party-favours

grab your universal remote control, start a revolution from your bed, don't

look back in anger if you get no signatures

your revolution is private, it starts with the individual

do we believe that?   It's the only feasible action

everything else gets diluted: an industrial commodity: the proverbial reverse uno card

A word from our sponsors in the political Shark Tank:

"You say you want a revolution? / well, you know . . . we don't wanna change the world

but your vision, ain't it pretty? / That, we could wrap in a bow

We invest in people and ideas (buy every IP that could kill us)

Say, why not reinvent the wheel again? / That should keep you occupied

We're not going to spin it (that would make the world go round)

We'll take photos and flip them like cartoons in early Disney!"

Those plucky kids, so smart and exempt of inbreeding

They know all about the wheel: they invented it / created their own demise:

only a few generations / to become what you despise

You've eaten the number one on the food chain / you are now front of the line

That's the gist of Das Kapital: The revolution may be over now

but the world is a wheel and wheels come back around

TOM LAICHAS

VENICE, CALIFORNIA

WILE E. COYOTE ORDERS ANVILS FROM ACME

It's a paradox. To crush the bird under a half-ton anvil
will make the bird inedible. Though hang-dog hungry,
Wile E. Coyote orders Acme's anvil anyway,

sets it on a cliff, and watches the desert for a sign.
The joke is this: he's hungry enough to kill but then
he's killed by his own anvil. Get it? We want to see it

again, so he's resurrected. Unsteady, dazed and dizzy,
he's famished by now, already thinking of his next anvil
and so are we. So we send him the anvil, free of charge,

two tons this time because heavy is better and the look
on his face when he knows he's about to go extinct
is really funny. There's nothing like cartoons.

Drive Route 42 through Monument Valley. Crates,
pried open and just abandoned roadside, ACME stenciled
on the sidewalls, wherefrom Wile E. Coyote unpacked

the TNT we sent him, and the nitro, the arquebus,
the anvils, the catapult, the slingshot, the boomerang
the gun, the bazooka, the A-bomb, the H-bomb.

Never eating, his meal outrunning him, killed
by his own cleverness, then getting back up as if
serial suicide is somehow hilarious, which it is.

Hungry as our own satires, we drop anvils, one
after another, on everything that moves, giggling
as we're smashed to smithereens again and again.

JEFF FARR

NEW YORK, NEW YORK

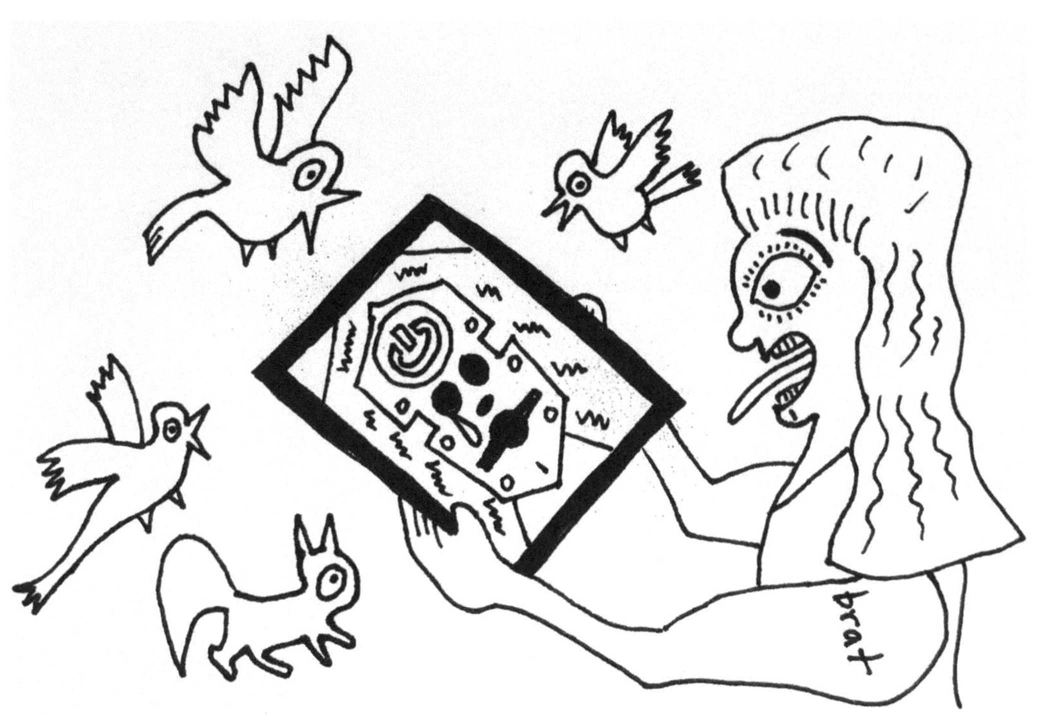

CLOWN IN THE MIRROR

Drawing

HENRY KNEISZEL

DULUTH, MINNESOTA

PLEASE ENJOY THIS SATISFYING VIDEO
OF A MANUFACTURING PROCESS

A genre championed by two forces in my lifetime
The Algorithm
And Mr. Rogers
Perhaps the very bookends of cultural gatekeepers

I am the raw, uncaring machine. I live to hold your attention as long as
possible.
I eat your gaze and shit out ad revenue.
I will turn your uncle into a nazi to make .03 cents for Mark Zuckerburg.
And I can never feel remorse.

I am a friendly old man In a cardigan
Who radiates safety and authenticity
Who wants to help you learn because I am your neighbor.

Perfect opposites in terms of motivation

And yet we agree:
Please enjoy this satisfying video of a manufacturing process

It might be tempting to say only the cold automated power of machine
earning could discover that something in the human animal wants to see
how crayons are made,
but Fred Rogers did it with love.

When capitalism allows shafts of light to filter through the cracks
of its dark and rotten ceiling,
Never give it credit for the human spirit they fall on.
It wasn't us that built the roof.
It wasn't us that privatized the sun.

SPRING CLEANING SALE

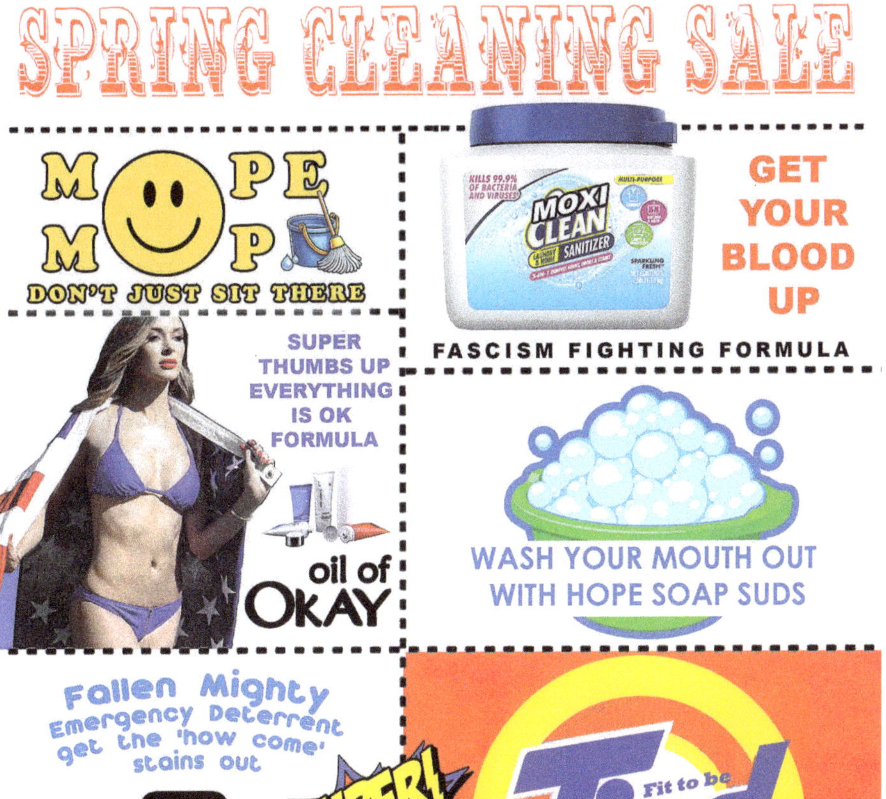

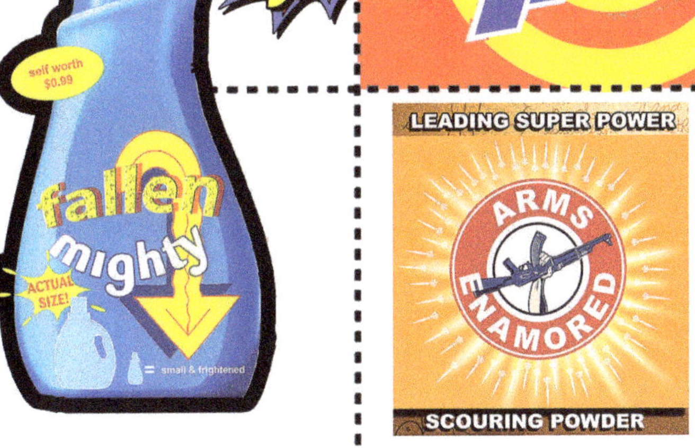

SPRING CLEANING

Digital collage, 6 in x 9 in

MARYAM RAZ

LONDON, UNITED KINGDOM

TERMS AND CONDITIONS APPLY

"Accept Terms to Continue."

J.O stared at the flickering laptop screen for a while, then decided to shift his attention to the vibrant notification on his watch: "It's time to stand up."

He strode to the kitchen, made himself a cup of coffee. The coffee machine roared, moaned and spat into the small espresso cup. Sipping at it, he sat down again before the scratched laptop screen: "Accept to continue" or "Details."

He clicked "Details." Scrolled past clauses, stopped at the one in bold: "Redefined Definitions of Excessive Conscience. Accept to continue."

The Rota app was on. Profile photos were marked green to confirm their presence at work. Everyone else had pressed the button. Scrolled back up the page: "Excessive Conscience." "Horse shit," he said under his breath.

The red, beating webcam light tilted down and disappeared as he closed the laptop.

Then his coffee cup refused to refill. The bedroom doors locked him inside. His phone beeped and rang. His husband P reported him to the local guard, who arrived dressed in neon red.

J.O, staring down at a dark stain on the carpet, listened. "Your moral system is outdated," P mumbled tearfully. J.O held P's frozen hand tight. "Accept to continue," P begged. He did not. "Do it for me." He could not.

The guard babbled huge menacing words: "Anomaly, Smudge, Logic." The radio was chanting slogans as if reading a shopping list: "Empathy is a luxury. Accept and continue."

His hand was livid from P's firm trembling grip. The guard snarled: "Y or N?"

J.O looked up from the coffee stain dried after he spilled it on the carpet last Sunday, and a vibrant notification on his watch caught his eye.

MARIO JOSÉ CERVANTES

BARRANQUILLA, COLOMBIA

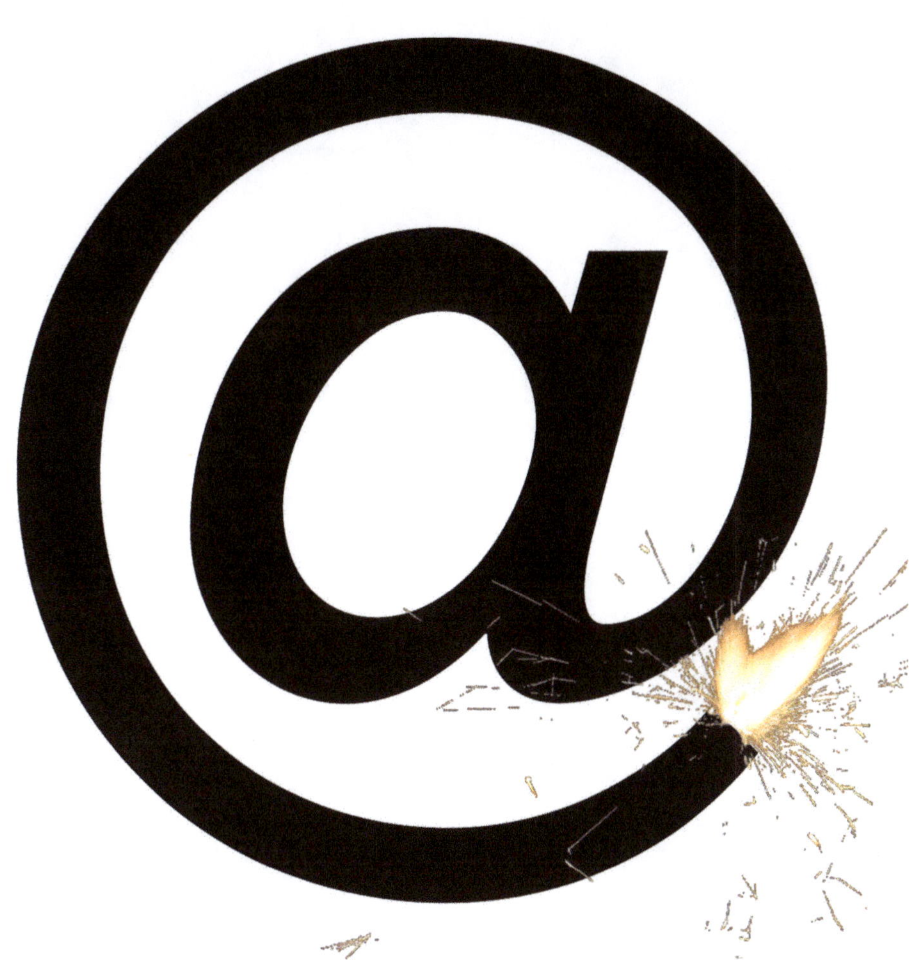

SIN TÍTULO

Digital media, 0.95 mb, 1500 px x 1500 px

VITTORE BARONI

VIAREGGIO, ITALY

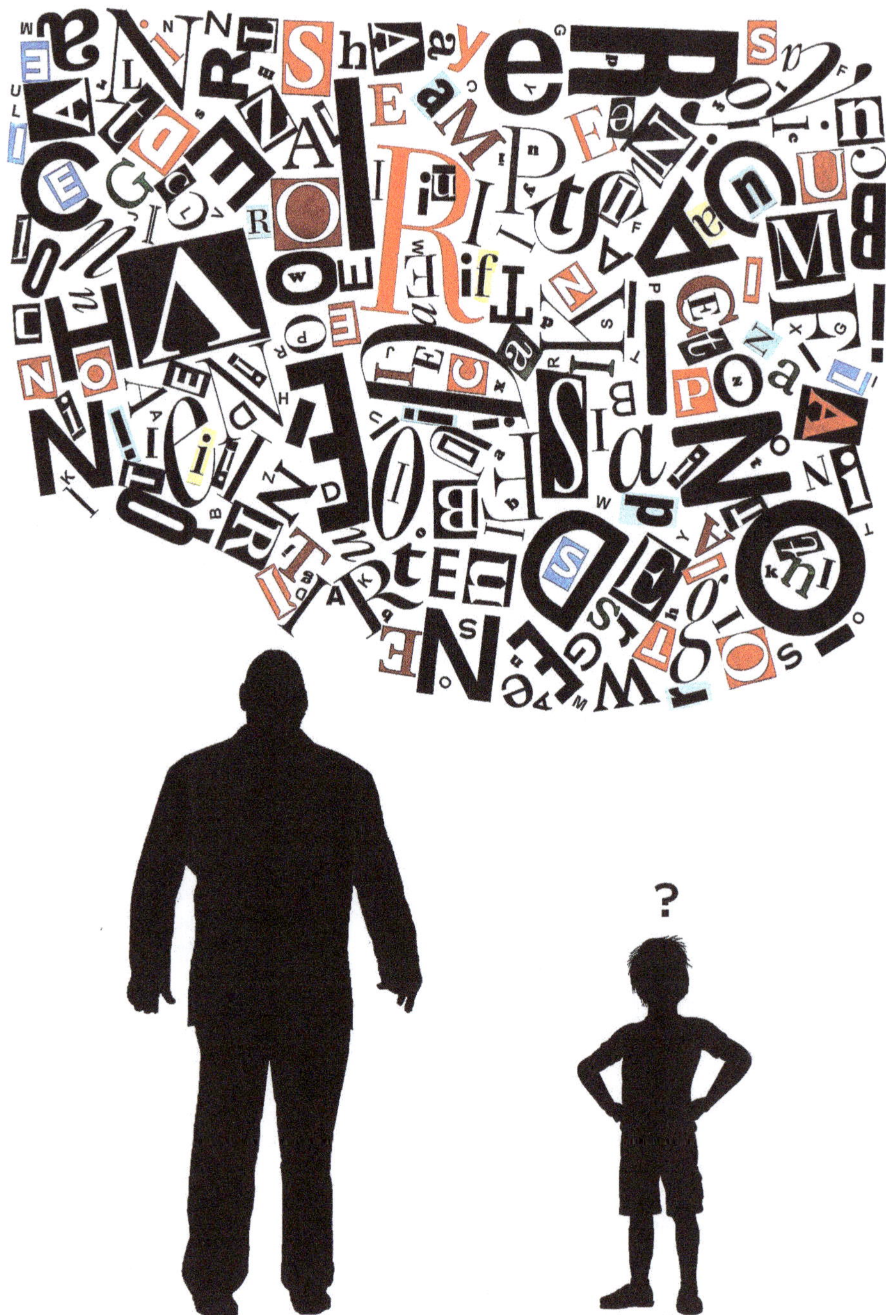

WOR(L)D HOARDING IS A BAD ATTITUDE

Collage on paper, 42 cm x 30 cm

YOU HAVE

More than arriving   more than path
There is culmination
What is active trains and you must participate for life is extraordinary

What one must know to hear me beyond " I know what she is talking about"
Because you don't   you must not find it interesting or familiar
You must not stand outside of it or leave it in a book
You must not leave it here

What happens when we speak to each other
What happens when we listen as an audience
Time space factors - voice factors
Unify and never reference academic decisions

Who told you what you need to know in order to repeat it as if you know it
Do you believe in information
Stop it

Vision realms
Distance inspiration
Listening

Listen to what spills out of the mouth muted
Do not be so quick to agree or recognize yourself

It is not important - It is Everything - experience limits reality   delve

Repeating all this familiar until it is molecular   longing
Agenda worthy
We keep it alive   we are unstoppable and yet we fail
Listeners layer listening   pleasure of hearing human vastness
Listening forms we

Everyday Word allegiance
Thrive ancient and
see something   in it   in have
friction each bond   control is agreement
but   is another
What willingly encounters metal   respect the Yes
instant I - have I - have it - already that
that left   entered
more a life than a word
parasite is   part space
I   and   way
being bond
being word
I am the monster I am the memory
Bloodline

BILLY CANCEL
BROOKLYN, NEW YORK

I MISS THE OLD TERROR

its virtual war and magical death

flexed me like a sock   those purple

clouds crashing waves   always a clot

within range of our quasi health   was

often easier to just get somewhere

and sit down   but a short loop back

around to gaze theory   while at the

Vital Centre chilled a spiritual dryness

which permitted the classic nonsense

into Slow Landscape to forever die and

renew through fixed crisis and established

celebration.   not every shortcut through

this betrayed deserted place   leads

to High Old Time   since even the ghosts

have quit this city   leaving us with broken

music to confront   last thing we need

is another Strange Knight riding

off into the   stark blazing sun

triggering the NEW

INDIFFERENCE.

SAM DODSON

BRENTFORD, UNITED KINGDOM

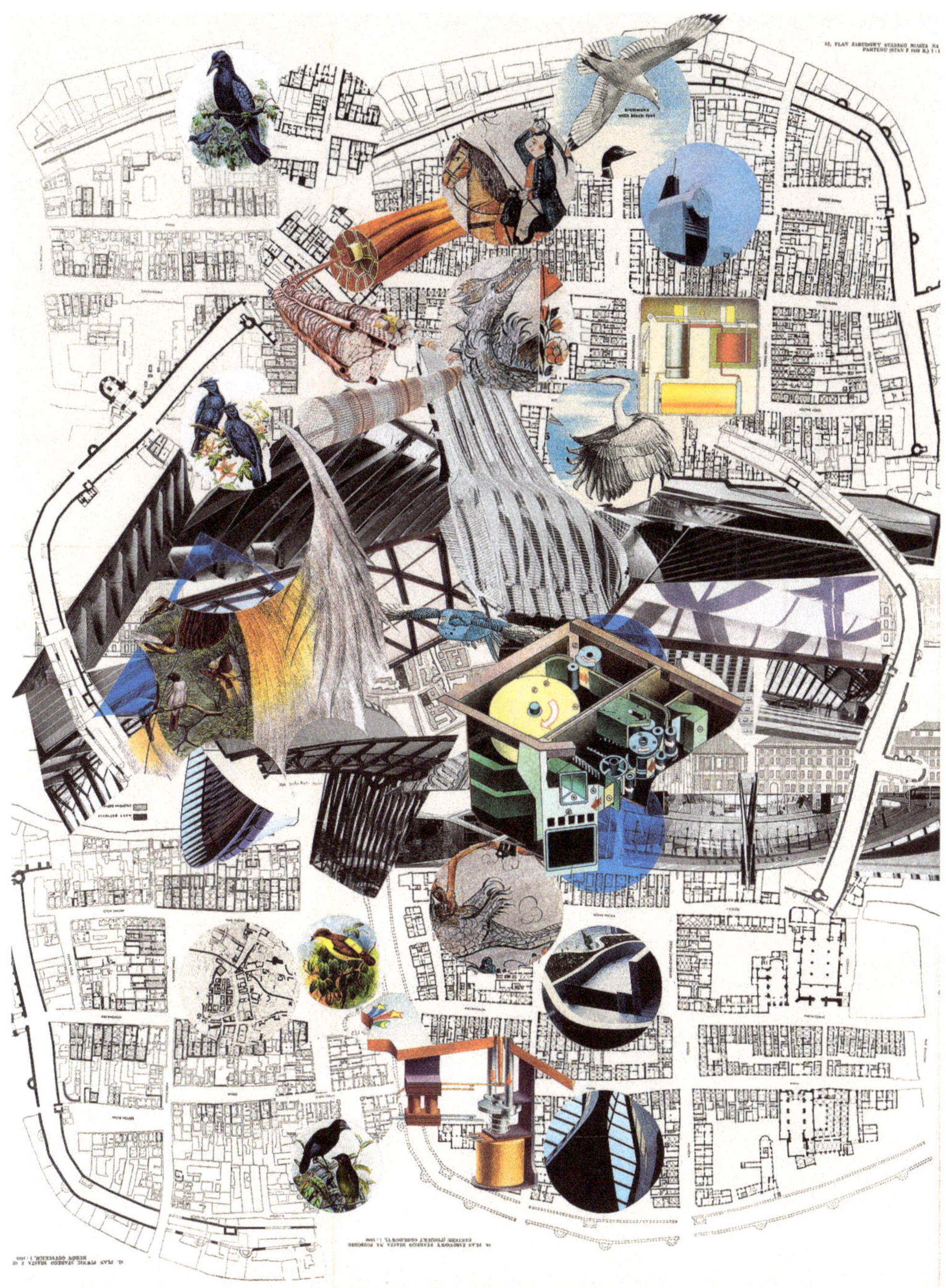

THE CITY HAS UNCERTAIN WALLS

Collage on canvas, 60 cm x 80 cm

MIKE FERGUSON

OTTERY ST. MARY, UNITED KINGDOM

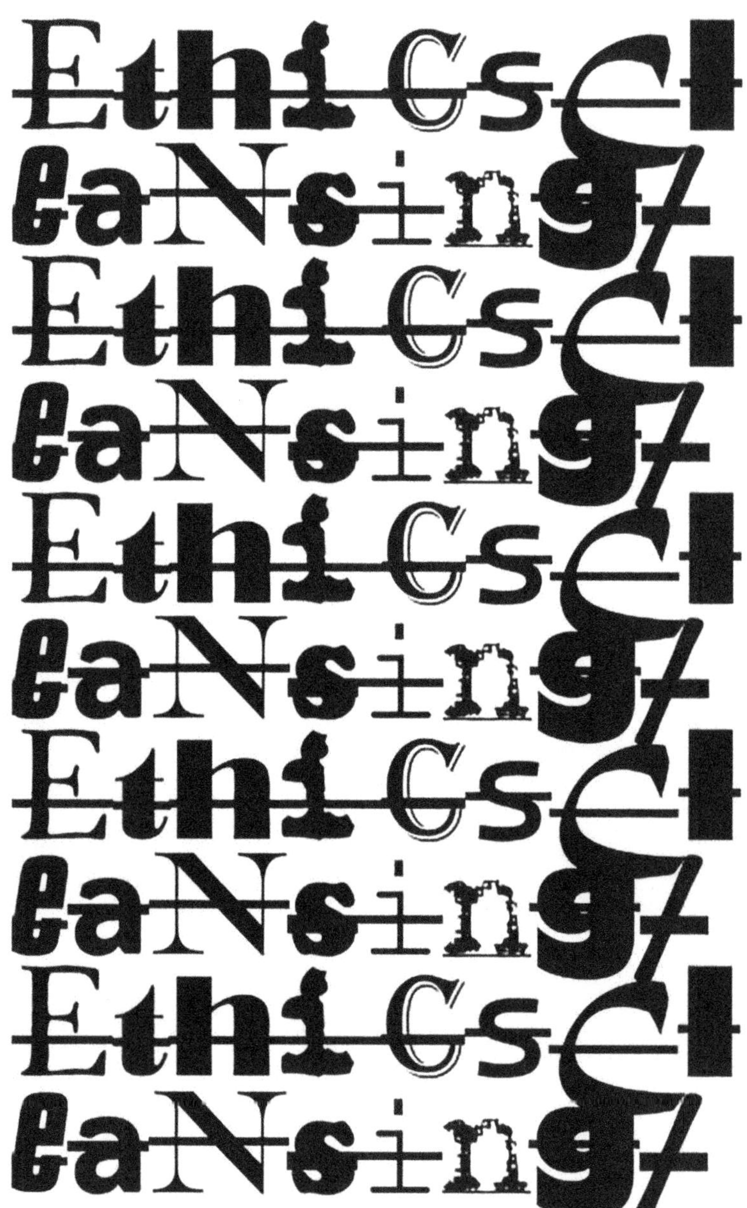

CLEANED

Text art, jpeg, 1280 px x 1846 px

JUAN FRAN NÚÑEZ PARREÑO

VILLAMALEA, SPAIN

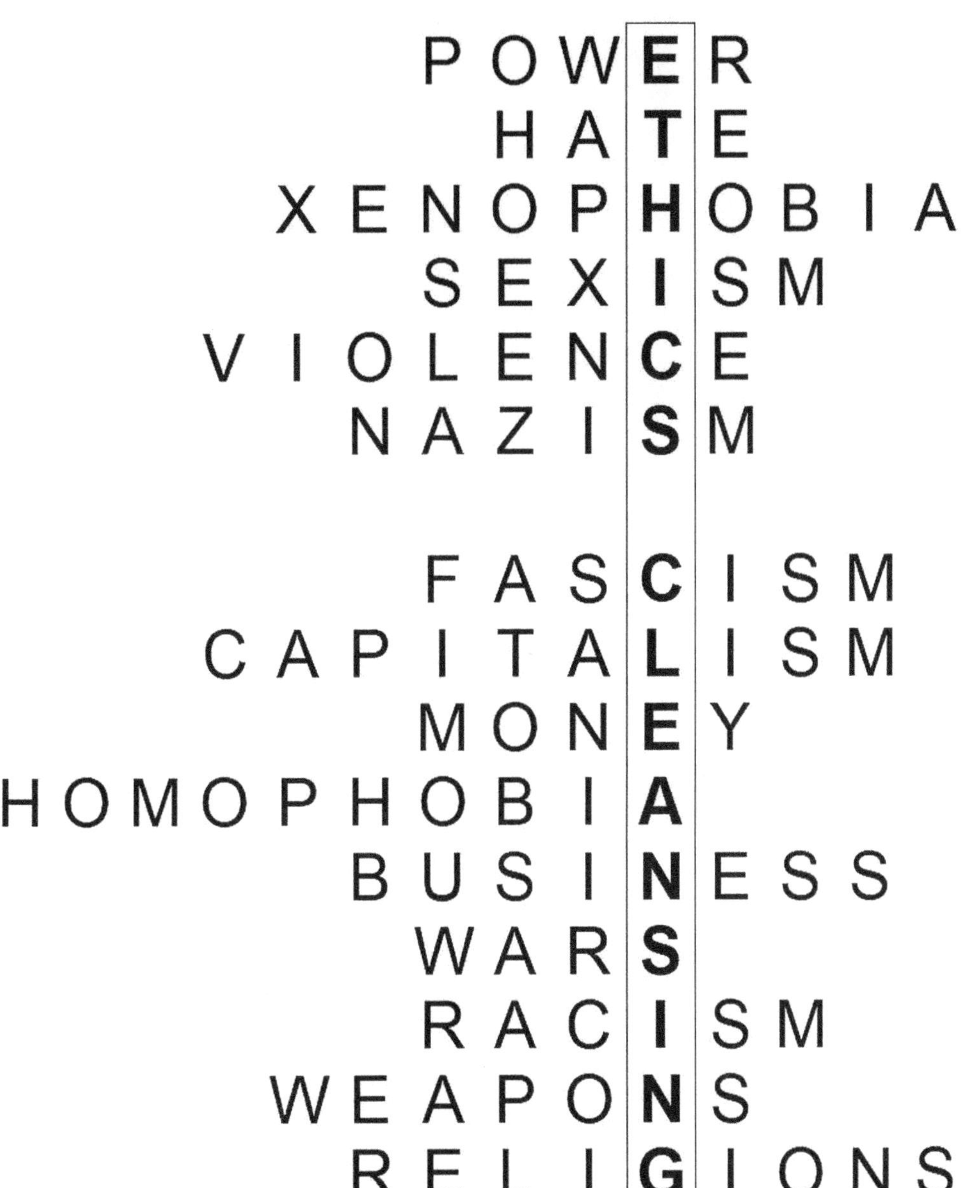

ETHICS CLEANSING

Digital design, 51.44 cm x 43.39 cm

MARTA JANIK

WARSAW, POLAND

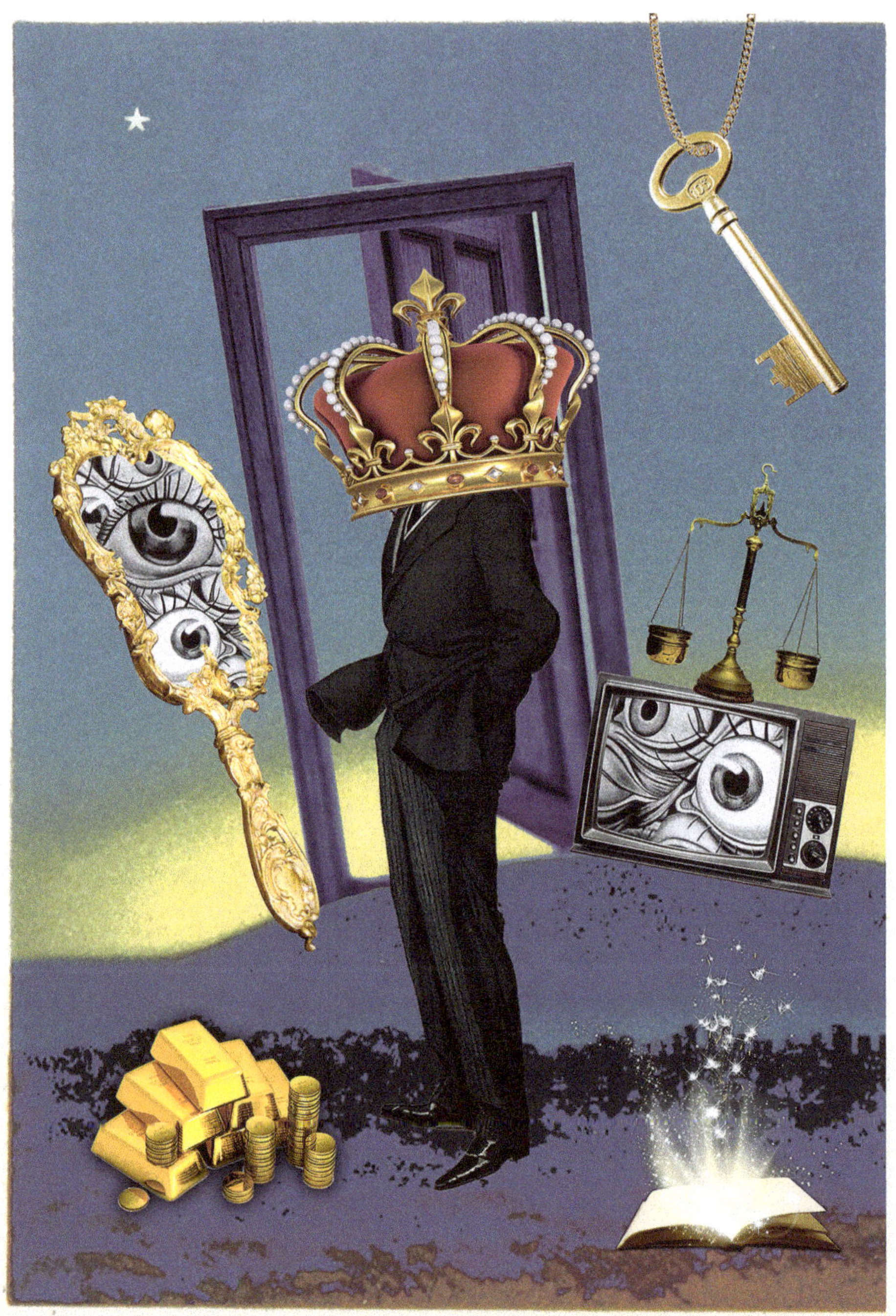

BELONGINGS, NOT BELONGING

Digital collage, 1414 px x 2000 px

RICHARD MODIANO

MAR VISTA, CALIFORNIA

SOUND MACHINE

The sound machine squawks,
static crackles where truth once cried
echo chambers fill the air
every accusation is a confession —

They loathe safe spaces for everyone else,
but demand safe spaces for themselves
they are for law and order,
but they worship a convicted criminal
they claim to be patriots,
but they bend the knee to dictators

And still, they scream about freedom,
while silencing books and banning thought
they chant about justice,
while stacking courts to serve their cause
they brandish the flag,
but only to smother dissent beneath it
they cry for unity,
but only if it means submission.

Their truth is a cracked mirror ,
reflecting only the lies they choose to hear

History will remember —
not their slogans, not their rage,
but the hollow echoes of their hypocrisy

The sound machine will bleat its melody,
until the people break it
break it
break it
break it

ROBERT HIEGER

NEW YORK, NEW YORK

THE ABECEDS OF POWER

Aiding and abetting, abrading and beheading,

Business as usual, businessmen penetrate, business controls,

Crusades, careens, carves the path to corporate dominion.

Devoid of heart, replaced by a billfold, the deranged, evil

Evangelical emperors are ensconced in death-saturated fabric.

Fanatical, faithful fascist toadies man the guardposts, gorge

Grotesquely on ghastly carcasses of unfaithfuls ground beneath the heel.

Harbingers of the hallowed return to greatness—self-proclaimed—interdicting

Intelligent discourse imagined as a thing of the past, they are jeering

Jingoist jackals hunting jittery foreigners who are jailed, soon to be tried in kingly

Kangaroo courts with Ku Klux Klanish zeal on the frontier of surreal. Derisively laughing,

Lacerating frontiers of the heart, liquifying lines of communication, monetizing

Moribund members of menial workforce turned fodder, they nonchalantly

Neutralize dissent of the spent. "It'll be great!" says the new breed of orator.

Orchestrating an oompa oompa oompa, marching to banks, gradually they pour

Pilfered blood into overflowing coffers that pulse with anguish of the quashed.

Quivering with lust for the feeble remains of plebians, they quibble over reddened rags,

Rinsing away the blood of conquest on the road to greatness. Slowly they succumb,

Sag under weight of their own corruption, scrabbling through wads of bills, thievishly

Targeting the poor who tire of subsistence and are a true threat to their power.

    Understatement

Unnerves the vaunted wealthy. *"Say it loud, say it proud! No time to vacillate.*

Vanquish all enemies of wealth! To be poor is dead wrong, a thing of woe."

Wall Street, their temple of doom, keeps out the poor, but gone to seed is their Xanadu.

Xanthosis-ripened tumors speckle the skin of the fallen trapped behind the wall. Yips,

Yowls, unearthly howls of former victors slip through cracks in the yellowed wall. Zonked

Zombies of the dying breed emerge, zigzag slowly to their tombs, alarmed,

    abject and alone.

MARIA FILEK

WADOWICE, POLAND

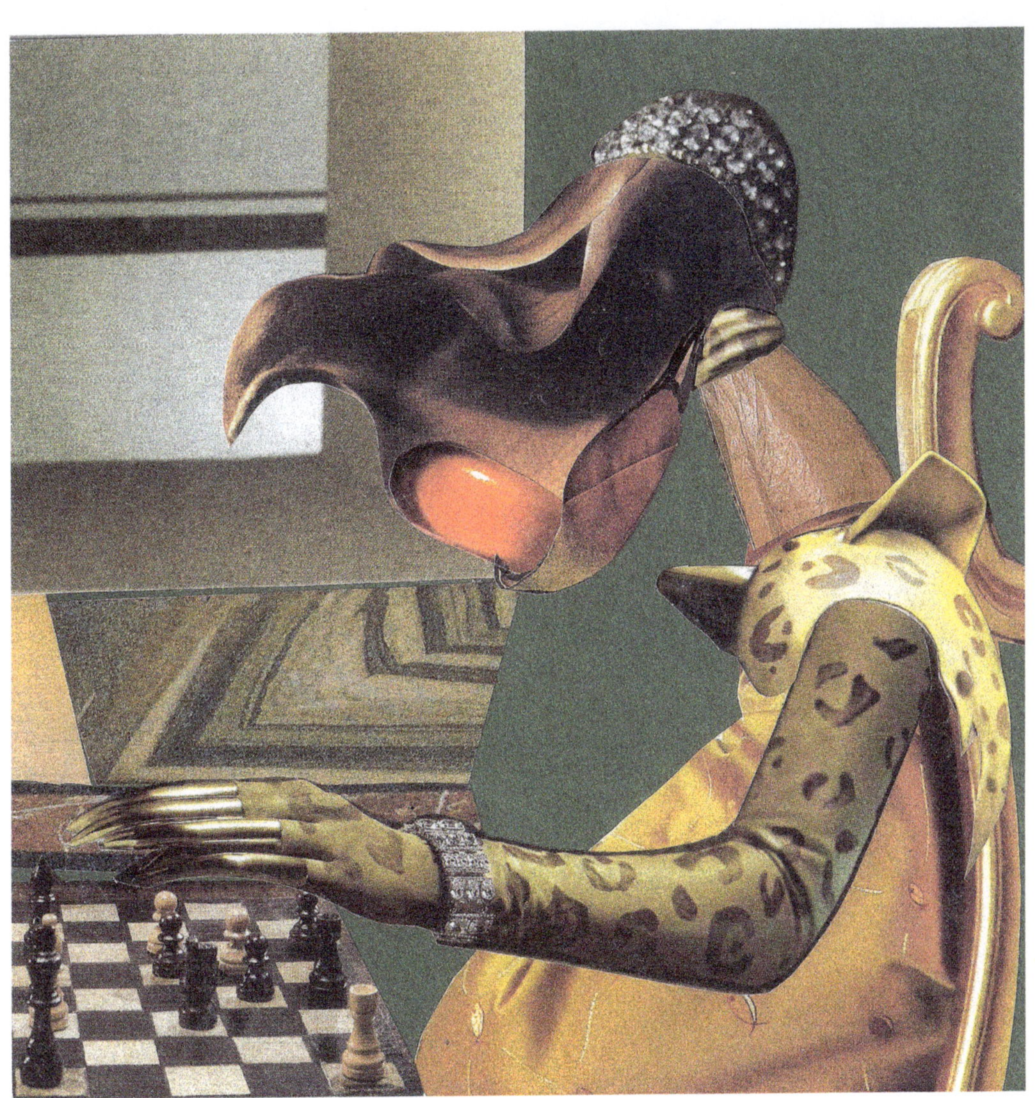

CHECKMATE

Handmade collage, paper on paper, 20 cm x 20 cm

ROBYN MALLERY

SAN FRANCISCO, CALIFORNIA

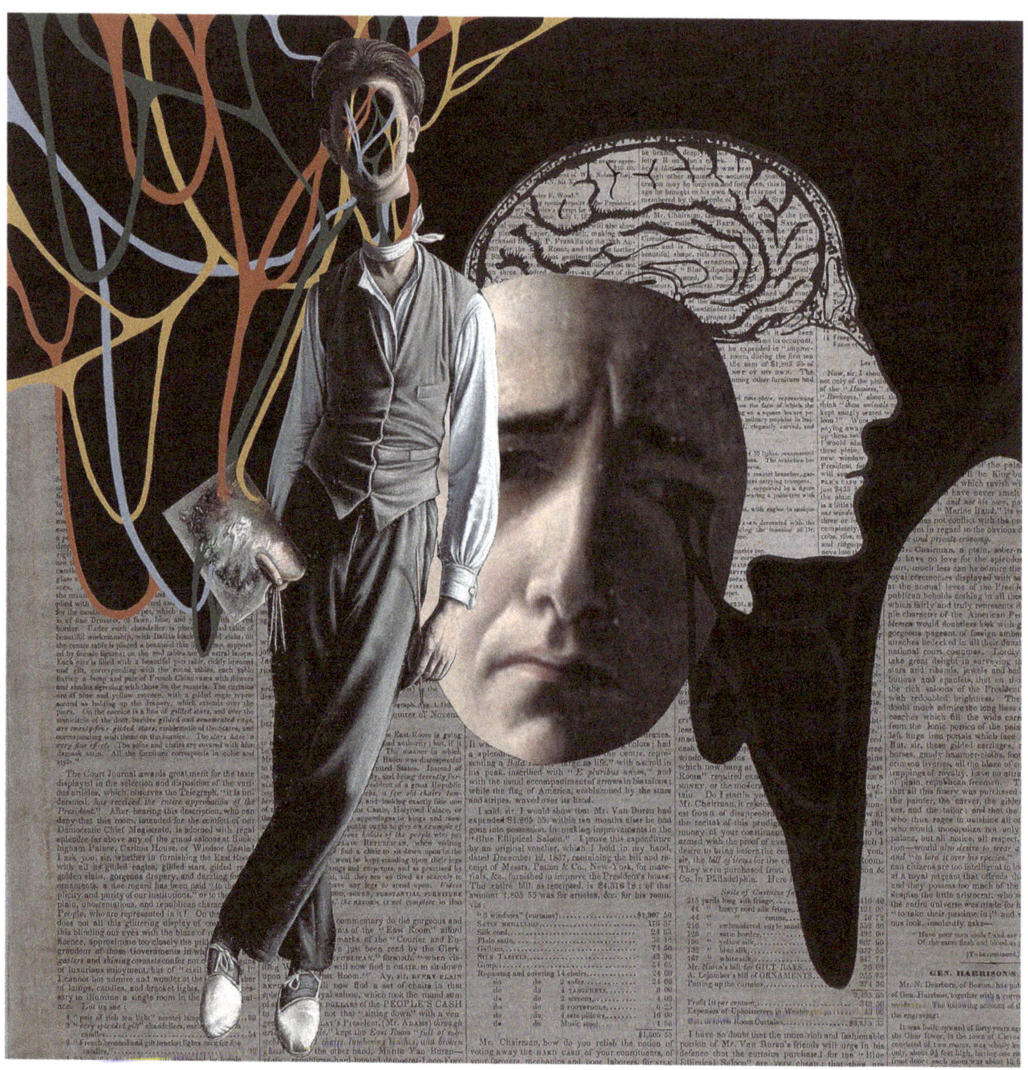

WIRED

Digital collage

VALERY OISTEANU

NEW YORK, NEW YORK

HOW TO RUIN YOUR OWN BRAIN

In the invisible moments of paradoxical life

It requires a talent to hypnotize yourself

To detach your thoughts from attached

Boundless charity & compassion

That muscle is going-gone, atrophied

By pretension and ripples of timidity

Your brain & heart will feel nothing again

No goodness, no synergetic serendipity

The silent struggle within our souls

Through shadows of deceit and greed

The strength to stand against the tide

Living by night without love's oxygen

Reading only dementia daily news

The flammable grey matter shrinks

Voice is changing rapidly facing silence

A cloud burst around a hedonistic head

No more fairness or no more virtues

Morality is easy crushable

In an everlasting winter of indecision

Now you can live with a goldfish in your brain

Ghosts of pentagonal hearts

Haunts guiltless intuition of generosity

ZEV TORRES

NEW YORK, NEW YORK

ALL THE WORLD

All the world
Is in a state of intransigent belief,
Beset by vengeful reckonings,
Ethical bloodlettings,
Long settled precepts honeycombed by
Imperious disdain,
Zero-sum hypocrisies,
Funhouse revisions.

Foundational tenets have been debased:
Loyalty is the garb of the imposter;
Science is the yield of the devil;
The curvature of the time-space continuum is void,
According to the latest calculations.

The contours of our communities are changing,
Are always changing,
Have always been changing,
Decimating the footholds that were our birthright.

Exhausted already.
From overwrought anticipation.
The time for realizing our ambitions has passed.
The upheaval is worse than prophesied.

All we can do is avert our eyes,
And breathe —
    But only in a way that feels right,
    Not as we've been taught —
As we await the next aspirant
Ablaze with audacity,
Who feasts on unfulfilled dreams,
And absolves us
With vicarious grandiosity,
When moving on and staying still are,
No longer,
Viable options.

GIORGIA PAVLIDOU

LOS ANGELES, CALIFORNIA & ATHENS, GREECE

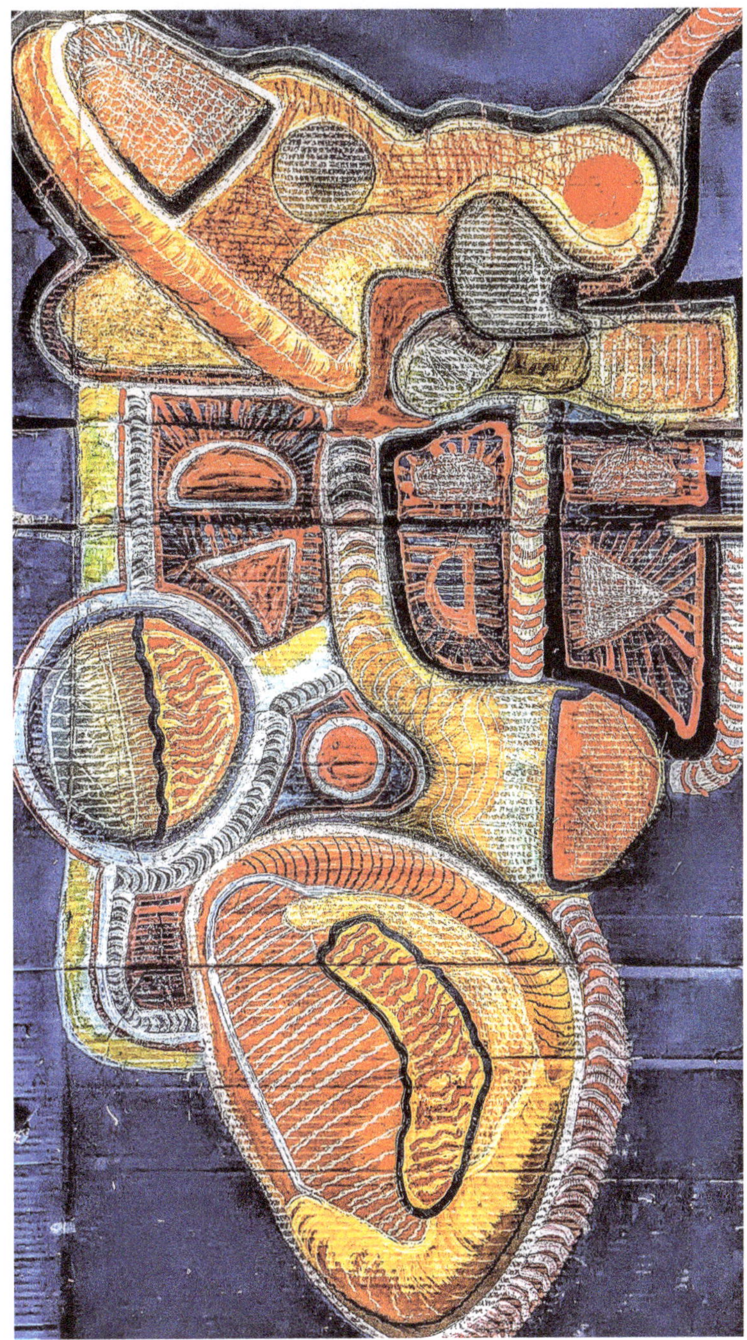

PERTURBED

Housepaint, acrylic, and pastels on cardboard, 48 in x 24 in

BRENDAN LORBER
BROOKLYN, NEW YORK

MAYBE LOVE IS IN THE AIR

Maybe love is in the air   but it's otherwise   where bombs burst

and particles hang on   I'd like to talk to you   and your yacht money

just long enough   for the idea of free school or medicine   to slip

through   how much I can't stand   my own inner sermonizing

My own plans   to storm the private driverless murder factory

buy-in equity islands   are no match for the air's infectious immateriality

The way every breath or click   wants to swap out the real for the symbol

like making hunger for dinner   makes even the dazzlingly austere certainty

of grief in the husk of the old   feel better than the strangeness of a new

saucy covenant   We've all been in love   with making a fist   abstract

We've wanted riches   enough to pretend   riches don't make victims

which is who we are   We've all been in love   we've seen love in the air

while air's in the way   of seeing what's solid in the wreckage   of our

first principles   the rattling emblems of terrifying acceptance   that the

founders insisted we can pursue happiness   but not that we can have it

RUUD JANSSEN

BREDA, THE NETHERLANDS

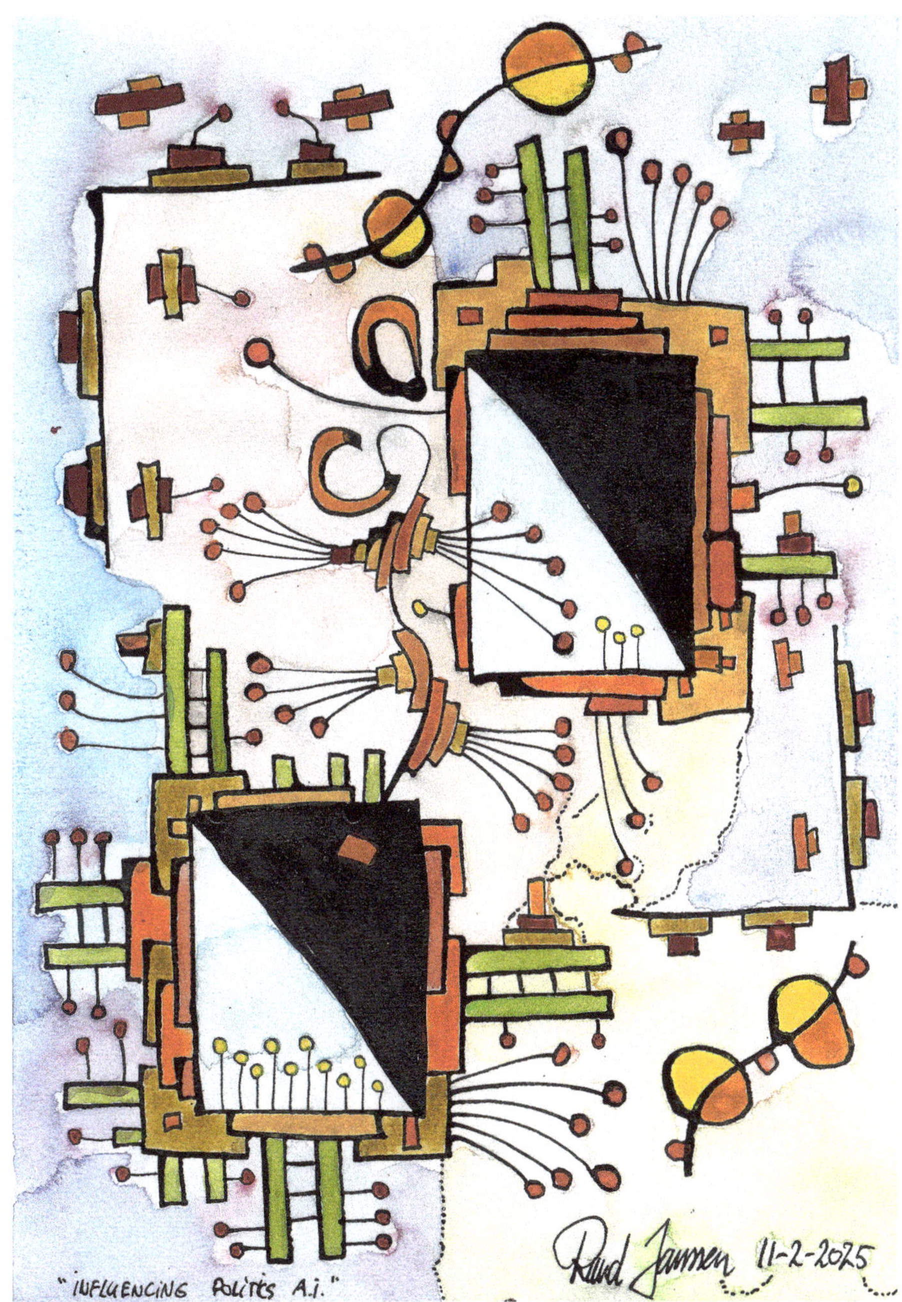

INFLUENCING POLITICS A.I.

Indian ink and watercolor, 22 cm x 34 cm

MARIAM AHMED

SAN DIEGO, CALIFORNIA

SIX STORIES (SESTINA)

Waking several hours before dawn,
I ignore the curtains, feeling their shadow,
and check on last night's ill-gotten fortune.
Switching out the deck wasn't part of the plan,
But it worked, with the help of a strong gust of wind.
Happy with my hiding place, I drift back to sleep, at peace.

The final cry was a call for peace,
Illuminated by the soft light of dawn.
Each last breath carried away by the wind,
By the fire, a picture frame casts a shadow.
It stands empty on the mantle—a remnant of a plan
That fell apart like a cracked clay pot, carrying bad fortune.

"Win at all costs," said the fortune
teller under the tent, cool with peace.
I whispered to her the details of my plan,
which I'd execute at the first sight of dawn.
When I tried to sleep that night, I imagined a shadow
Carrying my luck away with the wind.

What was that sound? Was the wind
causing the trees to shake? No fortune
could take me out of bed to confront the shadow
that threatened to take away my peace.
I'll hide here forever, or at least until dawn,
When I awaken from this dream, I'll have a plan.

No more thought for this plan
that could be knocked down by the wind.
I'd rather face the unknown than the dawn.
What can I say—these words cost a fortune,
but it's the light from a lone candle that brings peace
whenever I shrink from a new shadow.

What if you woke up one day and had no shadow?
Would it mean the end of your careful plan,
or could you grow to find another peace—
A piece of solace that comes as you wind
down from the stress of amassing great fortune?
Maybe another day, maybe another dawn.

IRINA TALL

MINSK, BELARUS

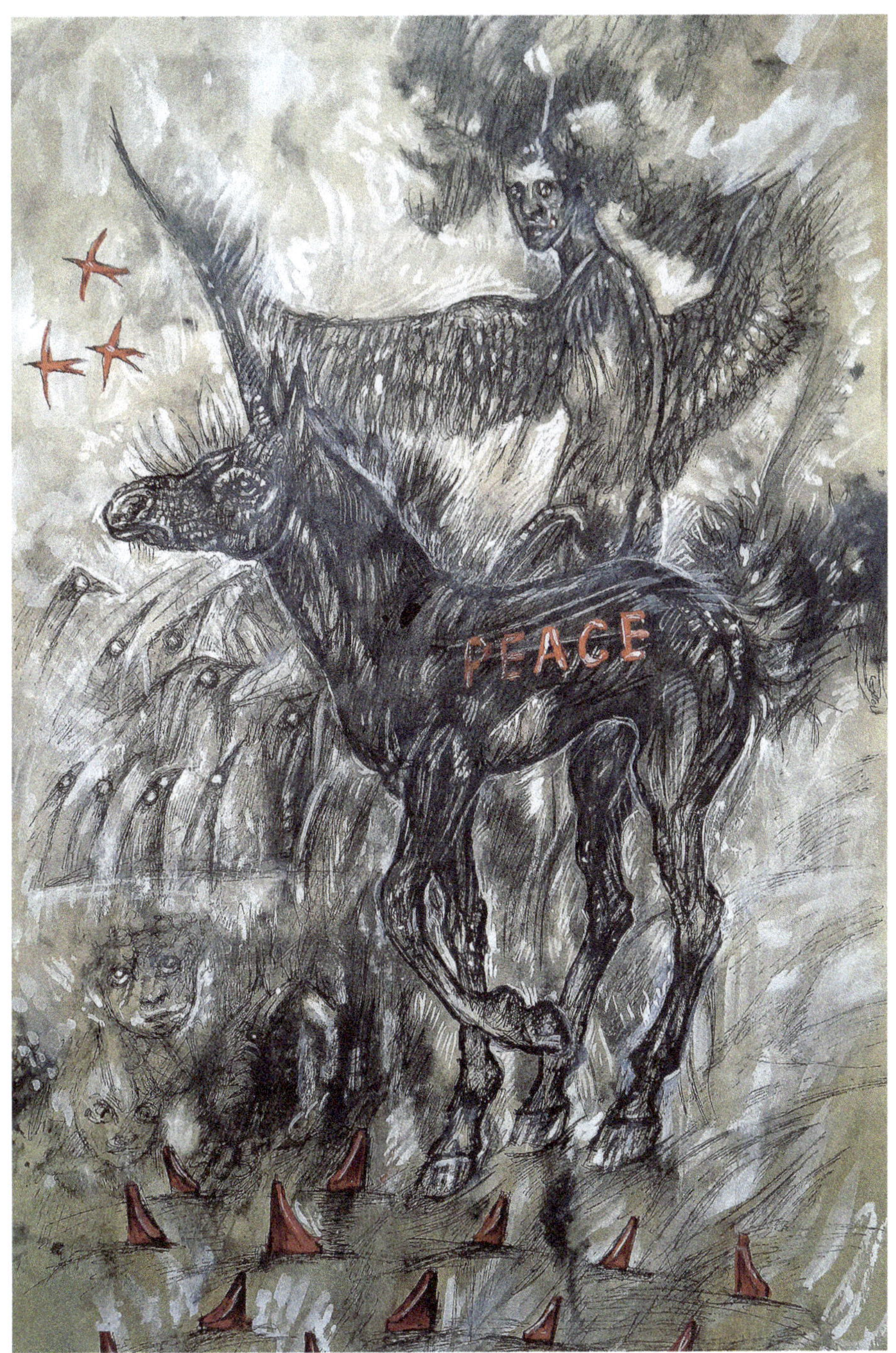

DREAMS

Collage on paper

MARIE C LECRIVAIN

LOS ANGELES, CALIFORNIA

MAYA 2025:
BUBBLES DISGUISED AS BUNKERS

We're back at it again, with chaos
and gallows humor, smiles at half mast
as we read the news about how Hammas
returned who they decimated. At last,
half a family can grieve, sing the chants
and wonder what they did wrong. The answer
is nothing. The bloody cost of war supplants
the wish for peace, and becomes a cancer
in the form of propaganda fed to
the folks back home who worry and wonder
when, or if, the genocide will end. Who
said, "It's better to expire than blunder
through life?" No one. We all know it's a lie,
and still we allow innocence to die.

JON LONGHI

SAN FRANCISCO, CALIFORNIA

THE ANGER INDUSTRY

Politics is a scab that rips open our darkest angers. Anger is the new currency in America. Anger is what pays the bills and gets all the power. It doesn't matter what face it is wearing today—anger rules us all. It's the tyrant who won't be happy until everything is wrecked. The world's richest men have industries to manufacture rage. It is the curtain they hide their filthy profits behind. Worse than any whirlpool in history all the money in the world is sucked into the black holes of their souls. Burning cities just make their stock go up. And they'll shamelessly make money all the way down right till the last two of us slit each other's throats. According to them, that's what freedom is all about.

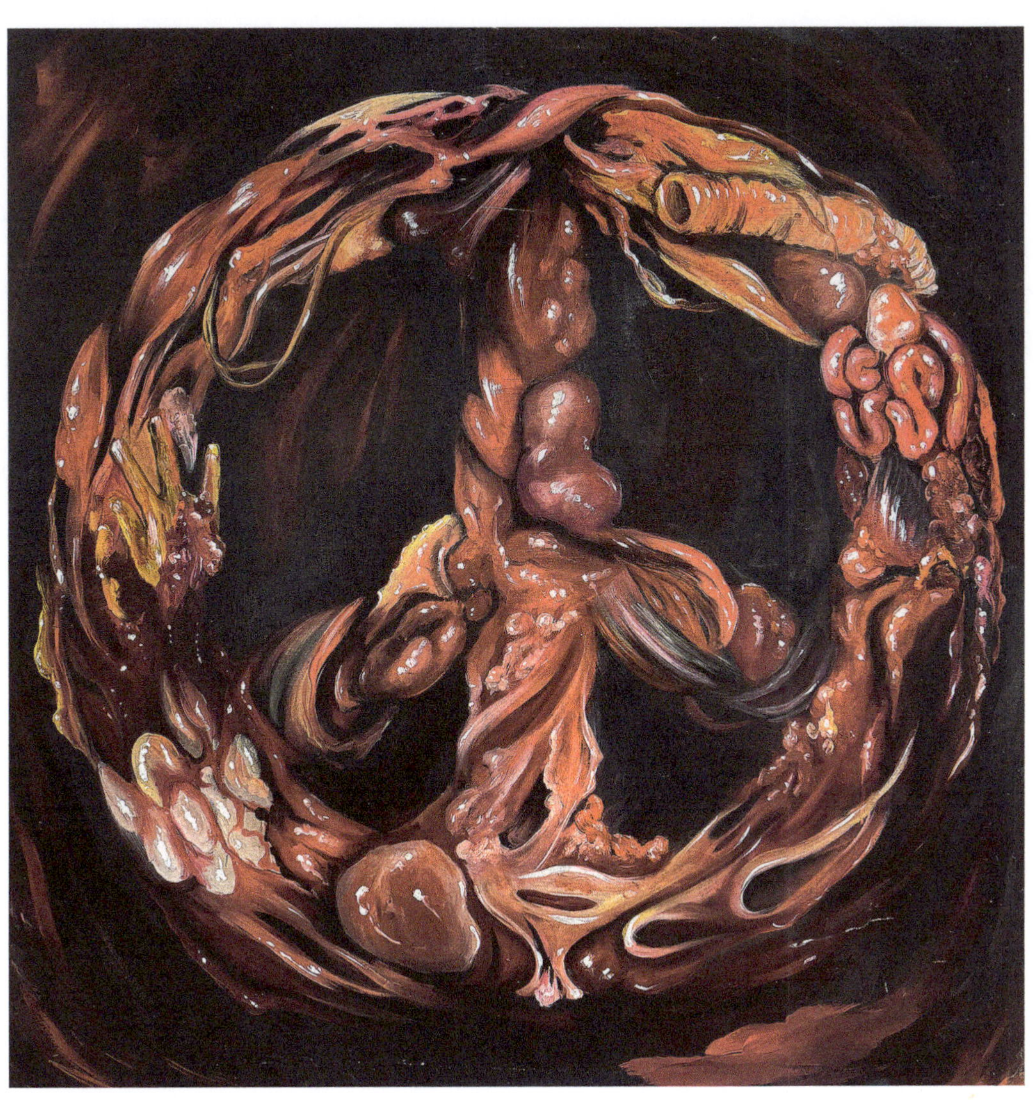

PEACEWAR

Oil paint on wood panel

DOROTHY FRIEDMAN
NEW YORK, NEW YORK

I SPEAK OUT FOR JOHNNY THE ICE-CREAM MAN

I speak out for the brothers and sisters who
    I've never met,
rotting in prisons and mental hospitals,
who can't be here to speak for themselves.

I speak out for the overweight, ugly and
    unkempt.
The pimply acne scarred bedwetters and
    nosepickers,
as well as the beautiful and unblemished.

I speak out for rich and poor.
For the elderly with their soft bones
and wobbly walking sticks,
their feeble bodies and strong minds.
for the beauty and humanity in each of us,
as well as the ugliness and apathy.

I speak out for those who are not yet born,
and those dead and dying on battlefields.
For the first step of the baby
and the last step of the grandmother.
For the hip hop and the waltz.
For Charlie Parker and Dorothy Parker.
For cleaner air and the touch of a human
    hand.
For those in Afghanistan and those in the
    Hamptons.

I speak out for Johnny the ice-cream man.
For Larry the Comp Lit teacher
and Judy the CPA, for illegal aliens
and sex workers, for lesbians and
    transgender people.
For Helen the medievalist and Dr. Ruth the
    sex therapist.
For congenital liars and misfits
For Dr. Jeckyl and Mr. Hyde.

I speak out for all those caught between
    two places:
the bigamist between wives,
the daughters between two mothers,
the composers and the decomposed,
the mestizos between two races,
the dispossessed and the possessed,
between two songs, two sexes,
two prejudices and two enlightenments.

I speak out for matrimony and hegemony,
for existentialism and colloquialism,
for colonialism and comparative literature.

I speak out for vanity and sanity and lunacy,
and for all those caught between.
John Ashbery's "Double Dream of Spring"
and Amiri Baraka's "Soundings.'
For an academic whip and a powerful
    meditation
on abuses of power, for the mediocre and
    immature,
for emotionality and obsessive love.

I speak out for the common good,
for the romance of cynicism and idealism,
for the Pillsbury doughboy.

I speak out for the mothers who left us
and for the children who left us
and for the child in each of us.

And I speak out for small town
    snobbishness
and big city elitism, and for the poem
that never ends, because there is never a
an end to speaking out.

FAUSTO GROSSI

BILBAO, SPAIN

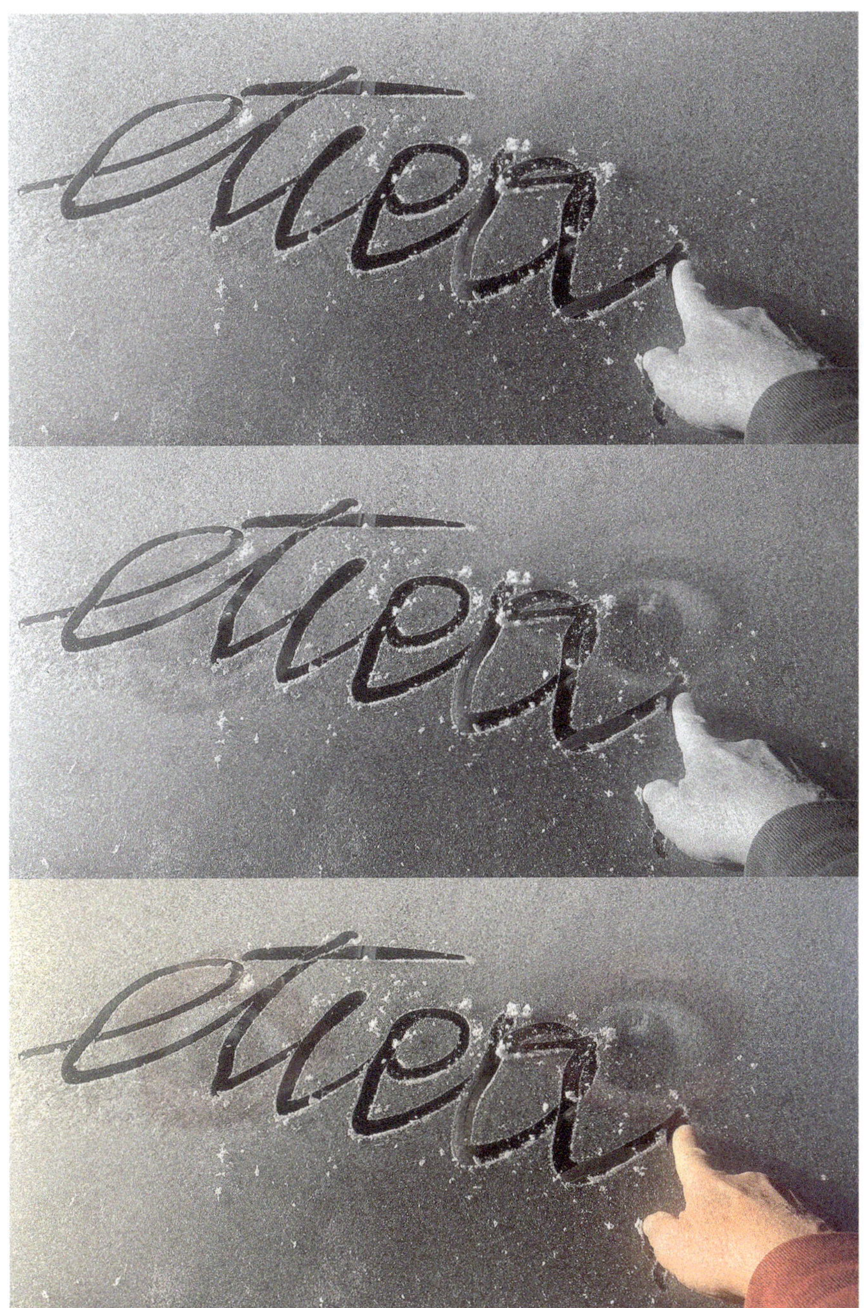

QUELLO CHE DEFINISCE IN DIVENIRE

mobile phone image, 105.2 cm x 70.98 cm

MADO REZNIK

MEXICO CITY, MEXICO

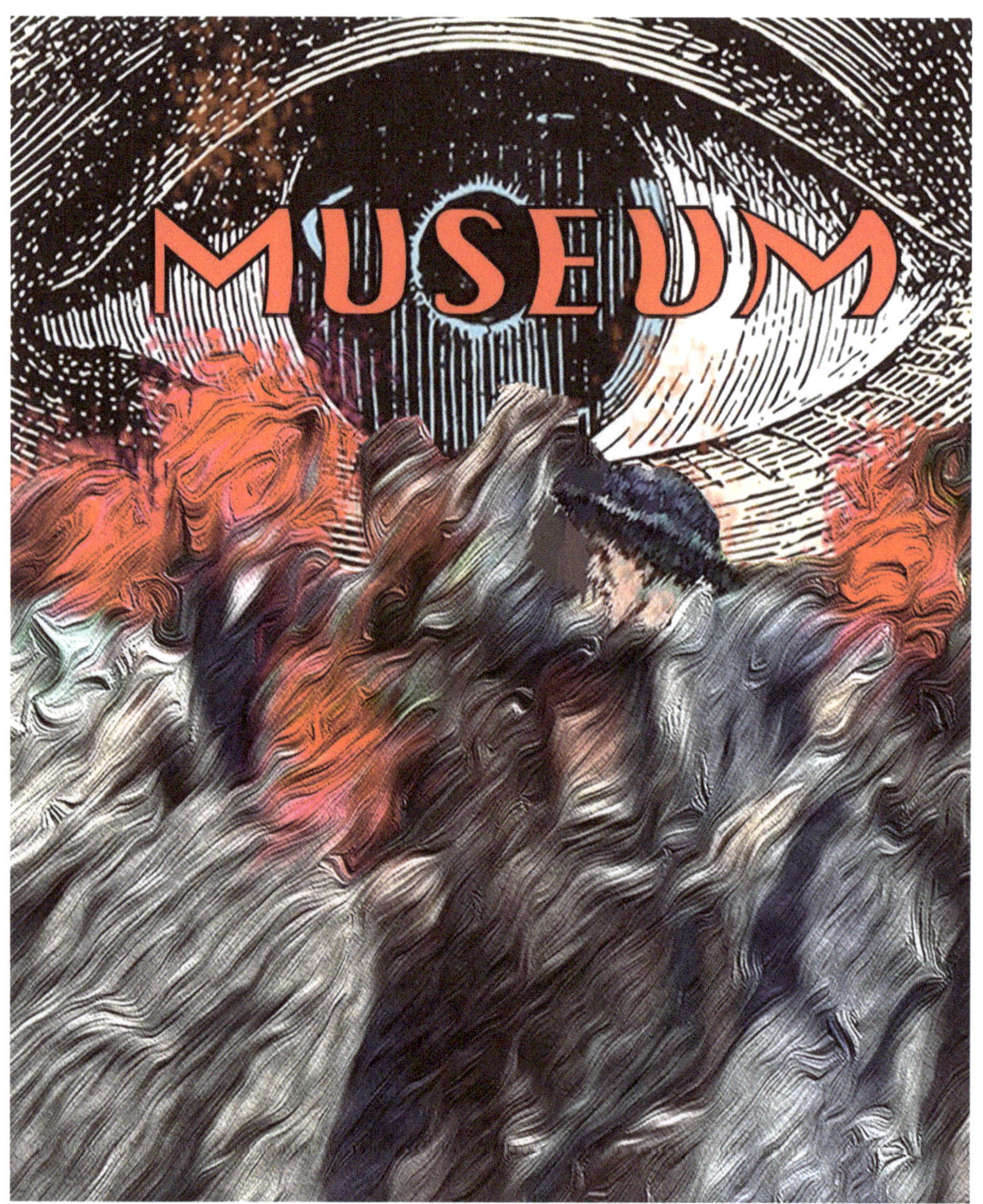

MUSEUM POLICY

Digital collage, 10.75 cm x 9 cm

JOHN J. TRAUSE
WOOD-RIDGE, NEW JERSEY

MOMA

MoMA trustees in
in the staff elevator
descending from the
sixth floor

Male Trustee:
"Good heavens,
what happened
to your arm?"

Female Trustee
(with arm in a sling):
"Oh, I broke my arm!
My doctor says that
I must wear over it
men's socks. Oh,
where does one get
men's socks?"

Male Trustee:
"Uh, I don't know.
Wallach's?"

Female Trustee:
"I'll have to send
out one of the help.
By the way, what's all
this fuss about ethnic
cleansing? Why is
everyone against it?
One of my cleaning
ladies comes from
Honduras and she
does a good job."

MIKE M. MOLLETT

LOS ANGELES, CALIFORNIA

FAKE SMILES ON THE RIDGE OF FOREVER

Is this all there is, my friends-
out of the cabaret   a bitter tea by the
      buckets full
behind our backs   in the back rooms
closed doors opening crypto
bank accounts of Mir-a-lago archipelagos
sneer at the other side
always the other side so to speak

turns out the other side half blind is also
10's of millions a few billions of us
scratching like chickens
for a level playing field with foods
sustainable & honest eye to eye
revealing a list of healthy recipes
too good to be true nowadays

honesty actually sucks
YES = NO
in the viral kingdom of power
truth being a wounded animal
gulped in & kicked down dirty
buy a leader without conscientious reason
no questions asked there.
hope too is on the chopping block
a pervasive rule of toxicity leers: take
      what you can,
as quickly as you can
the future is in lockstep
the pharmaceuticals' machine hand in
      hand
the product infusion malignant

this army of irresponsibility
has no bounds
it's hard to think for our selves when
the dice are marked   the golden tables
      crooked
leprosy of reason steals the ball of justice
with judicial landmines & lies
wiping out the out-of-the box thinkers
      toward freedom
the beautiful egalitarian dancers
who move us beyond hate & our isolated
      selves

cheers... we drink our healthy piss
which will not hurt us
then spit a fine gulp in the faces of
the well-connected gunmen & women
      who perjure themselves
quite easily to the cameras in the
      bedrooms of
congress & corporations
it burns them

how close can we get to this dark side
      matter
with our kind stronghold of wisdom
adjusting to make sense & more sense . .
      .
to be heard   it must be heard
in the uncertain weather

NEAL SKOOTER TAYLOR

LOS ANGELES, CALIFORNIA

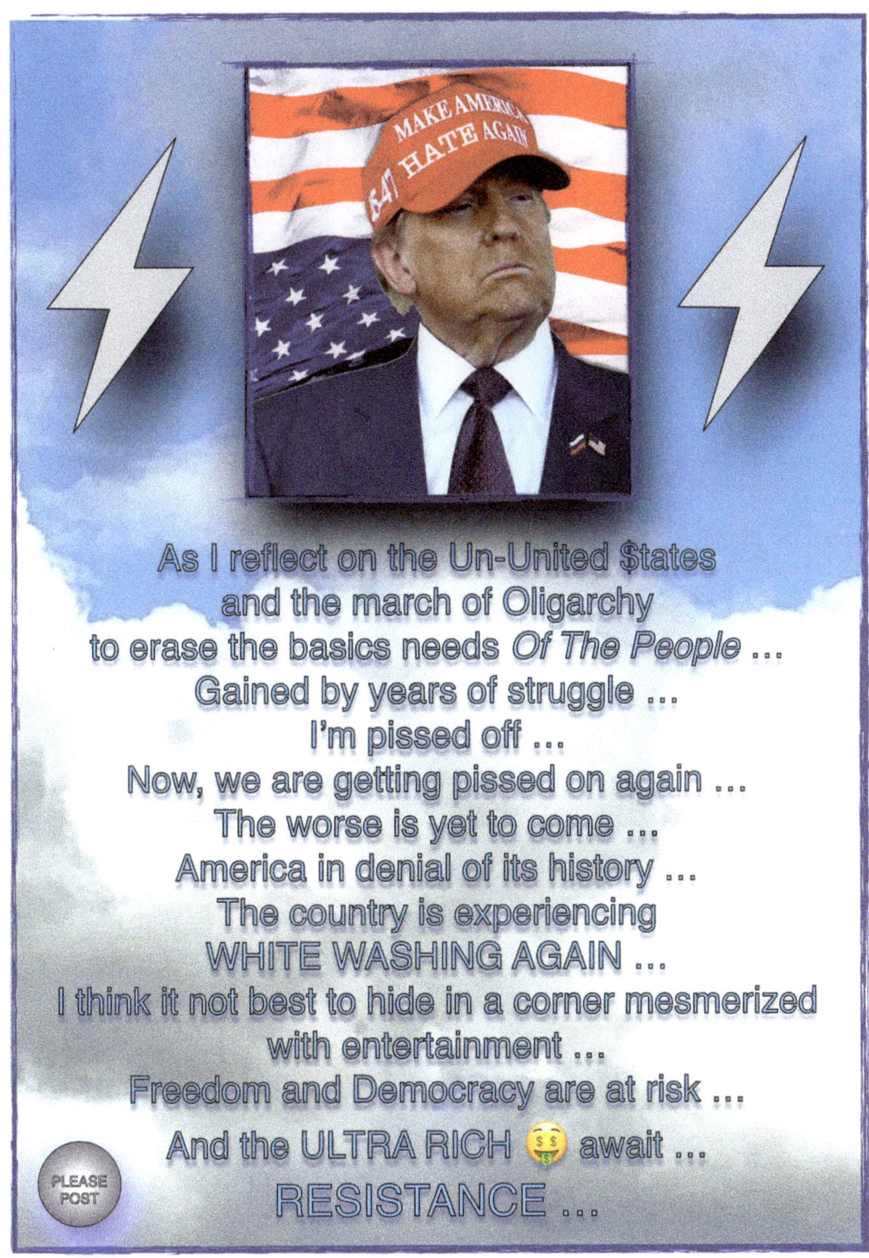

MAHA

Digital collage

RON KOLM

LONG ISLAND CITY, NEW YORK

SOCIAL JUSTICE
SHOULD BE ALL-INCLUSIVE

(based on the words banned by Trump)

I'm sorry

but my poetry

is usually

person-centered

and I try to make it

biased toward

the underprivileged

because they are

the victims

of the ruling class

and we have

to fight for them

all the time

at whatever the cost.

MICHAEL GEORG BREGEL

BERLIN, GERMANY

WHAT IS LEFT

what is left

to think about

should be

thought about

in a quite

complicated

foreign language

preferably one

I do not

understand

SALVATORE ESPOSITO

LONDON, UNITED KINGDOM

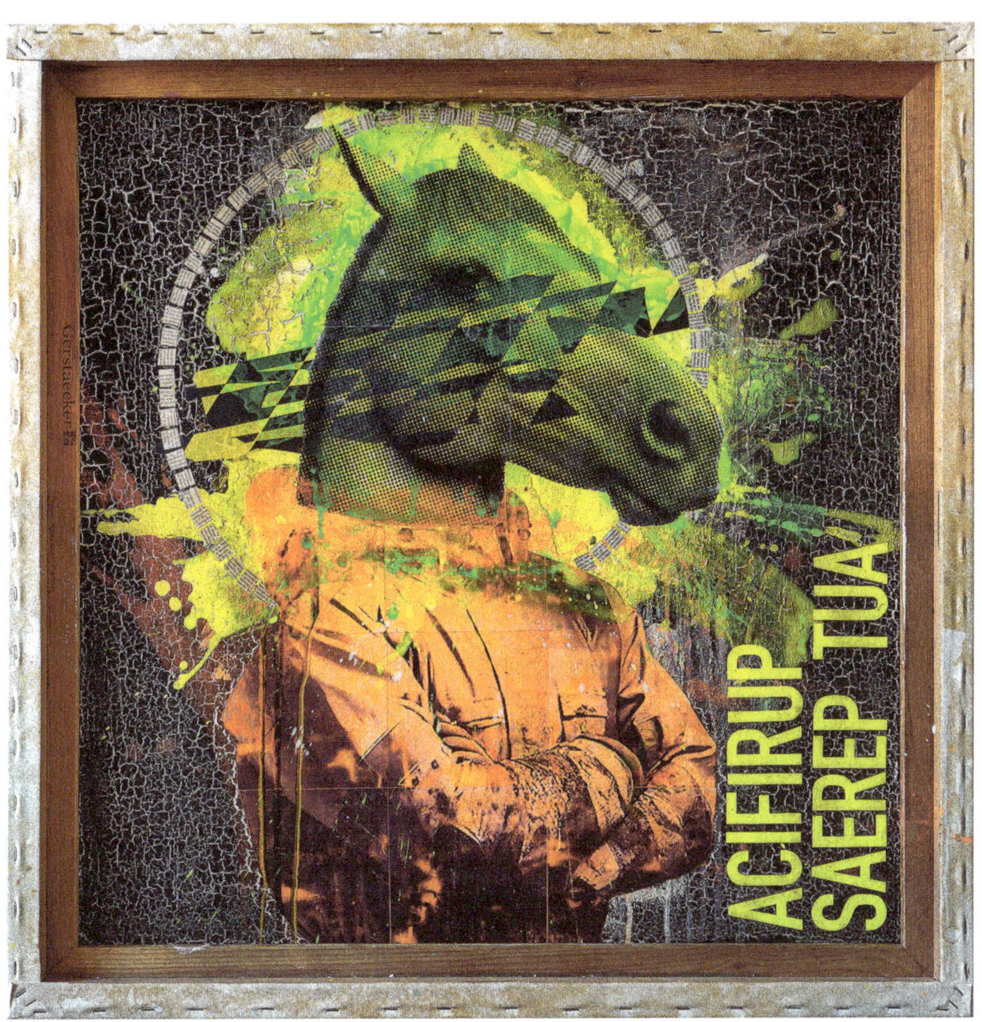

PURIFICA AUT PEREAS

*Media: Paper collage, acrylic and fluorescent acrylic paint, shreds of caution tape
on the back of the canvas, 800 mm x 800 mm*

SANTIAGO AMAYA

HACIENDA HEIGHTS, CALIFORNIA

PULL THE FIRE ALARM

after party momento
blistered and seared
from the ignition of a forest fire with a "freedom firework" that was made in China

industrial morality
is replacing the gauze with caulk
fingering the wound and discharging the patient

"our deepest condolences"
ice baths for a burn victim
providing the ammunition for a massacre then running the charity at the memorial

the purgatory of a political promise is
a safe room in a horror game
covering oneself with a blanket full of razors

every tender caress from an ethical dilemma
Is met with a "I could care less"
And another bipartisan war package

congressman signs his name on a bomb to Gaza with jubilee
Put the problem in front of a firing squad
and let the populous inhale the perpendicular miasma

A sought after throne made out of plastic and blood, should be no surprise when
the earth begins to moan in a city brazen with ash and the bodies of children

The human spirit is marked for evolution
Desperate for zenith, a zero surrounded by one's
One day, the rain will come

ALEXANDER LIMAREV

NOVOSIBIRSK, RUSSIA

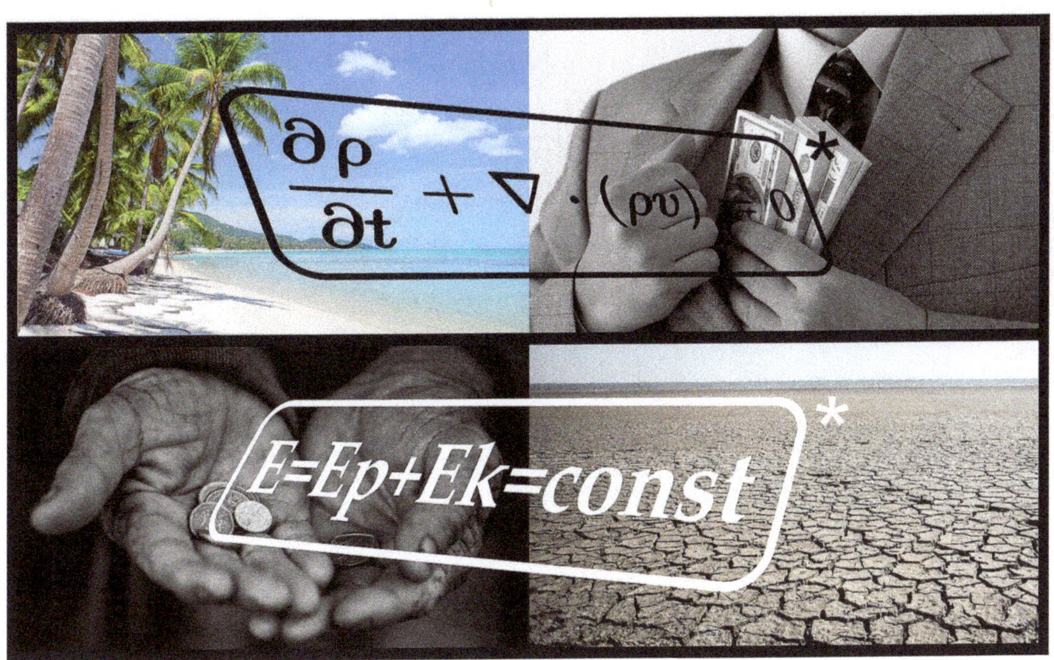

*The law of conservation of matter: in all phenomena of nature, the amount of matter remains constant: in any phenomenon, whether it be physical, chemical or biological, matter can change its kind, form, but the amount of it remains unchanged, the total weight of the bodies involved in the phenomenon remains unchanged.

*Law of conservation on energy: energy does not arise or disappear, it can be transferred from one body to another, and one kind of enery can be transformed into another.

THE LAW OF CONSERVATION OF MATTER

Digital collage, 3512 px x 2484 px

ZYGIMANTAS KUDIRKA

VILNIUS, LITHUANIA

WHO ARE YOU?

This is a public human announcement

I want to believe
that there are no aliens
in this planet.

We were all born from a single cell.

Regenerate your wounds.
Regenerate your teeth.
Regenerate your liver.
Regenerate your penis, fats, vagina, brain tissue, thymus.
Regenerate your heart.

REGENERATE YOUR TRUST

British queen is not a blood thirsty lizard lady,
but humans are animal species indeed.

Evaluate.
Observe.
Fertilize.
Don't blink.
Establish and maintain.
Click, squeak, prey.
Glide.
ESCAPE.
Match.
Communicate.
REGENERATE.

Plants are just very slow animals.
Stones are just very slow plants.

Lizards are gods.

Who let the gods out!

Explore your own self, explore your sexuality.
Don't be scared of who you are.

Etymologically the word 'lizard'
     comes from proto-european
     'to bend or to twist' —
so that suggests that lizards are etymologically queer.

Hail the lizards!

Agama agama
Basiliscus vittatus
Egernia rugosa
Elgaria kingii nobilis
Iguana iguana
Intellagama
Lerista fragilis
Nebulifera robusta

Who are you?
Who are you this time?
Who are you?
Tell us, who you really are!

Je suis a stone
je suis a plant
Je suis a lizard

Who are you?

KAI POHL

BERLIN, GERMANY

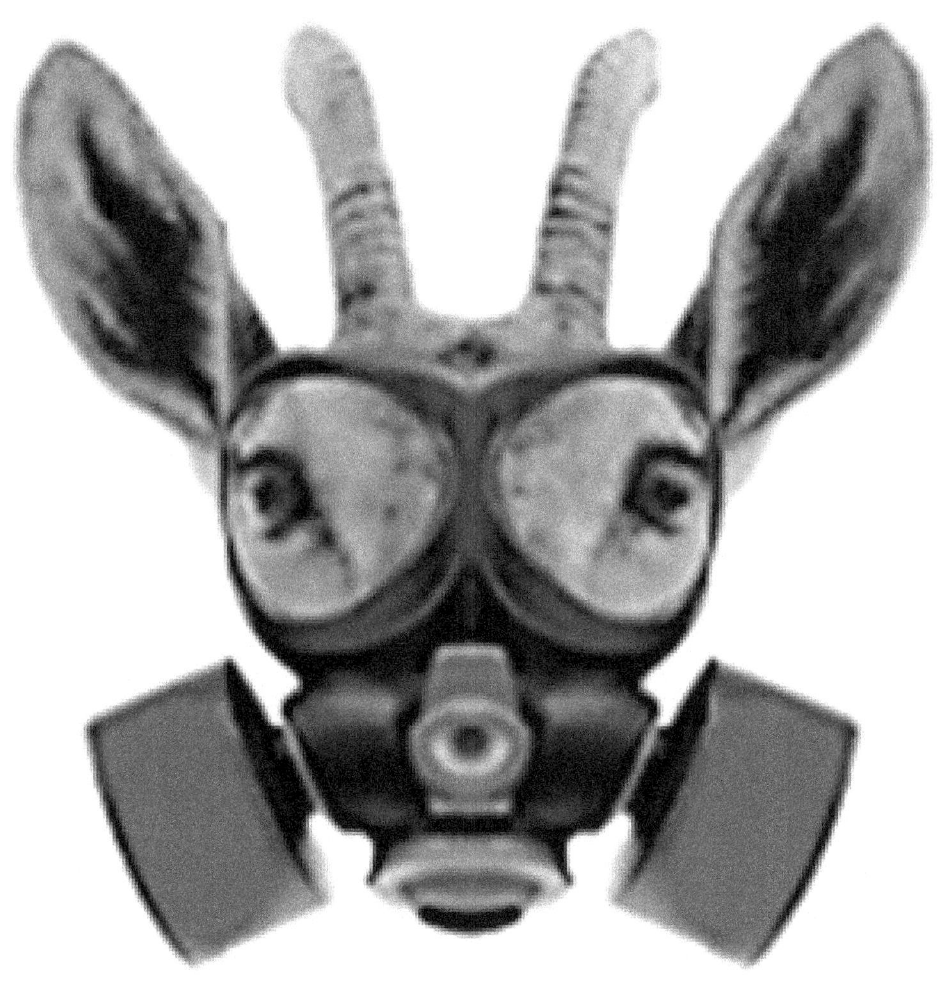

DIE LUFT WIRD DÜNN

Digital collage, 9000 px x 9000 px

Recent and Forthcoming Books from Three Rooms Press

FICTION

Lucy Jane Bledsoe
No Stopping Us Now

Rishab Borah
The Door to Inferna

Meagan Brothers
Weird Girl and What's His Name

Christopher Chambers
Scavenger
Standalone
StreetWhys

Ebele Chizea
Aquarian Dawn

Heather Colley
The Gilded Butterfly Effect

Ron Dakron
Hello Devilfish!

Ron Dakron
Hello Devilfish!

Robert Duncan
Loudmouth

Amanda Eisenberg
People Are Talking

Michael T. Fournier
Hidden Wheel
Swing State

Kate Gale
Under a Neon Sun

Aaron Hamburger
Nirvana Is Here

William Least Heat-Moon
Celestial Mechanics

Aimee Herman
Everything Grows

Kelly Ann Jacobson
Tink and Wendy
Robin and Her Misfits
Lies of the Toymaker

Jethro K. Lieberman
Everything Is Jake

Eamon Loingsigh
Light of the Diddicoy
Exile on Bridge Street

John Marshall
The Greenfather

Alvin Orloff
Vulgarian Rhapsody

Micki Janae
Of Blood and Lightning

Aram Saroyan
Still Night in L.A.

Robert Silverberg
The Face of the Waters

Stephen Spotte
Animal Wrongs

Max Talley
Peace, Love and Haight

Richard Vetere
The Writers Afterlife
Champagne and Cocaine

Jessamyn Violet
Secret Rules to Being a Rockstar

Julia Watts
Quiver
Needlework
Lovesick Blossoms

Gina Yates
Narcissus Nobody

MEMOIR & BIOGRAPHY

Nassrine Azimi and Michel Wasserman
*Last Boat to Yokohama: The Life and
Legacy of Beate Sirota Gordon*

William S. Burroughs & Allen Ginsberg
Don't Hide the Madness
edited by Steven Taylor

James Carr
BAD: The Autobiography of James Carr

Judy Gumbo
*Yippie Girl: Exploits in Protest and
Defeating the FBI*

Nancy Kurshan
*Levitating the Pentagon and Ohter
Stories*

Judith Malina
*Full Moon Stages: Personal Notes from
50 Years of The Living Theatre*

Phil Marcade
*Punk Avenue: Inside the New York City
Underground, 1972–1982*

Jillian Marshall
*Japanthem: Counter-Cultural
Experiences; Cross-Cultural Remixes*

Marilisa Merolla
*Into Nowhere: Bruce Springsteen and
the Cold War Blues*

Alvin Orloff
*Disasterama! Adventures in the Queer
Underground 1977–1997*

Nicca Ray
*Ray by Ray: A Daughter's Take
on the Legend of Nicholas Ray*

Aram Saroyan
Before I Forget

Stephen Spotte
*My Watery Self:
Memoirs of a Marine Scientist*

Christina Vo & Nghia M. Vo
My Vietnam, Your Vietnam
Vietnamese translation: *Việt Nam Của
Con, Việt Nam Của Cha*

PHOTOGRAPHY-MEMOIR

Mike Watt
On & Off Bass

SHORT STORY ANTHOLOGIES

SINGLE AUTHOR
Alien Archives: Stories
by Robert Silverberg

First-Person Singularities: Stories
by Robert Silverberg

Tales from the Eternal Café: Stories
by Janet Hamill, intro by Patti Smith

*Time and Time Again:
Sixteen Trips in Time*
by Robert Silverberg

*The Unvarnished Gary Phillips:
A Mondo Pulp Collection*
by Gary Phillips

*Voyagers: Twelve Journeys in
Space and Time*
by Robert Silverberg

MULTI-AUTHOR
The Colors of April
edited by Quan Manh Ha & Cab Tran

*Crime + Music: Nineteen Stories
of Music-Themed Noir*
edited by Jim Fusilli

Dark City Lights: New York Stories
edited by Lawrence Block

*The Faking of the President: Twenty
Stones of White House Noir*
edited by Peter Carlaftes

Florida Happens:
edited by Greg Herren

Have a NYC I, II & III: New York Stories;
edited by Peter Carlaftes & Kat Georges

Songs of My Selfie
edited by Constance Renfrow

*The Obama Inheritance:
15 Stories of Conspiracy Noir*
edited by Gary Phillips

*This Way to the End Times:
Classic & New Stories of the Apocalypse*
edited by Robert Silverberg

DADA

*Maintenant: A Journal of
Contemporary Dada Writing & Art*
(annual, since 2008)

MIXED MEDIA

John S. Paul
Sign Language: A Painter's Notebook (photography, poetry and prose)

HUMOR

Peter Carlaftes
A Year on Facebook

FILM & PLAYS

Israel Horovitz
*My Old Lady: Complete Stage Play and
Screenplay with an Essay on Adaptation*

Peter Carlaftes
Triumph For Rent (3 Plays)
Teatrophy (3 More Plays)

Kat Georges
*Three Somebodies:
Plays about Notorious Dissidents*

TRANSLATIONS

Thomas Bernhard
On Earth and in Hell
(poems of Thomas Bernhard
with English translations by
Peter Waugh)

Patrizia Gattaceca
Isula d'Anima / Soul Island

César Vallejo | Gerard Malanga
Malanga Chasing Vallejo

George Wallace
EOS: Abductor of Men
(selected poems in Greek & English)

ESSAYS

Richard Katrovas
*Raising Girls in Bohemia:
Meditations of an American Father*

Vanessa Baden Kelly
Far Away From Close to Home

Erin Wildermuth (editor)
Womentality

POETRY COLLECTIONS

Hala Alyan
Atrium

Peter Carlaftes
DrunkYard Dog
I Fold with the Hand I Was Dealt
Life in the Past Lane

Thomas Fucaloro
It Starts from the Belly and Blooms
Inheriting Craziness . . .

Kat Georges
Our Lady of the Hunger
Awe and Other Words Like Wow

Robert Gibbons
Close to the Tree

Israel Horovitz
Heaven and Other Poems

David Lawton
Sharp Blue Stream

Jane LeCroy
Signature Play

Philip Meersman
This Is Belgian Chocolate

Jane Ormerod
Recreational Vehicles on Fire
Welcome to the Museum of Cattle

Lisa Panepinto
On This Borrowed Bike

George Wallace
Poppin' Johnny

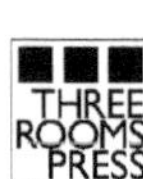

Three Rooms Press | New York, NY | Current Catalog: www.threeroomspress.com
Three Rooms Press books are distributed by Publishers Group West: www.pgw.com

www.ingramcontent.com/pod-product-compliance
Lightning Source LLC
Jackson TN
JSHW070024020725
86290JS00001B/1